Pleasures of the Prose:
Journalism and Humour

EDITED BY
Richard Lance Keeble and David Swick

Published 2015 by Abramis academic publishing

www.abramis.co.uk

ISBN 978 1 84549 662 3

© Richard Lance Keeble and David Swick 2015

All rights reserved

This book is copyright. Subject to statutory exception and to provisions of relevant collective licensing agreements, no part of this publication may be reproduced, stored in a retrieval system, or transmitted in any form or by any means, without the prior written permission of the author.

Printed and bound in the United Kingdom

Typeset in Garamond 11pt

This book is sold subject to the conditions that it shall not, by way of trade or otherwise, be lent, re-sold, hired out, or otherwise circulated without the publisher's prior consent in any form of binding or cover other than that which it is published and without a similar condition including this condition being imposed on the subsequent purchaser.

Abramis is an imprint of arima publishing.

arima publishing
ASK House, Northgate Avenue
Bury St Edmunds, Suffolk IP32 6BB
t: (+44) 01284 700321

www.arimapublishing.com

The Editors

Richard Lance Keeble, Professor of Journalism at the University of Lincoln since 2003, has written and edited more than 30 books on a wide range of topics: including peace journalism, literary journalism, investigative reporting, practical newspaper reporting skills, the coverage of US/UK militarism and the secret state, and George Orwell. In 2011, he was given a National Teaching Fellowship, the highest award for teachers in higher education in the UK, and in 2014 he received a Lifetime Achievement Award from the Association for Journalism Education.

David Swick is associate director of journalism at the University of King's College in Halifax, Nova Scotia, Canada. He teaches writing courses to undergraduates and Master's students. A journalist for more than 20 years before entering academia, Swick's media work includes hour-long documentary Ideas programmes and foreign correspondence for Canada's national CBC Radio, scriptwriting television documentaries, dozens of magazine articles, nearly 2,000 newspaper columns, and one non-fiction book. He has won two major fellowships and judged Canada's CBC Literary Awards, national music awards, the Junos, and National Magazine Awards.

Contents

Introduction: Getting Seriously Funny over Journalism
Richard Lance Keeble and David Swick — 1

Section 1. Humour in Journalism, Yesterday and Today

1. 'There is Always Room for One More Custard Pie': Orwell's Humour
Richard Lance Keeble — 10

2. Humour and its Role in the Early Decades of the *New Yorker*
Mathilde Roza — 26

3. Leading with Humour: How the Mainstream is Adapting to Market Pressures
Miki Tanikawa — 41

4. *Swimming in a Sea of Death*: Reviewers Respond to a Journalist's Work of Mourning With Humour
Carolyn Rickett — 54

5. Russell Brand: The Compassionate Humorist
Sarah Niblock — 70

Section 2: The Witty Ways of Literary Journalists

6. The Savage Wit of Hunter S. Thompson
Garry Whannel — 86

7. Sarcasm, Satire and Irony: The Literary Journalism of Three Spanish Women
Novia D. Pagone — 97

8. Humour in Mexican Illicit Drug Trade-Related *Crónicas*: A Way of Pointing the Finger at Injustice
Ave Ungro — 110

Section 3: The Politics of Being Funny

9. A Mirror and a Pen: Millôr Fernandes's Legacy and the Role of Humour in Brazilian Journalism
Nicolás Llano Linares — 124

10. Humour and Identity in Catalonia: The Role of the Satirical Press
Rhiannon McGlade — 138

11. Monarchy, Army and Catholic Church in the Spanish Satirical Press: From Franco's Death to the first Socialist Government (1975-1982)
Josep Lluís Gómez-Mompart, with Dolors Palau-Sampio, José Luis Valhondo-Crego and María Iranzo-Cabrera 155

12. Once Upon a Time in Manila: Managing Marcos and Martial Rule through Humour
Amy Forbes 169

Introduction: Getting Seriously Funny over Journalism

Richard Lance Keeble and David Swick

So finally, an academic text – with an international focus – examining humour in print and online journalism! As far as we know, this is the first such text: and that says a lot about both the media industry and journalism teaching in higher education across the globe. Why has humour (so much a part of everyday communication and the pleasure of media consumption) been so marginalised in the academy?

According to Tony Harcup (2015), author of a number of texts on communication ethics, alternative media and journalism practice and theory:

> I suspect humour is largely ignored in academic literature on journalism because academics are either more interested in exploring the 'fourth estate' role of journalism or because they feel that research into 'serious' journalism will be taken more seriously (by peers and/or their bosses) than something that might be dismissed as froth. Possibly both. In contrast, the memoirs of journalists and ex-journalists are often full of humour.

Harcup also includes a brief note on 'humour' in his *Dictionary of Journalism* (2014: 129): 'Humour: A funny element within a potential story that increases its chances of being selected as news, even if the subject matter is not particularly serious or important.'

The Canadian award-winning author, actor, playwright and journalist, Mark Leiren-Young, (2015) is blunt: 'Most academics wouldn't know funny if it hit them in the face with a banana cream pie.' Sue Joseph, author and Senior Lecturer in Journalism and Creative Writing at the University of Technology, Sydney, commented: 'Perhaps we all take ourselves too seriously to do this!' And for Chris Frost (2015), author of a range of textbooks on media ethics and newspaper production skills, important factors are time and money. He said: 'I certainly think humour can be a powerful journalistic tool but its use requires skill and time. It's a shame that so few writers are given the time to apply it these days.'

Mark Leiren-Young also has the rare privilege of running a module (called 'Finding the Funny') on journalism and humour at the University of Victoria, Canada. Session titles include 'That's not funny! Or is it? What's funny? What isn't? What's taboo? What, if anything, should be taboo?: A look at comedy and censorship', 'Why did the caveman cross the road? History of humour... From Aristophanes to YouTube' and 'Canadian comedy, eh. We'll talk about Canada's coolest export – other than hockey and beer'. Students keep a humour journal and complete a range of practical assignments. For instance, one briefing runs: 'A funny thing happened ... Tell a funny story ... Something true with a comic spin. 500 words ... Bonus marks for delivering via audio (i.e. sound cloud). Extra bonus for delivering via video (i.e. YouTube or Vimeo).' Leiren-Young warns that humour travels to controversial, sensitive areas most academics may wish to avoid: 'It's a minefield. I opened my first class on humour with a blanket warning that at some point in the term I expected there to be something that would offend, upset or disturb everyone in the class.'

Indeed, the slaughter of *Charlie Hebdo* journalists and cartoonists in Paris in January 2015 by Islamic fanatics was a terrible (though somewhat extreme) reminder of the dangers humorous/mocking/satirical media can face. Chapters in the section of *Pleasures of the Prose* focusing on the politics of humorous journalism highlight other instances when writers were attacked, jailed and censored.

This text concentrates on humour in print and online journalism in a range of countries including Brazil, Britain, Spain, Mexico, the Philippines and the United States of America. There is already a substantial literature on cartoons and television 'comedic, satirical journalism' (of, say, Jon Stewart, Steven Colbert and John Oliver in the US; Rick Mercer in Canada; Mark Thomas and Chris Morris in the UK; John Clarke in Australia). But given the ways in which the various media platforms (print, online, broadcasting, social media, Twitter, YouTube) interact today – and with personnel constantly moving across them – it is difficult to study print and online separately. Inevitably a number of chapters here acknowledge the overlaps in humour across the various media platforms, as does Leiren-Young in his teaching programme.

Humour and the journalistic imagination

A special section of *Pleasures of the Prose* focuses on the humour of literary journalists. Indeed, much recent academic study has been focusing on global literary journalism and the various elements that make up the 'journalistic imagination' (see Hartsock 2000; Keeble and Wheeler 2007; Bak and Reynolds 2011; Keeble and Tulloch 2012 and 2014). Accordingly, the ways in which journalists exploit literary techniques – such as the use of humour, descriptive colour, character sketches, dialogue, eye-witness observations, a wide range of tones (ironic, satirical, sarcastic, mocking, witty, aggressively macho, confessional, reverential, sexually provocative and so on) – are both analysed, critiqued and celebrated. Literary journalism, in effect, asserts that journalism is as worthy of attention as a literary genre as, say, the works of Jane Austen and Aleksandr Solzhenitsyn.

Humour, then, is being increasingly studied as part of literary journalism programmes internationally, in relation to the work, say, of the Irish Myles na gCopaleen, the Swede Moa Martinson, the Finn Veikko Ennala, the Indian N. K. Narayan, Britons Charles Dickens, George Orwell, Evelyn Waugh, Martin Amis, Clive James, John Diamond, Lynn Barber, Mark Steel; Canadians Allan Fotheringham, Stephen Leacock and Will Ferguson; Americans Mark Twain, Dorothy Parker, Robert Benchley, Art Buchwald, James Thurber, Gore Vidal[1] – and so on. Long may these initiatives continue…

On that positive note, let's begin our detailed examination of the contents of each chapter and the various important themes they capture.

Humour in the press, yesterday and today

Pleasures of the Prose begins with a brief historical section, focusing first on the humour of George Orwell (1903-1950), the celebrated author of *Animal Farm* (1945) and *Nineteen Eighty-Four* (1949). For many this may appear a surprising choice. Orwell has tended to be associated with gloom and dystopian nightmares. D. J. Taylor, in his award-winning biography, has a chapter devoted to 'Orwell's failure' (2003: 318-321) which starts: 'Orwell was obsessed by the idea of failure. Life, he once wrote, was on balance a succession of defeats, and only the very young or the very foolish believed otherwise.'

Yet here Richard Lance Keeble highlights the lighter side of Orwell's personality, his fascination with humour – and the humorous elements in his journalism. For instance, *Homage to Catalonia* (1962 [1938]), his eye-witness account of fighting alongside Republican militiamen during the Spanish civil war, is infused throughout with a droll, self-deprecating wit: military cynicism mixed with military know-how, according to Keeble. Moreover, humour and high spirits were the constant ingredients of the eighty 'As I Please' columns Orwell contributed to *Tribune*, the leftist journal, between 1943 and 1947.

Keeble even stresses the ironic and satiric humour which, he argues, runs all through Orwell's *Nineteen Eighty-Four*. He suggests Bernard Crick provides one of the most perceptive analyses of the novel when he talks of it as being inspired by 'satiric rage' (2007: 147). Finally Keeble looks at some of the many occasions when humour was the subject of Orwell's writings: as in describing the seaside postcards of Donald McGill 'with their endless succession of fat women in tight bathing-dresses and their crude drawing and unbearable colours' (Orwell 1965 [1941]: 142), and in his book reviewing and essays on writers such as Charles Dickens, Rudyard Kipling, Jonathan Swift, Mark Twain and P. G. Wodehouse. Significantly, in 'Lear, Tolstoy and the Fool' (1947), Orwell celebrates Shakespeare's exuberance, his vitality and love of life, bawdy jokes and riddles – comparing all that with Tolstoy's dull puritanism.

Introduction

How useful is the notion of the 'court jester' to an understanding of contemporary journalistic humour? During the Middle Ages, one of the most important roles at courts throughout Europe (and in India, Persia and China) was occupied by the jester. Often known as 'licensed fools' their crucial function was to mock their employer. Queen Elizabeth the First (who ruled between 1558 and 1603) was said to have even rebuked one of her fools for not being severe enough in his mockery of her. Fools, clowns and jesters all appear in Shakespeare's plays: Feste, the jester in *Twelfth Night*, is even described as 'wise enough to play the fool' (Otto 2001). As Tim Crook, Professor in Media and Communication, at Goldsmiths, University of London, argues: 'The mocking journalism of humour can be traced back, perhaps, to the role of the clown in the medieval King and Queen's court – dramatised so effectively in the Shakespeare canon and during the Renaissance age. And it was to be famously theorised and ritualised by Baldasare Castiglione in his *Book of the Courtier* (of 1528) which itself was satirised in England.'

All this tells us a lot about the importance of humour and mockery – not only in Britain but in all societies. Elites know they will always be mocked and attacked – but clever are those elites who control the mockery. The court jester system did just that. Today, intriguingly, a modern version of the court jester system operates, in both the political and cultural spheres, and while there is no formal licensing, a subtler – and hence more powerful – unwritten licensing system helps define the limits of acceptable debate in many contemporary societies (see Keeble 2014). Orwell certainly never aspired to be a member of any 'elite court' – and this, in part, helps explain the vitality and authenticity of his satires – and the richness of his journalism.

Next, Mathilde Roza examines the distinctive wit associated with the *New Yorker*, founded by Harold Ross in 1925 and still regarded as one of the most influential forces in the history of American humour. Roza argues that the humorous, often sardonic mood of cleverness that gave the magazine its special identity strongly relied on an aura of 'sophistication', described by Yagoda as 'knowing, a trifle world-weary, prone to self-consciousness and irony, scornful of conventional wisdom or morality, resistant to enthusiasm or wholehearted commitment of any kind, and incapable of being shocked' (2000: 57).

Miki Tanikawa keeps our attention focused on the US in exploring a range of literary devices journalists there use to introduce humour into their opening paragraph/s (known as leads in the US, intros in the UK). In a detailed content analysis of the *International Herald Tribune* (now the *International New York Times*), which draws much of its editorial content from *The New York Times*, he then aims to identify in quantitative data the range of soft, featury intros and the percentages of humorous intros. He argues that much of this 'featurisation' of the news intro is part of 'an inevitable push to make journalism more engaging, readable and fun for the audience as traditional news outlets battle to keep their brand of journalism alive and competitive'.

After his mother, the celebrated American writer and film maker, Susan Sontag (1933-2004), died, David Rieff – an acclaimed investigative journalist, author and literary editor – reflected on the final months of her life in a memoir, *Swimming in a Sea of Death: A Son's Memoir* (2008). Here, Carolyn Rickett draws attention to a range of dissenting critiques in newspapers and online publications that refused to be constrained by either Rieff's literary lineage or the pathos of his prose. Instead, these selected reviews, according to Rickett, 'employed unanticipated humour and wit to appraise and question the motivation and merit of his memoir'. Drawing on Billig's notion that 'humour and seriousness remain inextricably linked' (2005: 243) and Eakin's ideas relating to narratives and the construction of identity, Rickett argues that her selected reviewers 'are able to hold in creative tension the seeming polar opposites of the memoir's memorialising and grim content with their own honed and reflexive journalistic wit'.

Finally in this section, Sarah Niblock brings us up-to-date with a detailed exploration of the idiosyncratic and witty interventions in journalism by the maverick UK celebrity, broadcaster, film star and 'revolutionary' Russell Brand. According to Niblock, Brand resides on the margins of class and gender, offering himself as a fascinating point of contemplation. 'His self-referential, soul-bearing humour in which he describes his exploits in excruciating detail beckons identification with him. His rock star looks and disarmingly camp manner have attracted legions of female fans and he even recounts his womanising with unflinching, self-deprecating honesty.' She concludes:

> Brand's engaging, immersive style highlights to journalists that their industry's relationship with its audiences has changed, even if their professional notions of what it is have not. He challenges journalists – if they are to transmit journalism's relevance to younger audiences – to revisit the standards and assumptions of their professional practice. Perhaps instead of attacking him, they might start to think about what he is saying.

The witty ways of literary journalists
Garry Whannel opens our section on the humour of literary journalists, exploring the wit of Hunter S. Thompson, the lonely high-priest of gonzo, which emerged out of the New Journalism movement in the United States in the 1950s and 1960s (see Wolfe and Johnson 1973).

Thompson's style included raw field notes, documents, conversations, editors' notes, and author interviews to augment more honed prose. Gonzo placed the writer at the centre and, according to Nick Nuttall, required 'fierce subjectivity' (2007: 136). Indeed, American novelist Tom Wolfe called Hunter S. Thompson the greatest comic writer of the 20th century (McKeen 2008: 360). Whannel concentrates on his 'most elaborate and successful work of journalism', the day-by-day coverage of the 1972 presidential election campaign, which appeared first as a series of features in the music journal *Rolling Stone*, and subsequently in book form as *Fear and Loathing on the Campaign Trail '72*. According to Whannel:

'Gonzo cannot exist without humour. This is more than just the voice of the prankster, the parodist, the joke-teller or the caricaturist at work. It has to do with comic vision.' He concludes:

> Thompson's writing was always situated between fact and fiction, actuality and fantasy, journalism and polemic. In his early writing the caustic wit had yet to find a consistent voice. In the later work, the focus became more diffuse and only on occasion could it hit its targets with forensic accuracy. ... He utilised a savage wit to smash through the conventions of politeness and respect that characterised political journalism, reminding his readers of the venal and corrupt motives of the power-seekers.

Next Novia Pagone examines the ways in which humour – and, of course, talent – gave women writers entrance to the mainstream editorial pages in Spain, beginning in the mid-1970s. Moreover, Pagone shows how, through essays, columns and interviews on topics as diverse as immigrant labour, abuses in prisons, dating services, and elections, humour helped establish and expand the presence of female perspectives in the public sphere. In particular, Pagone focuses on three women journalists – Maruja Torres, Rosa Montero, and Empar Moliner – whose work 'used irony and satire as key ingredients in making their sociocultural and political critiques effective and accessible'. She ends on an optimistic note, arguing that 'the rich tradition that began in the 1970s with humour magazines such as *Hermano Lobo* and *Por Favor*, and continued with increased freedom in mainstream publications, has taken root and will continue to be a valuable source of social and political criticism in the future'.

Ave Ungro's chapter focuses on a strikingly original theme: namely humour in Mexican literary journalism as it relates to the illicit drug trade. In particular, Ungro analyses the humorous discursive expressions in contemporary Mexican *crónicas*, a type of human interest story, and the ways in which humour has helped Mexican *cronistas* – the authors of the *crónicas* – explore the complex patterns of Mexican power structures. She concludes that in the *crónicas* we often see 'a harsh critique of economic gain at the expense of human integrity, and frank judgement of the controversial attitude towards the illicit drug trade as a form of entertainment. *Cronistas* can find or use humour in a variety of topics; there are no thematic boundaries to the expression of humour'.

The politics of being funny

Millôr Fernandes (1923-2012) was a journalist, cartoonist, dramatist, translator and visual artist whose influence extended throughout Brazil's cultural scene. Millôr – as he was commonly known – is the subject of Nicolás Llano Linares's chapter. Millôr's journalistic work during the military dictatorship (1964-1985) is examined, namely on *Pif-Paf* magazine (May-August 1964), an unconventional, independent enterprise that used humour to critically dissect the country's political system, and later on *O Pasquim* (1969-1991), an alternative weekly magazine often considered the main vehicle for independent, countercultural and alternative voices, at a time when censorship and political persecution were common.

Much of Millôr's work was strictly focused on Brazil's changing political context. Linares argues that the array of themes and genres he explored made him a truly universal writer. 'He saw humour not as a genre, but as a tool, a resource, an apolitical stand on life in general.' In the end, Millôr Fernandes was not the best humorist in the country, but only 'the funniest person of the funniest family of the funniest city of the most mishandled country in the world'.

The international spread of the chapters continues as Rhiannon McGlade introduces readers to the satirical press in Catalonia, charting its rise to prominence from the nineteenth century until the end of the Spanish civil war (1936-1939), focusing on two publications of the time: *L'Esquella de la Torratxa* (1872-1939) and *Papitu* (1908-1937). She concludes:

> The satire directed at the institutions most associated with the right – the Church and the Nationalist army – was based on underlining the Church's lack of ethics and the incompetence of the Rebels, as opposed to the Republican side, who were typically depicted as strong, righteous defenders of liberty. These themes remained fairly constant in the satirical press throughout the war and demonstrate how humour can be used to highlight the unsatisfactory behaviour of the out-group in order to amplify the superiority of the in-group.

Josep Lluís Gómez-Mompart, Dolors Palau-Sampio, José Luis Valhondo-Crego and María Iranzo-Cabrera keep our focus on Spain, this time on the period between General Franco's death in 1975 until the formation of the Socialist government in 1982. In particular, they consider the work of journalists on the progressive liberal *Hermano Lobo* (1972-1976), the anarchist-popular *El Papus* (1973-1987), the communist libertarian *Por Favor* (1974-1978), and the moderate left *El Jueves* (since 1977). They show how these journals threw an ironical and satirical spotlight on the political and economic power-holders and managers rather than the politics of the state apparatus.

> To avoid fines, impounding, and suspensions, threats which remained enshrined in the Franco regime's Press Law until 1977, and also as a result of certain routines acquired by journalists who feared reprisals from the Head of State and the Army, the self-controlled, trade-off style of humour was aimed at a public that knew how to read between the lines.

Finally, the spotlight falls on Manila, capital of the Philippines. Here Amy Forbes explores in detail the ways in which print and television journalist Ninez Cacho-Olivares used humour, fairy tales and fables in her columns in *Bulletin Today* to outwit the censors during the dictatorship of Ferdinand Marcos (1965-1986). Forbes argues that Olivares's most successful pieces were those where she laments her own inadequacies, in understanding both herself and the goings-on in government and society. She portrays herself as confused and in need of her friendly psychiatrist. Olivares, herself now a newspaper publisher, ends an interview with Forbes in a defiant mood: 'I'm very comfortable with presidents who hate me. I have been very consistent in being an adversary. I always have an adversarial stance. It's the role of the press. I don't praise if they're doing their jobs right. I will always be contrarian. Someone's gotta do it.'

Note
[1] There is a brief section on humour in the *Encyclopedia of American Journalism*, edited by Stephen L. Vaughn, New York and Abingdon, Oxon: Routledge pp 215-216

References

Bak, John S. and Reynolds, Bill (2011) *Literary Journalism across the Globe: Journalistic Traditions and Transnational Influences*, Amherst and Boston: University of Massachusetts Press

Crick, Bernard (2007) *Nineteen Eighty-Four*: Context and Controversy, Rodden, John (ed.) *The Cambridge Companion to George Orwell*, Cambridge: Cambridge University Press pp 146-159

Crook, Tim (2015) Email correspondence with author, July 2015

Frost, Chris (2015) Email correspondence with the author, July 2015

Harcup, Tony (2014) *A Dictionary of Journalism*, Oxford, Oxford University Press

Harcup, Tony (2015) Email correspondence with author, July 2015

Hartsock, John C. (2000) *A History of American Literary Journalism: The Emergence of a Modern Narrative Form*, Amherst: University of Massachusetts Press

Keeble, Richard Lance (2014) Rajiv Chandrasekaran's *Imperial Life in the Emerald City*: Beyond the court jester? Keeble, Richard Lance and Tulloch, John (eds) *Global Literary Journalism: Exploring the Journalistic Imagination, Vol. 2*, New York: Peter Lang pp 139-151

Keeble, Richard Lance and Tulloch, John (2012) *Global Literary Journalism: Exploring the Journalistic Imagination, Volume 1*, New York: Peter Lang

Keeble, Richard Lance and Tulloch, John (2014) *Global Literary Journalism: Exploring the Journalistic Imagination, Volume 2*, New York: Peter Lang

Keeble, Richard and Wheeler, Sharon (2007) *The Journalistic Imagination: Literary Journalists from Defoe to Capote and Carter*, London: Routledge

Leiren-Young, Mark (2015) Email correspondence with the author, July 2015

McKeen, William (2008) *Outlaw Journalist: The Life and Times of Hunter S. Thompson*, London: Aurum

Nuttall, Nick (2007) Cold-blooded journalism: Truman Capote and the non-fiction novel, Keeble, Richard and Wheeler, Sharon (eds) *The Journalistic Imagination: Literary Journalists from Defoe to Capote and Carter*, London: Routledge pp 130-144

Orwell, George (1962 [1938]) *Homage to Catalonia*, Harmondsworth, Middlesex: Penguin

Orwell, George (1962 [1941]) The art of Donald McGill, *Decline of the English Murder and Other Essays*, Harmondsworth: Penguin pp 142-154

Otto, Beatrice (2001) *Fools are Everywhere*, Chicago: University of Chicago Press

Taylor, D. J. (2003) *Orwell: The Life*, London: Chatto & Windus

Yagoda, Ben (2000) *About Town: The New Yorker and the World it Made*, New York: Scribner

Section 1: Humour in Journalism, Yesterday and Today

'There is Always Room for One More Custard Pie': Orwell's Humour

Richard Lance Keeble

Introduction: Failure but also fun

George Orwell was a very complex character full (like most of us) of contradictions. Critics of his life and works have often associated him with failure, pessimism, guilt and the terror of torture. The very word 'Orwellian' has come to be associated, in part, with the gloom, authoritarianism and oppressiveness of the Big Brother society as described in his celebrated dystopian novel *Nineteen Eighty-Four* (1949), where the state invades the most private aspects of the individual's life.

According to Richard Rees, Orwell sought refuge in 'failure, failure, failure' (cited in Davison 2011: x). And significantly, of his schooldays at St Cyprian's, Eastbourne (1911-1916), which he revisited later in life in the ironically titled essay 'Such, such were the joys' (2001 [1960]), he wrote: 'Failure, failure, failure – failure before me, failure ahead of me – that was by far the deepest conviction that I carried away' (ibid: 400). His novels certainly tend to end rather gloomily. As Alok Rai comments in his significantly titled text *Orwell and the Politics of Despair* (1998: 148): 'It is, of course, remarkable that every single one of Orwell's novels is about failed rebellions, secessions.' Indeed, Flory, in *Burmese Days* (1934), ends up disgraced and committing suicide. Dorothy, the anti-heroine of *A Clergyman's Daughter* (1935), escapes from her 'prison' to a new dawn only to find herself back in the soul-destroying routine from which she thought she had freed herself. George Bowling, in *Coming up for Air* (1939), ends his trip down memory lane finding the pond where he used to fish built over – and the site of a rubbish dump. *Nineteen Eighty-Four* ends with the terrible rat torture scene and with Winston Smith meekly submitting to his torturer, O'Brien, and these grim words: 'He loved Big Brother.'

Géraldine Muhlmann even highlights the way in which *Down and Out in Paris and London* (1933) ends in the failure of his remarkable exercise in participant observation: 'I should like to know people like Mario and Paddy and Bill the moocher, not from casual encounters, but intimately; I should like to understand what really goes on in the souls of the *plongeurs* and tramps and Embankment sleepers. At present I do not feel that I have seen more than the fringe of poverty' (2008: 201). D. J. Taylor, in his award-winning biography, has a whole chapter devoted to 'Orwell's failure' (2003: 318-321) which begins: 'Orwell was obsessed by the idea of failure. Life, he once wrote, was on balance a succession of defeats, and only the very young or the very foolish believed otherwise.'

This chapter will examine the other side of Orwell. It will seek to explore his character as revealed in his writings and described by his biographers – and identify the lighter aspects of his personality. It will also look at his profound fascination with wit as a subject to explore – and the humorous elements in his writings.

The lighter side of Orwell's personality

A number of Orwell's biographers have tended to downplay his humorous side. Christopher Hitchens (2002: 127) says of Orwell's first published novel *Burmese Days*: 'As is customary with Orwell, there are very few jokes and they are extremely dry.' Lucas (2003: 76) has five entries on his pessimism and talks of him being in 1945 'lost in his pessimism'. Indeed, Lucas is rather dismissive about the writer's sense of irony, commenting: 'Orwell had a sense of irony, even if it was no more than naming his dog Marx.' D. J. Taylor (2003: 461), under 'characteristics', highlights his love of animals, sense of failure, love of nature, paranoia, self-pity and unworldliness – but there is no mention of humour. Bowker (2003: 489) lists his misogyny and sadism – but likewise ignores his humour.

Other commentators, however, have seen a different Orwell. In his 'Introduction' to *George Orwell: A Life in Letters*, Peter Davison (2011: xiv) recalls how David Astor, Orwell's great friend and editor of the *Observer*, told him how he would telephone Orwell when he felt depressed and ask to meet him in a local pub because he knew Orwell would make him laugh and cheer him up. Myers (2000: 34) talks of Orwell having a 'sophisticated sense of humour' and that he 'relished the absurd'. At Eton:

> One of his star turns was to go around inquiring about the religions of new boys and naming a series of extinct creeds. 'Are you Cyrenaic, Sceptic, Epicurean, Cynic, Neoplatonist, Confucian or Zoroastrian?' he would ask a bewildered youngster. 'I'm a Christian.' 'Oh,' said Eric, 'we haven't had that before.'

Jeffery Myers (ibid: 267) also shows how Orwell ('the old colonial policeman'), in a review of *The Hamlet* in 1940, wittily puts down the American novelist William Faulkner by describing characters as if they were a primitive tribe in a remote corner of the earth: '…people with supremely hideous names – names like Flem Snopes and Eck Snopes – sit about on the steps of village stores, chewing tobacco, swindling one another in small business deals, and from time to time committing a rape or a murder.'

Bernard Crick throughout his biography is deeply sensitive towards Orwell's lighter side. For instance, he reports (1980: 222) one of the boys at the Hawthorns High School for Boys, in Hayes, Middlesex, where Orwell taught in the early 1930s, remembering his 'inward laughter'. While fighting with the Trotskyist POUM militia against General Franco's fascists in Spain 1936-1937, his friendship with Georges Kopp grew 'because they had a similar sardonic humour' which 'helped to pass the time away' (ibid: 322). Later (ibid: 359), a fellow patient at Preston Hall sanatorium, Aylesford, Kent, in 1938 is quoted remembering Orwell in 'fits of laughter. Catching my eye, he beckoned me over, having been amused by two large caterpillars performing antics on the long stems of grass'. Crick adds: 'He appears like some Buddhist monk laughing at the aptness of the small things of creation.'

And Malcolm Muggeridge (ibid: 420) remembers speaking to Orwell about his time at the BBC 1941-1943 – with authors reading their 'gems of Western culture' with a view to enthusing folk in India and South-East Asia for the Allied cause. 'When I delicately suggested that this may well have failed to hit its target, the absurdity of the enterprise struck him anew and he began to chuckle, deep in his throat, very characteristic of him and very endearing.' In 1945 (ibid: 505), Orwell's friend Celia Kirwan enjoyed reading 'Old George's Almanac' in the Christmas number of *Tribune* as an example of his comic self-mockery. The article predicts a whole series of appalling disasters for 1946: 'Gazing into my crystal, I see trouble in China, Greece, Palestine, Iraq, Egypt, Abyssinia, Argentine and a few dozen other places. I see civil wars, bomb outrages, public executions, famines, epidemics and religious revivals. An exhaustive search for something cheerful reveals that there will be a slight improvement in the regimes of Spain and Portugal and that things will not go too badly in a few countries too small or remote to be worth conquering.' But he ends sardonically: '1946 will still be appreciably better than the last six years' (Anderson 2006: 271).

Not surprisingly, then, Orwell's diaries are full of witty observations, humorous anecdotes and high spirits. While down-and-out with the hop-pickers in Kent in September 1931, he records with clear delight the 'uproarious scenes' on Saturdays 'for the people who had money used to get well drunk and it needed the police to get them out of the pub. I have no doubt the residents thought us a nasty vulgar lot, but I could not help feeling that it was rather good for a dull village to have this invasion of cockneys once a year' (Orwell 2009: 17).

In March 1936, while researching the condition of the northern English working class for his book *The Road to Wigan Pier* (1937), Orwell stayed with the Grey family at 4 Agnes Terrace, Barnsley. He records 'Mr G.' talking about his war experiences, especially the malingering he witnessed when he was invalided with an injury to his leg. One man feigned insanity and got away with it: 'For days he was going around with a bent pin on a bit of string, pretending to be catching fish. Finally he was discharged and on parting with G. he held up his discharge papers and said: "This is what I was fishing for'" (ibid: 58).

The humour in *Homage*

Homage to Catalonia (1962 [1938]) is celebrated as a vivid, deeply personal account of his time on the frontlines in the Spanish civil war of 1936-1937 (though it actually sold only 700 copies during his lifetime) (see Hunter 1984). Orwell wrote the book in a state of 'white hot anger' during the second half of 1937, and this helps account partly for the extraordinary freedom of his writing, its flair, outspokenness, its creative, imaginative, literary richness – and its use of an eclectic range of literary techniques (see Keeble and Tulloch 2012 and 2014). It is reportage – but it also amounts to art. As Orwell commented in 'Why I write' (1970 [1946]): 'What I have most wanted to do throughout the past ten years is to make political writing into an art.' Indeed, drawing on the work of Max Saunders (2010), Nick Hubble (2012: 36) argues that *Homage* amounts to a 'prime example' of the genre of autobiografiction, cleverly blending two well-established forms – autobiography and fiction. Orwell actually had rather a low opinion of journalism – considering it 'mere pamphleteering' – and a horror of the 'subworld of freelance hackery' (Keeble 2007a: 6). Yet, as Peter Davison stresses in the 'Introduction' to the collection of Orwell's journalism (2014: 2): 'Although Orwell continued to the end of his days to strive for success as a novelist, three of his nine "books" are the product of his journalism in a form in which he excelled: documentary reportage: *Down and Out in Paris and London*, *The Road to Wigan Pier* – and *Homage to Catalonia*.'

One of *Homage*'s most striking aspects is the range of literary genres and tones Orwell incorporates into the text. For instance, there are profiles (of individuals, cities, groups), sections of very direct, personal, emotional writing (conveying an earnestness to describe authentic/real experience); elements of background description, generalising comment and personal commentary, together with eye-witness reportage informed by a social political awareness. In addition, there is a journalistic emphasis on the extraordinary and the contradictory; confessional writing; a practical, down-to-earth awareness/sensibility; press content analysis/critique, and political analysis (however reluctant). Amidst all this flowering of the journalistic imagination, it's easy to marginalise the important role humour plays in the book.

Throughout the reportage is infused with a droll, self-deprecating wit: military cynicism mixed with military know-how. Of his time on the frontline fighting for the Trotskyite POUM militia against Franco's forces, he wrote: 'It is curious, but I dreaded the cold much more than I dreaded the enemy' (op cit: 21). On the Russian gun he wrote: 'Its great shells whistled over so slowly that you felt certain you could run beside them and keep up with them' (ibid: 83). Of the fat Russian agent, he says: 'I watched him with some interest for it was the first time that I had seen a person whose profession was telling lies – unless one counts journalists' (ibid: 135). And notice his brilliantly down-beat, anti-heroic description of being shot through the neck on 20 May 1937, a model of journalistic clarity and conciseness drawn from personal experience:

> The whole experience of being hit by a bullet is very interesting and I think it is worth describing in detail. ... Roughly speaking it was the sensation of being at the centre of an explosion. ... Not being in pain I felt a vague satisfaction. This ought to please my wife, I thought, she had always wanted me wounded which would save me from being killed when the great battle came (ibid: 177).

He assumes he is about to die and continues: 'It is very interesting to know what your thoughts would be at such a time. My first thought, conventionally enough, was for my wife. My second was a violent resentment at having to leave this world which, when all is said and done, suits me so well' (ibid: 178). He adds: 'No one I met at this time ... failed to assure me that a man who is hit through the neck and survives is the luckiest creature alive. I could not help thinking that it would be even luckier not to be hit at all' (ibid). He describes a cathedral as 'one of the most hideous buildings in the world'. 'I think the anarchists showed bad faith in not blowing it up when they had the chance' (ibid: 214).

Chapter 11 includes a detailed account of the fighting in Barcelona in May 1937 (after the government ordered the anarchists to surrender their arms), which he viewed from a roof overlooking the main avenue, the Ramblas – and the distorted coverage of the events in the Spanish and British press. But notice his droll, dead-pan debunking of the lofty claims of history:

> When you are taking part in events like these you are, I suppose, in a small way, making history and you ought by rights to feel like a historical character. But you never do because at such times the physical details always outweigh everything else. Throughout the fighting I never made the correct 'analysis' of the situation that was so glibly made by journalists hundreds of miles away. What I was chiefly thinking about was not the rights and wrongs of this miserable internecine scrap but simply the discomfort and boredom of sitting day and night on that intolerable roof and the hunger which was growing worse and worse. ... If this was history it did not feel like it... (ibid: 134).

Amidst all the horror of trench warfare (when it flares up), Orwell also manages to inject some humour into his narrative. For instance, Orwell is involved in a rare attack on the Fascist lines and sees 'a shadowy figure in the half-light' (ibid: 90). He continues:

> I gripped my rifle by the mall of the butt and lunged at the man's back. He was just out of my reach. Another lunge: still out of reach. And for a little distance we proceeded like this, he rushing up to the trench and I after him on the ground above, prodding at his shoulder-blades and never quite

getting there – a comic memory for me to look back upon, though I suppose it seemed less comic to him (ibid).

Pleasure of reading 'As I Please' columns

I personally cannot read the eighty wonderful 'As I Please' columns Orwell contributed to *Tribune*, the leftist journal, between 1943 and 1947 without constantly smiling at his wit and high spirits. Through the columns Orwell was, in effect, defining a new kind of radical politics:

> It involved reducing the power of the press barons, facing up to racial intolerance, defending civil liberties. Yet it also incorporated an awareness of the power of language and propaganda, a celebration of the joys of nature and an acknowledgement of the cultural power of Christianity. Above all, it recognized the extraordinary richness of the individual's experience … (Keeble 2007b: 113).

Humour and high spirits were the constant ingredients of the columns. For instance, on 24 December 1943, he critiqued 'the pessimists': there was Petain (French 'chief of state' in the Vichy regime, 1940-1944) preaching 'the discipline of defeat'; Sorel (the French philosopher, supporter of the far-right) denouncing liberalism; Berdyaev (the Russian theologian) 'shaking his head over the Russian revolution'; Beachcomber (the columnist) 'delivering side-kicks at Beveridge in the *Express*'. Above all, he denounced 'their refusal to believe that human society can be fundamentally improved' (Anderson 2006: 73). His tone was constantly shifting – from ironic self-effacement to de-mystification and debunking. In his 7 January 1944 column (ibid: 80), he mocked the ruling classes in this way:

> Looking through the photographs in the New Years Honours List I am struck (as usual) by the quite exceptional ugliness and vulgarity of the faces displayed there. It seems to be almost the rule that the kind of person who earns the right to call himself Lord Percy de Falcontowers should look at best like an overfed publican and at worst a tax-collector with a duodenal ulcer … What I like best is the careful grading by which honours are always dished out in direct proportion to the amount of mischief done – baronies for Big Business, baronetcies for fashionable surgeons, knighthoods for tame professors.

On 4 February 1944, in typical idiosyncratic style, he chose to link a comment on trouser ends (of all things) to the war effort in this highly original way (Anderson op cit: 94):

> Announcing that the Board of Trade is about to remove the ban on turn-up trouser ends, a tailor's advertisement hails this as 'a first instalment of the freedom for which we are fighting'. If we are really fighting for turned up trouser ends I should be inclined to be pro-Axis. Turn-ups have no function except to collect dust and no virtue except that when you clean them out you occasionally find a sixpence there … I would like to see

clothes rationing continue until the moths have devoured the last dinner jacket and even the undertakers have shed their top hats. I would not mind seeing the whole nation in dyed battledress for five years if by that means one of the main breeding points of snobbery and envy could be eliminated.

Humour amidst dystopian gloom in *Nineteen Eighty-Four*

Ironic and satiric humour runs all through Orwell's gloomy dystopian masterpiece, *Nineteen Eighty-Four* (1949). Bernard Crick, in one of the most perceptive analyses of the novel, talks of it as being inspired by 'satiric rage' (2007: 147). He identifies seven broad satiric themes:

- The division of the world at the Tehran conference in 1943 by Stalin, Roosevelt and Churchill.

- The mass media and proletarisation (now termed 'dumbing down').

- Power-hunger and totalitarianism – particularly in the depiction of the torturer O'Brien who is shown driven mad by the hunger for power.

- The corruption of language in the drive towards Newspeak.

- The destruction of any objective history and truth by the Ministry of Truth.

- The view (well-known at Orwell's time) of James Burnham (1941) that capitalism and communism will converge through managerialism.

Crick argues convincingly (ibid: 148-149) that the novel is 'plainly a satire on hierarchical societies in general'. 'Orwell's satire is so consistent that the dictator is actually called "Big Brother". "Big Brother is watching you," but not watching over you as a brother should.' Moreover, Crick suggests that a positive ending can be seen to the otherwise darkly pessimistic text if the end is considered not with the anti-hero Winston Smith loving Big Brother but at the conclusion of the appendix titled 'The Principles of Newspeak'. Here we are told that translations into Newspeak of writers such as Shakespeare, Milton, Swift, Byron and Dickens were going slowly so the 'final adoption of Newspeak had been fixed for as late a date as 2010'. Crick concludes (ibid: 158): 'If we read *Nineteen Eighty-Four* as Swiftian satire, this is as good to say "this year, next year, sometimes, never". Colloquial language, the common people and common sense will survive the most resolute attempts at total control.'

There is also satiric humour in Orwell's decision to give the room where Winston is tortured the number 101 – after his office at 55 Portland Place, London where he worked for the BBC's Eastern Service from 1941-1942 (Myers 2000: 214). Bowker (2003) also reflects on the fact that the name of O'Brien happened to be the codename of Hugh O'Donnell, the KGB handler of David Crook who was keeping a close eye on Orwell in Spain (Keeble 2012: 154). He concludes that Orwell was oblivious to this and so 'the fact that the character in *Nineteen Eighty-Four* who first wins the confidence of Winston Smith and then betrays him is given the name O'Brien must be one of the strangest coincidences in literature' (ibid: 219). But Orwell had close connections with the spooks and probably went to the continent in 1945 as part of some kind of intelligence mission for David Astor (Keeble 2012). So he may well have found out this information about O'Donnell through his contacts. If so – what a wonderful satiric jibe!

Sexy, seaside postcards, Sancho Panza and the subversive role of humour
Moreover, humour was a constant subject in Orwell's writings. Orwell virtually invented the discipline of Cultural Studies with his commentaries on so many of the manifestations of popular culture (usually considered too trivial and unworthy of attention by the intellectual and cultural elite) which fascinated him – crime novels, boys' weeklies, women's magazines, cups of tea, Woolworth's roses, common lodging houses and handwriting. In one of his most celebrated essays – published in Cyril Connolly's *Horizon* in September 1941 – he examined the seaside postcards of Donald McGill 'with their endless succession of fat women in tight bathing-dresses and their crude drawing and unbearable colours' (Orwell 1965 [1941]: 142).[1] As Peter Marks observes (2011: 122):

> Orwell treats the postcards seriously, as valuable sociological evidence of ideas and cultural forces at work in society. The postcards reflect and reinforce certain stereotypes and conventions (marriage only benefits the woman; all drunken men have optical illusions) that individually might be dismissed as crass, but that collectively, especially given how popular they are, suggest unconsciously accepted customs and attitudes embedded in national culture.

The presumption is that highbrow *Horizon* readers will not be acquainted with the postcards, so he begins by providing an explanatory overview: 'They are a *genre* of their own, specializing in very "low" humour, the mother-in-law, baby's nappy, policemen's-boot type of joke and distinguishable from all the other kinds by having no artistic pretensions' (ibid: 142, italics in the original). The tension in the text emerges from Orwell's ambivalent attitude to the postcards: his intellectual side is fascinated by them, his puritan side is appalled. He writes: 'Your first impression is of overpowering vulgarity. This is quite apart from the ever-present obscenity, and apart also from the hideousness of the colours. They have an utter lowness of mental atmosphere which comes out not only in the nature of the jokes but, even more, in the grotesque, staring blatant quality of the drawings' (ibid: 143). Just as physically Orwell adventured into 'low' life with his stint as a hotel *plongeur* in Paris and travels with tramps and hop-pickers (as narrated in *Down and Out in Paris and London*), here he is exploring 'low' culture.

He lists three of their typical 'Max Millerish', music hall-type jokes. For instance: 'I like seeing experienced girls home.' 'But I'm not experienced.' 'You're not home yet!' He then provides a 'rough analysis of their habitual subject-matter'. Theoretical abstraction was never part of Orwell's repertoire; his essays are never buried in endless references which encumber so much of academic writing but they are bursting with original, lively, clearly expressed ideas.[2] So the subjects of sex, home life, drunkenness, WC jokes, inter-working class snobbery and stock figures are covered in some detail. He observes both the visible – and (equally interesting) the invisible: 'Foreigners seldom or never appear. The chief locality joke is the Scotsman, who is almost inexhaustible. The lawyer is always a swindler, the clergyman always a nervous idiot who says the wrong thing' (ibid: 146).

Orwell moves on from the specifics to discuss the broader social and class aspects of the postcards. Their particular brand of humour can only have meaning, he argues, in relation to a 'fairly strict moral code' (ibid: 148). And he is able to reassure his highbrow readers that jokes about nagging wives and tyrannous mothers-in-law 'do at least imply a stable society in which marriage is indissoluble and family loyalty taken for granted' (ibid: 149). Finally, Orwell's brilliant, inventive coda uses the 'vulgar' postcards as a platform on which to pronounce, quite profoundly, on the complexities of the human condition and the social function of jokes. The postcards 'give expression to the Sancho Panza view of life' (ibid: 151).

Speaking directly to his readers (having flattered them with passing references to Bouvard and Pécuchet, Jeeves and Wooster, Bloom and Dedalus, Holmes and Watson) he continues:

> The Don Quixote-Sancho Panza combination ... is simply the ancient dualism of body and soul in fiction form ... Evidently, it corresponds to something enduring in our civilization, not in the sense that either character is to be found in a 'pure' state in real life, but in the sense that the two principles, noble folly and base wisdom, exist side by side in nearly every human being. If you look into your own mind, which are you, Don Quixote or Sancho Panza? Almost certainly you are both. There is one part of you that wishes to be a hero or a saint, but another part of you is a little fat man who seeks very clearly the advantages of staying alive with a white skin. He is your unofficial self, the voice of the belly protesting against the soul (ibid: 151-152).

Orwell's imagined audience is clearly male: here he appears to concede the argument to his feminist critics who highlight his sexism and even misogyny (for instance, see Patai 1984; Campbell 1984) when he talks of 'little fat man'; later on he addresses his reader as being 'unfaithful to your wife' (ibid: 152). But he goes on to conclude, somewhat aphoristically: 'Codes of law and morals, or religious systems never have much room in them for the humorous view of life. Whatever is funny is subversive, every joke is ultimately a custard pie' (ibid). But is Orwell right here? Orwell, in stressing the subversive role of humour, is clearly reveling in being the dissident, the controversialist, the maverick. For Gordon Bowker, such views follow on from his belief that all art is propaganda (Bowker 2003: 321). But not all jokes play this role. For instance, the wit and mockery of the court jester in the Middle Ages essentially served the interests of the court, while today sexist, racist, ageist jokes merely reinforce dominant prejudices.³ But Orwell's conclusion is both profound and witty – in a droll, downbeat sort of way: 'On the whole, human beings want to be good, but not too good, and not quite all the time' (ibid: 154).

'Every joke is a tiny revolution': Orwell on writers' humour

Orwell's fascination with humour was also reflected in his book reviewing and essays on writers such as Charles Dickens, Rudyard Kipling, Jonathan Swift, Mark Twain and P. G. Wodehouse. Significantly, in 'Lear, Tolstoy and the Fool' (1947), Orwell celebrates Shakespeare's exuberance, his vitality and love of life, bawdy jokes and riddles – comparing all that with Tolstoy's dull puritanism. In his celebrated essay on Dickens (1962 [1940]: 137), which combines a detailed study of an essentially literary subject with a critique of contemporary political attitudes (Marks 2011: 94), he returns to his theme of the 'subversive' role of humour, suggesting that Dickens's constant wish to preach a sermon was 'the final secret of his inventiveness':

> For you can only create if you can *care*. Types like Squeers and Micawber could not have been produced by a hack writer looking for something to be funny about. A joke worth laughing at always has an idea behind it, and usually a subversive idea. Dickens is able to go on being funny because he is in revolt against authority, and authority is always there to be laughed at. There is always room for one more custard pie (emphasis in the original).

In his study of Rudyard Kipling (1965 [1942]: 45-62), Orwell is keen to highlight his comic style. He suggests that in his soldier poems, especially Barrack-Room Ballads, there is an 'underlying air of patronage' (ibid: 51). 'Kipling idealizes the army officer, especially the junior officer, and that to an idiotic extent, but the private soldier, though lovable and romantic, has to be comic. He is always made to speak in a sort of stylized Cockney, not very broad but with all the aitches and final "g's" carefully omitted' (ibid).

Orwell is even able to display his polymathic knowledge of (and highly opinionated views on) English humorous writing in his 1,884-word essay 'Funny not vulgar' (first published in the *Leader*, on 28 July 1945). Notice the striking, rhetorical opening and the massive build-up of data:

> The Great Age of English humorous writing – not witty and not satirical, but simply humorous – was the first three quarters of the nineteenth century. Within that period lie Dickens's enormous output of comic writings, Thackeray's brilliant burlesques and short stories, such as 'The Fatal Boots', … Surtees's *Handley Cross*, Lewis Carroll's *Alice in Wonderland*, Douglas Jerrold's *Mrs Caudle's Curtain Lectures*, and a considerable body of humorous verse by R. H. Barham, Thomas Hood, Edward Lear, Arthur Hugh Clough, Charles Stuart Calverley and others. Two other comic masterpieces, F. Anstey's *Vice Versa* and the two Grossmiths' *Diary of a*

Nobody, lie only just outside the period I have named. And, at any rate until 1860 or thereabouts, there was still such a thing as comic draughtsmanship, witness Cruikshank's illustrations to Dickens, Leech's illustrations to Surtees and even Thackeray's illustration of his own work (Orwell 1970 [1945]: 324).

With typical provocation, he next argues that Britain has produced no writing of any value in the twentieth century while comic verse has lost all its vitality (ibid: 324-325). For a laugh, people are more likely to go to a music hall or a Disney film or buy a few Donald McGill postcards than resort to a book or periodical. Orwell is concerned to understand what causes laughter (so drawing his readers into this educational process) but without resorting to any obscure theoretical abstractions. So he returns to his favourite theme of the subversive role of humour:

> A thing is funny when – in some way that is not actually offensive or frightening – it upsets the established order. Every joke is a tiny revolution. If you had to define humour, you might define it as dignity sitting on a tintack. Whatever destroys dignity, and brings down the mighty from their seats, preferably with a bump, is funny. And the bigger the fall, the bigger the joke (ibid: 325).

Today, he suggests, humorists are 'too genteel, too kind hearted and too consciously lowbrow'. 'P. G. Wodehouse's novels or A. P. Herbert's verses seem always to be aimed at prosperous stockbrokers whiling away an odd half hour in the lounge of some suburban golf course. They and all their kind are dominated by an anxiety not to stir up mud, either moral, religious, political or intellectual' (ibid). Yet, significantly, Stefan Collini has taken particular offence at Orwell's constant critique of British intellectuals (as in this essay) and intellectual theorising. He writes (2007: 350):

> Orwell probably did more than any other single writer in the middle of the twentieth century to shape and harden attitudes towards intellectuals in Britain. His iconic status both as the courageous truth-teller and as the champion of the individual in the face of totalitarian tendencies of modern states has meant that his writings have helped shape a semantic field in which freedom, honesty, and plain speech are contrasted with tyranny, ideological fashion and pretension and in which the term 'intellectuals' is strongly associated with the latter of these two poles.

Orwell's interests in politics, humour and the broader social impacts of literature come together in his essay 'In defence of P. G. Wodehouse' (first published in the journal *Windmill*, then being edited by Kay Dick and Reginald Moore, in 1945). The famous comic writer, and creator of Bertie Wooster and Jeeves, had been captured by the Germans while living in Belgium in 1940, and taken to Germany where he had made a series of broadcasts. He was promptly damned as a traitor in the British press, libraries withdrew his books, and the BBC banned his lyrics (Marks 2011: 137). He was then moved to Paris 'under some kind of house arrest' (Bowker 2003: 324). Orwell had been introduced to Wodehouse by Malcolm Muggeridge – who was keeping an eye on him for British intelligence – while in Paris during his stint reporting on the closing months of World War Two for David Astor's *Observer* and *Manchester Evening Post* (Keeble 2001 and 2012).[4] Orwell states his defence of the writer near the opening, suggesting that 'the events of 1941 do not convict Wodehouse of anything other than stupidity' (Orwell 1998 [1945]: 53). Some were arguing that Wodehouse was mocking the British aristocracy. Nonsense, says Orwell:

> On the contrary, a harmless old-fashioned snobbishness is perceptible all through his work. Just as an intelligent Catholic is able to see that the blasphemies of Baudelaire or James Joyce are not seriously damaging to the Catholic faith, so an English reader can see that in creating such characters as Hildebrand Spencer Poyns de Burgh John Hanneyside Coombe-Crombie, 12th Earl of Dreever, Wodehouse is not really attacking the social hierarchy. Indeed, no one who genuinely despised titles would write of them so much. Wodehouse's attitude towards the English social system is the same as his attitude towards the public-school moral code – a mild facetiousness covering an unthinking acceptance (ibid: 57).

As Marks summarises Orwell's argument, Wodehouse essentially remained 'a comedian foolishly playing for laughs in a time of grave danger, a political naïf, a puppet for the cynically manipulating German propaganda machine' (op cit: 138).

Wit and the common toad
One of my favourite pieces of Orwellian journalism, which never fails to amuse me, is his essay 'Some thoughts on the common toad' (Orwell 1980 [1946]: 744-746). It shares many of the characteristics of the numerous 'As I Please' columns he wrote for the leftist journal *Tribune*, where he was literary editor between 1943 and 1947, which featured surprisingly idiosyncratic, 'ordinary' subject matter (Keeble 2007b: 103). These were all deliberately distant in tone and style from the heavy diet of political polemic and policy analysis that filled the rest of the journal's pages (Anderson 2006: 26). For instance, he would expand on a passing comment of a barmaid, deconstruct the advertisements in women's magazines, answer a reader's query or set a brain-teaser. But his 'common toad' column captures Orwell's love of animals, the changing of the seasons and the extraordinarily intense way in which he observed nature. As Meyers comments, he combined 'close observation and unusual facts with tenderness for a repulsive creature' (2000: 225). He starts the column with a gentle, witty dig at Anglo-Catholics, saying that 'after his long fast, the toad has a spiritual look, like a strict Anglo-Catholic towards the end of Lent' (Orwell 1980 [1946]: 744). He continues:

> I mention the spawning of the toads because it is one of the phenomena of spring which most deeply appeals to me, and because the toad, unlike the skylark and the primrose, has never had much of a boost from the poets.[5]

So here is the ever maverick Orwell delighting in speaking out for one of the forgottens of the animal kingdom. From this unlikely source his prose then flows on to a critique of capitalism, no less – and a celebration of life and the pleasure principle! He writes:

> Is it wicked to take a pleasure in spring and other seasonal changes? To put it more precisely, is it politically reprehensible, while we are groaning, or at any rate ought to be groaning, under the shackles of the capitalist system, to point out that life is frequently more worth living because of a blackbird's song, a yellow elm tree in October, or some natural phenomenon which does not cost money and does not have what editors of left-wing newspapers call a class angle (ibid: 745-746).

And he ends on an elegiac note – his prose soaring almost into a form of poetry:

> The atom bombs are piling up in the factories, the police are prowling through the cities, the lies are streaming from the loudspeakers, but the earth is still going round the sun, and neither the dictators nor the bureaucrats, deeply as they disapprove of the process, are able to prevent it (ibid: 746).

Conclusion

At the start of this chapter, I noted how Orwell's novels tended to end rather gloomily. Yet Orwell knew that stories which conclude on a down-note are far more likely to provoke thought than those which end up-beat. Stories with happy endings (as Hollywood knows only too well) so often leave you feeling OK with the world, the *status quo*. Orwell constantly challenged and questioned the *status quo*. And he knew instinctively that society was largely built on narratives of success, finding it difficult to confront and speak about failure. For Orwell failure was an intrinsic, important part of life (see Keeble 2012: 6).

Failure, as Terry Eagleton says, was Orwell's forte (see Davison 2011: ix). But then, as this chapter has argued, so too was fun.

Notes

[1] Donald McGill was to be held in a police cell in Lincoln in May 1954 (for an hour) while awaiting trial over the obscene publication of a stick of rock (appearing in a cartoon like a ginormous penis). He was fined £50, had costs of £25 to pay plus his own higher legal costs. While he had prepared a defence, he pleaded guilty on legal advice. See Kennedy, Maev (2004) Exhibition marks 50 years of holding back the sauce, *Guardian*, 22 May. Available online at http://www.theguardian.com/uk/2004/may/22/arts.artsnews, accessed on 21 February 2015. See also Barrell, Tony (2012) May the sauce be with you, 26 February, *Sunday Times Magazine* pp 52-55

[2] This absence of references and footnotes might be due to the fact that Orwell neither enjoyed nor endured a conventional university education

[3] Today, the role of the 'court jester' is played by mainstream comedians, journals (such as *Private Eye* in the UK) and corporate journalists. See Keeble, Richard Lance (2014) Rajiv Chandrasekaran's *Imperial Life in the Emerald City*: Beyond the court jester? Keeble, Richard Lance and Tulloch, John (eds) *Global Literary Journalism: Exploring the Journalistic Imagination Vol 2*, New York, Peter Lang pp 139-154

[4] Muggeridge later became a close friend of Orwell, attended his funeral – and later became editor of *Punch* (1953-1957), broadcaster and Christian convert. He wrote on the Wodehouse saga (1968: 92): 'The Germans, in their literal way, took his works as a guide to English manners and actually dropped an agent in the Fen country wearing spats. This unaccustomed article of attire led to his speedy apprehension. Had he not been caught, he would, presumably, have gone on to London in search of the Drones Club, and have thought to escape notice in restaurants by throwing bread about in the manner of Bertie'

[5] Orwell had a certain fascination for copulating creatures. In his diary entry for 2 February 1936, he writes: 'For the first time in my life saw rooks copulating. On the ground, not in a tree. The manner of courtship was peculiar. The female stood with her beak open and the male walked round her and it appeared as though he was feeding her' (Orwell 2009: 48). Interestingly, Davison records that Orwell had originally written 'copulating' in *Road to Wigan Pier*: but being considered too explicit it was first changed to 'courting' and finally to 'treading' (ibid: 49)

References

Anderson, Paul (2006) *Orwell in* Tribune: *'As I Please' and Other Writings 1943-7*, London: Politico's

Bowker, Gordon (2003) *George Orwell*, London: Little, Brown

Burnham, James (1941) *The Managerial Revolution: What is Happening in the World*, New York: John Day Co.

Campbell, Beatrix (1984) *Wigan Pier Revisited: Poverty and Politics in the 80s*, London: Virago Press

Collini, Stefan (2007) *Absent Minds: Intellectuals in Britain*, Oxford: Oxford University Press

Crick, Bernard (1980) *George Orwell: A Life*, Harmondsworth, Middlesex: Penguin Books

Crick, Bernard (2007) *Nineteen Eighty-Four*: Context and controversy, Rodden, John (ed.) *The Cambridge Companion to George Orwell*, Cambridge: Cambridge University Press pp 146-159

Davison, Peter (ed.) (2011) *Orwell: A Life in Letters*, London: Penguin

Hitchens, Christopher (2002) *Orwell's Victory*, London: Allen Lane/Penguin Press

Hubble, Nick (2012) Orwell and the English working class: Lessons in autobiografiction for the Twenty-First Century, Keeble, Richard Lance (ed.) *Orwell Today*, Bury St Edmunds: Abramis pp 30-45

Hunter, Lynette (1984) *George Orwell: The Search for a Voice*, Milton Keynes: Open University Press

Keeble, Richard (2001) Orwell as war correspondent: A reassessment, *Journalism Studies*, Vol. 2, No. 3 pp 393-406

Keeble, Richard (2007a) Introduction: On journalism, creativity and the imagination, Keeble, Richard and Wheeler, Sharon (eds) *The Journalistic Imagination: Literary Journalists from Defoe to Capote and Carter*, London: Routledge pp 1-14

Keeble, Richard (2007b) The lasting in the ephemeral: Assessing George Orwell's As I Please columns, Keeble, Richard and Wheeler, Sharon (eds) *The Journalistic Imagination: Literary Journalists from Defoe to Capote and Carter*, London: Routledge pp 100-115

Keeble, Richard Lance (2012) Orwell, *Nineteen Eighty-Four* and the spooks, Keeble, Richard Lance (ed.) *Orwell Today*, Bury St Edmunds: Abramis pp 151-163

Keeble, Richard Lance and Tulloch, John (2012) *Global Literary Journalism: Exploring the Journalistic Imagination Volume 1*, New York: Peter Lang

Keeble, Richard Lance and Tulloch, John (2014) *Global Literary Journalism: Exploring the Journalistic Imagination Volume 2*, New York: Peter Lang

Lucas, Scott (2003) *Orwell*, London: Haus Publishing

Muggeridge, Malcolm (1968) *Tread Softly for you Tread on My Jokes*, London: Fontana

Muhlmann, Géraldine (2008) *A Political History of Journalism*, Cambridge: Polity Press

Rai, Alok (1988) *Orwell and the Politics of Despair*, Cambridge: Cambridge University Press

Myers, Jeffery (2000) *Orwell: Wintry Conscience of a Generation*, New York/London: W. W. Norton and Company Ltd

Orwell, George (1962 [1938]) *Homage to Catalonia*, Harmondsworth, Middlesex: Penguin

Orwell, George (1962 [1940]) Charles Dickens, *Inside the Whale and Other Essays*, Harmondsworth, Middlesex: Penguin Books pp 80-141

Orwell, George (1962 [1941]) The art of Donald McGill, *Decline of the English Murder and Other Essays*, Harmondsworth: Penguin pp 142-154

Orwell, George (1965 [1942]) Rudyard Kipling, *Decline of English Murder and Other Essays*, Harmondsworth: Penguin pp 45-62. First published in *Horizon*, February

Orwell, George (1970 [1945]) Funny not vulgar, Orwell, Sonia and Angus, Ian (eds) *The Collected Essays, Journalism and Letters, Vol. 3: As I Please*, Harmondsworth: Penguin Books pp 324-329

Orwell, George (1998 [1945]) In defence of P. G. Wodehouse, Davison, Peter (ed.) *The Complete Works of George Orwell*, Vol. XVII pp 53-61. First published in *Windmill*, No. 2, July 1945

Orwell, George (1970 [1946]) Why I write, *Collected Essays, Journalism and Letters*, Vol. 1, Harmondsworth, Middlesex: Penguin Books 1970 pp 23-30. First published in *Gangrel*, No. 4

Orwell, George (1947) Lear, Tolstoy and the fool, *Polemic*, No. 7, March. Available online at http://www.orwell.ru/library/essays/lear/english/e_ltf, accessed on 28 August 2014

Orwell, George (2001 [1960]) Such, such were the joys!, *Orwell's England* (texts selected by Peter Davison), London: Penguin Books pp 362-408. First published, posthumously, in 1952 in the *Partisan Review* in the US

Orwell, George (2009) *The Orwell Diaries* (edited by Peter Davison), London: Penguin Books

Orwell, George (2010) *A Life in Letters* (selected by Peter Davison), London: Penguin Books

Orwell, George (2014) *Seeing Things As They Are: Selected Journalism and Other Writings* (selected by Peter Davison), London: Harvill Secker

Patai, Daphne (1984) *The Orwell Mystique: A Study in Male Ideology*, Amherst: University of Massachusetts Press

Rai, Alok (1988) *Orwell and the Politics of Despair*, Cambridge: Cambridge University Press

Saunders, Max (2010) *Self-Impression: Life Writing, Autobiografiction, and the Forms of Modern Literature*, Oxford: Oxford University Press

Taylor, D. J. (2003) *Orwell: The Life*, London: Chatto & Windus

Humour and its Role in the Early Decades of the *New Yorker*

Mathilde Roza

The *New Yorker*, founded in 1925, holds an important position as one of the most influential forces in the history of modern American humour. Even though the magazine offered more and more seriousness in the fields of journalism, verse and short fiction as the years went by, during the first two decades of its existence it was 'universally and unanimously' taken as a humorous weekly (Yagoda 2000: 54). Its 'wit' has become legendary. In both 'art' – the magazine's term for its cartoons, drawings and cover designs – and in writing, Harold Ross's magazine of urban sophistication initiated a standard and spawned a tradition of humorous writing that was undeniably its own and came to be referred to as the '*New Yorker* school' or '*New Yorker* tradition' of humour. Hailed as the 'home office of American humor' (Baker 1993: 107), the magazine's founding has been widely, if too conveniently, hailed as the milestone event which launched modern American humour and forever separated it from 'native' American humour – the vernacular tradition of folk and frontier humorists, the 'crackerbox philosophers', and the humorists of the old Southwest (Hill 1963: 170).

Within this account of *New Yorker* humour, strong emphasis has been placed on what contemporary critics have termed 'Little Man humour', a strand of laughter that specialised in 'tales of neurotic little men driven insane by jumbo women and modern life – especially things technical and commercial' (Lee 2000: 6). Although the humorists mainly responsible for creating this *New Yorker* trademark – Robert Benchley, James Thurber, Sid Perelman and, to a lesser extent, E. B. White – have become justly famous, their work represents only one manifestation of the humorous worldview that the *New Yorker* shared with its audience and by which it defined itself. During the 1930s, the dominance of this comic type was a source of irritation even to the *New Yorker* editors themselves. Thus, in 1937, when *New Yorker* staff member and parodist Wolcott Gibbs was about to hand over his position as fiction editor to Gustave Lobrano, Gibbs drew up a document of several pages in which he advised his successor on what to expect and how to respond (Thurber 1959: 112-117).[1] In addition to such recommendations as 'On the whole we are hostile to puns' (ibid: 116) and 'Try to preserve an author's style if he is an author and has a style' (ibid: 117), Gibbs warned Lobrano to be suspicious of 'such words as "little", "vague", "confused", "faintly", "all mixed up"', adding: 'The point is that the average *New Yorker* writer, unfortunately influenced by Mr Thurber, has come to believe that the ideal piece is about a vague, little man helplessly confused by a menacing and complicated civilization' (ibid: 113).

In fact, comic prose in the *New Yorker* was highly diverse in form, contents and style. As the magazine's current editor David Remnick, celebrating the *New Yorker*'s ninetieth birthday, recently observed: 'Wit ran through every corner of the magazine, from its satirical profiles to its clever criticism' (Remnick 2015). This chapter looks at the various manifestations of humorous *New Yorker* prose in its first two decades. Specifically, it seeks to reveal the significance of the magazine's many comic utterances as the means by which it gave shape and expression to its highly recognisable yet elusive identity and managed to consolidate an ever-growing base of committed readers.

Defining the *New Yorker*'s humour

From the moment the *New Yorker* established itself as a cultural and commercial success, the magazine's character, its special brand of humour and its formula for success have fascinated critics and scholars. So much so, in fact, that critic Stanley Edgar Hyman noted in the early 1940s: 'The *New Yorker* is unique of its kind, and it is this rather terrifying uniqueness that regularly fascinates critics and reviewers, so that no critical season is complete without at least one learned article attempting to define what makes the *New Yorker* tick' (Hyman 1942: 90). The bulk of material on the *New Yorker* has only grown since the magazine's records became available to the public through a gift to the New York Public Library in 1991. Since then, several scholars have researched the records systematically to unravel the magazine's identity through its publishing operations, its networks, decision-making processes and editorial practices.

The archive has given rise to important studies such as Thomas Kunkel's biography of Harold Ross, *Genius in Disguise* (1995) and his edited collection of Ross letters, *Letters from the Editor: The New Yorker's Harold Ross* (2000); Mary F. Corey's study of the *New Yorker* at mid-century, *The World Through a Monocle* (1999); Ben Yagoda's critical and cultural history of the *New Yorker* as institution from 1925 to 1999, *About Town: The New Yorker and the World it Made* (2000); and Judith Yaross Lee's study of the magazine's first five years, *Defining New Yorker Humor* (2000). These scholarly works represent a sharp departure from the earlier anecdotal (and often extremely funny) descriptions of Harold Ross and his magazine which, as one study observes, took 'an impish delight' in making Ross and the *New Yorker* seem like 'a much more arcane and esoteric enterprise than it actually was' (Holmes 1972: 131-132). Here, for instance, is Thurber describing Ross entering the meeting-room before a staff meeting: 'Ross would saunter in, sometimes with the expression of a man who has heard an encouraging word but oftener with the worried brow of a bloodhound that is not only off the scent but is afraid it's losing its sense of smell' (Thurber 1959: 74). Humorist Corey Ford, to take another example, paints an amusing picture of Ross as a highly improbable candidate – an image that was often repeated -- for the position of founding editor of the sophisticated 'smart magazine':

> Ross seldom laughed aloud. If something amused him, his upper body heaved spasmodically a couple of times and his heavy lips parted in a broad silent grin, showing large teeth with a gap in the center. ... He looked like a bucolic bumpkin, his features plain to the point of being homely, his big hands flailing in all directions to bolster his inarticulate speech. Often he would leave a sentence unfinished, and fling both arms aloft in utter futility. ... His language was a curious admixture of roundhouse oaths and bits of antiquated slang ... After a tirade, his mobile face would light with sheepish amusement and he would sigh, 'God, how I pity me' (Ford 1967: 112, 113).

While such accounts provide a memorable impression of the centrally important role that humour played in these professionals' lives, the archival research on the actual processes – personal, cultural and professional – that shaped the *New Yorker* as a cultural phenomenon have now been described in detail and de-mystified.

To a large degree, scholarly work suggests, the magazine's witty commentaries, cartoons, criticisms and responses to New York metropolitan culture provided a mirror to an audience eager to see the many facets of city life – often their own – reflected, recognised and commented on in word and image. In ways that allowed room for laughter, often involving parody, irony or satire, readers of the *New Yorker* were shown ways of seeing themselves, and the other. Crucially, the *New Yorker*'s ascension coincided with the rise of a large and newly affluent urban population which had left provincial America, seeking a new life in New York City, and for whom 'identity was up for grabs' (Corey 1999: 5). The *New Yorker* provided directions to this group, as Corey explains:

> Cut loose from the traditional ties of family and place, separated from farms and shops and face-to-face communications of small-town America, these men and women acquired distinction by the company they kept and the commodities they accumulated (ibid).

To these 'novice metropolitans' (ibid), the *New Yorker*, with its ample attention to class and the corresponding issues of life-style, spending-power and sophistication, provided an indispensable guide. Scholars on middlebrow culture further point to the magazine's importance as one of several 'apparatuses for learning "high culture" that appeared in the US from the 1890s onwards' (Tracy 2010: 40). Capitalising on 'the new and growing obsession with cultural legitimacy', the *New Yorker*, as well as its competitor *Vanity Fair*, performed a pedagogical function in which they mediated 'their authoritative role by taking up the tone of a friend' (ibid: 40-41). The fact that the *New Yorker*'s 'primary method' in creating this aura of friendliness was 'a cutting sense of humor' had the crucial effects of downplaying this pedagogical function and suggesting to readers that they, in fact, 'might already belong to the upper crust' (ibid: 41). An excellent example is Corey Ford's 1925 series on 'Creative Art' in New York, which reviewed urban phenomena such as clothes lines, broken windows, doodles on napkins and scribbles on telephone booths as legitimate means of artistic self-expression. In 'Laundry Art: Study in Wash', for instance, Ford presents 'the remarkable collection of Alfred J. Tuesday' who 'began work without any serious feeling for Art whatsoever', and discusses such items as 'a landscape entitled: "How to Get to Our House, Jim, You Can't Miss It" [which] gives an interesting perspective of Long Island, and part of Quebec, on a clear day with no static' (Ford 1925: 22). The success of Ford's parodies relied on readers' familiarity with both modern experimental art and the debates surrounding it: non-understanding readers were indirectly instructed to brush up on certain matters if they, too, wanted to laugh along.

The same principle applied to the magazine's 'Newsbreaks' – reprints of comical errors or unusual news items from publications across the United States, followed by the *New Yorker*'s response. The 'Newsbreaks' operated on the principle of providing laughter at the expense of others: they 'subtly but surely fed a sense of superiority on the part of the readers, and from the start the *New Yorker*'s appeal to many was a clubby sense of not so much social but verbal privilege: to belong, you had to "get" the jokes' (Yagoda 2000: 49). The 'Newsbreaks', too, often tested readers' cultural knowledge, flattering those who kept abreast of contemporary developments. The one below, from 1933, for instance takes the literary rivalry between Ernest Hemingway and William Faulkner as common knowledge. The piece is responding to a review of Faulkner's work that, curiously, had the author's name all wrong:

> William Faught, according to this critic, shows in his own experience the advantages of a well-developed technique. His work, *As I lay Dieing* [sic], never quite satisfied anyone because it was rather hysterical and lacked technique ... but in his latest work Faught satisfies the reader, because he has achieved a real technique – *Theta Sigma Phi Matrix*. And need take no sass from Ernst Heminpeffer (*New Yorker*, 27 May 1933 p. 45).

In this way, *New Yorker* humour played a key role in fostering and confirming a sense of identity and belonging for a metropolitan audience at a time of social flux. Simultaneously, and in a similarly paradoxical fashion, humour served to downplay the importance of belonging to the elite. Thus, the magazine frequently and self-consciously thumbed its nose at high society, even as it paraded its many attractions in an ever-increasing number of advertisements of luxury goods and comfortable lifestyles.

In fact, the magazine's predilection for (self-)mockery and mild derision was immediately communicated (and then immortalised) through its very first front cover: the *New Yorker* announced its arrival by presenting a top-hatted dandy – famously christened 'Eustace Tilley' by Corey Ford (McGrath 1993: 134) – haughtily scrutinising a butterfly through his monocle. Created by graphic artist Rea Irvin, and reprinted for each anniversary issue, the cover image offered a brilliant evocation of the magazine's outlook and identity: curious but aloof, it would scrutinise its immediate environment with an eye for unexpected detail. Yet all the while, the cover also suggested, the observing party itself would not escape the magazine's ironic gaze. This self-consciousness about status, identity and belonging could likewise be observed in such departments as 'Are You a New Yorker?' and in cartoons. As Yagoda comments (2000: 64): 'A 1928 cartoon by Leonard Dove asked, succinctly and eloquently, the question on everyone's mind. A society lady, relaxing on the beach, turns to a questionable-looking gentleman, wearing a boater and munching a banana, and says, "Excuse me, are you one of us?"'

'Not for the Old Lady in Dubuque': The start of the *New Yorker*

In addition to resonating with the nation's social and demographic shifts, the early *New Yorker* appeared at a time, as humorist Corey Ford described it, when laughter was 'was belly-deep and uninhibited' (1967: 133). Ford continued:

> The early Twenties marked the peak of comic writing in this country, a flowering of satire and parody and sheer nonsense that has never been equalled before or since, a galaxy of our greatest funnymen gathered together at one transcendental moment like a configuration of planets which would not occur again in a lifetime (ibid: 2).

Humorists were numerous, highly active and enjoyed respect as cultural commentators and as producers of much laughter. In her study of 1920s Manhattan, *Terrible Honesty*, Ann Douglas likewise draws attention to the era's thirst for extravagant emotion and drama, referring to the group of sharp-witted professional writers gathered in New York as 'the most theatrical generation in American annals' (1995: 55). Critic Edmund Wilson, too, defined his generational group as lacking in seriousness and dubbed them the 'All-Star Literary Vaudeville', identifying his peers as 'comic monologuists, sentimental songsters and performers of one-act melodramas' (1952: 247). Humour and theatre flowered and bloomed and did so along with New York City itself, which was rapidly growing into its new role as the nation's leading cultural centre. As a result, many 'wits converged, like so many worms, on the Big Apple', as Blair and Hill put it in their classic *America's Humor* (1978: 405).

In an early response to the new forms of humour, Carl van Doren referred to them as 'town wits' who responded to the new and constant need for information and entertainment demanded by metropolitan societies (1923: 308). Their work modernised and urbanised the traditionally 'rural' American forms of vernacular humour. Of these, the highly influential members of the Algonquin Round Table, a relatively small group of professional humorists who worked as journalists, columnists, critics, playwrights and in other literary or cultural professions – and of which Harold Ross was a member – became the most famous. Surrounded by wit, Ross became increasingly convinced of the feasibility of founding a new humorous weekly.

Faced with stiff competition emanating from the booming industry of magazine publishing, Ross was aware of the necessity to create a magazine that would be recognisably distinct from those already in circulation, particularly the two national comic weeklies *Life* and *Judge*, the sophisticated *Smart Set*, and the more recently established *College Humor*, *American Mercury* and *Vanity Fair*. To this end, Ross introduced a number of innovations, the most important of which stemmed from his decision to give his magazine a local rather than a national orientation. This revolutionary move – an idea that his friends at the Algonquin Table, also known as the Vicious Circle, had scoffed at (Ford 1967: 113-114) – established itself firmly in his mind when, during his tenure as co-editor of *Judge* he was forced to reject a funny piece by Corey Ford. Ford, whose many contributions were to be of great importance to the *New Yorker*'s survival in its first years (Lee 2000: 258), described the incident in the typical anecdote-of-Ross-as-the-unpromising-hero style:

> One day I brought in an article about New York's snow-removal problems, and Ross had to turn it down because its appeal was too limited for national circulation. 'That's the trouble with this goddam magazine,' he squawked, striding up and down his office. 'If it went after a local audience it would get local advertising.' He glared at me as though it were my fault. 'Why should a New York restaurant or theater or perfume shop spend money for an ad that would be wasted on the rest of the country? There's enough revenue right here in this city to support a smart magazine weekly.' He carried his argument to the top, but the publishers laughed at him (Ford 1967: 112).

In addition to the enormous benefit of lending thematic coherence to his magazine, a local focus would open the door wide to New York advertisers who were now offered a select group of buyers on a platter – an instance of target marketing uncustomary in the early 1920s (Lee 2000: 35-36). In the fall of 1924, after extensive comparative research, Ross composed a document of about 700 words which he sent out to prospective subscribers and investors. Its now well-known opening paragraph ran as follows:

> The *New Yorker* will be a reflection in word and picture of metropolitan life. It will be human. Its general tenor will be one of gaiety, wit and satire, but it will be more than a jester. It will not be what is commonly called highbrow or radical. It will be what is commonly called sophisticated, in

that it will assume a reasonable degree of enlightenment on the part of its readers. It will hate bunk (cited in Yagoda 2000: 38).

In another famous paragraph, Ross identified his target audience as follows:

The *New Yorker* will not be edited for the old lady in Dubuque. It will not be concerned in what she is thinking about. This is not meant in disrespect, but the *New Yorker* is a magazine avowedly published for a metropolitan audience and thereby will escape an influence which hampers most national publications (ibid).

The prospectus is a centrally important document by which to understand the magazine's goals, its humour and its development. During its formative period, as detailed studies such as the ones by Yagoda and Lee reveal, the magazine came increasingly to approximate the intuitive ideals formulated in this early document. Its importance underscores the perception of Ross as the 'genius in disguise' of Kunkel's monograph (1995), rather than the underdeveloped and 'totally inappropriate figure' from Aspen, Colorado, who, 'weighted down by huge pockets of ignorance, ... had to be coddled and gingerly outmaneuvered by staffers' (Douglas 1993: 132). This negative view of Ross was dominant for several decades although it was sometimes contested. A special *New Yorker* issue of *Studies in American Humor* of the mid-1980s, for example, credited the founding editor with the creation of a tone and mode that constituted 'an undeniable *New Yorker* brand of humor – witty, droll, lively of style, and appropriately urbane. That all the writers and cartoonists seemed to fall under the magazine's spell is a tribute to the ruling passion and editorial guidance of Ross' (Kesterton 1984: 7).

Voices in a crowd

As Kesterton suggested, another striking characteristic of the early *New Yorker* was the degree to which individual personalities were subordinated to that of the magazine. Ross, as Yagoda observes, 'had a newsman's conception of the magazine as somehow transcending the individuals who contributed to it' (2000: 43). As a result, the *New Yorker* listed no contributors' names in its table of contents (it only began to do so in 1969); its editorial departments were anonymous; writers signed their articles at the end rather than announce their identity at the beginning and frequently used pseudonyms or initials only. Consequently, readers had to leaf through the entire magazine, hunting for names, if they wanted to find out who had contributed to a particular issue. When Ross, in 1936, received the suggestion to change the latter practice he responded with typical force of conviction:

I am violently against any such change. I think it would be a foolish mistake, would violently impair the whole personality of the magazine. I don't think there's any argument in favor of it whatsoever. I have noticed lately considerable interest in several such radical proposals. I am against them all. My definite conviction is this: the format of the *New Yorker* is all right; it's been adequately proven all right by several years of signal success. All attempts to 'high power' the magazine ought to be kicked in the teeth (cited in Yagoda 2000: 42-43).

The subordination of the individual contributor to the collective – at its most clearly visible in the use of the editorial 'we' – contributed vastly to the formation of an 'in-group' of *New Yorker* writers and readers. At the same time, paradoxically, the many voices that together constituted the *New Yorker* were noticeably different in tone, subject matter and style and retained an individual and personalised outlook. In fact, as Yagoda and Lee also argue, the magazine featured a vast array of 'talking' voices (Yagoda 2000: 70-71; Lee 2000: 247n.). The emphasis on 'talk' in the *New Yorker*, the impression of the magazine as a chorus of voices, was created in the editorial departments but also by the magazine's inclusion of humorous writing that explicitly leaned on oral phenomena: interior or dramatic monologues, dialogues (often using dialect) and overheard 'snippets of conversation in the crowds' that were highly popular prose features in the *New Yorker*'s pages from the start (Lee 2000: 243-256).

Short pieces, sympathetic in tone, often used dialect. For instance, Arthur Kober featured the dialogue of two workers gossiping about an over-achieving colleague: 'At the next meetin' I'm goin' to make a motion that because he din keep to his pledge dooly recorded in th' minutes, that he don' deserve no present thereby. And you second my motion' (Kober 1929: 26). Zelda Popkin's series 'Reflections of More or Less Silent New Yorkers' introduced to readers the thoughts of a bus conductor or taxi driver as, for instance: 'Just come back from Brooklyn. Now I gotta go to the Bronx. Never hang round 42nd St again. Forty-second Street's no place for pick-ups' (Popkin 1926: 103). And John O'Hara's telephone conversation 'Spring 3100', including the phrase 'Wukkan I do fya?', showed how dialect could cause all kinds of problems of communication (O'Hara 1928). Written in the present tense, and focused on local people and situations, these talking voices gave a sense of immediacy and direct contact to readers and helped foster a community.

Although transplanted to an urban environment, these voices represent not a rupture with, but a continuation of the vernacular mock-oral tradition – with its distinctive tones of voice and attitude, and its emphasis on tall tales, common talk and experience-based anecdotes. Ross's decision to orient his magazine locally rather than nationally thus influenced the way in which the magazine continued the tradition of American humour. As Lee observes: 'The rural tradition of local color humor found new zest in the *New Yorker*'s urban topics, especially in mock-oral prose humor' (Lee 2000: 60). As a result, the *New Yorker* (its metropolitan focus and its urban sophistication notwithstanding), provided a small-town feeling and represented New York as a city that one could encompass, get to know, and feel at home in, whether you were a native or a so-called 'out-of-towner'.

The humorous, often sardonic mood of cleverness that gave the magazine its singular overarching identity, however, was created at the editorial, institutional, level. It was this aura of urban *savoir-faire* and sophistication – created by staff writers, underscored by the advertisements and offered to both sexes – that contained all the *New Yorker* voices, and held them together. Difficult to define, 'sophistication' as it appeared in the *New Yorker* has been succinctly described by Yagoda as 'knowing, a trifle world-weary, prone to self-consciousness and irony, scornful of conventional wisdom or morality, resistant to enthusiasm or wholehearted commitment of any kind, and incapable of being shocked' (2000: 57). This attitude of sophistication, applied to create laughter, propelled the 'Newsbreaks' and a plethora of other *ad hoc* departments such as the 'Overheard Department', 'Raised Eyebrow Department' or 'Answers to Hard Questions Department' that were created by the magazine's staff (especially E. B. White); and, above all, to the magazine's opening department, 'The Talk of the Town.' As a department, 'Talk of the Town' constituted what Ross had referred to in his prospectus as 'a jotting down in the small-town newspaper style of the comings, goings and doings in the village of New York' (cited in Yagoda 2000: 39). It concerned itself with the city's daily events but was distinguished from the newspapers by being 'less "who-what-when-where-why" conscious', as one the magazine's earliest 'Talk' writers, Robert Coates, described it (Coates 1961). Written in an 'informal yet knowledgeable conversational tone' (Roza 2011: 159), the editorial department departed from a generally comic and confidently ironic view of metropolitan life, and frequently displayed either a tone of fond amusement or bemusement at the spectacle of urban life. The examples below aptly illustrate the magazine's ironical style and its treatment of the city as a small-town source of humour:

> In this commercial age, anything free deserves prominent mention. We refer, in this instance, to a free show which has recently been instituted by a dentist on Park Avenue and not far from the Vanderbilt Hotel. He has obligingly leased the ground floor of one of the remodeled houses in that section, and when the steam heat is working, opens the window and permits passers-by to inspect his patients. It is an excellent idea ('Talk of the Town', *New Yorker*, 6 November 1926).

Or, in the same issue:

> Much praise must go to the Anti-Fifth Avenue Association for its notable accomplishments on Madison Square. For many weeks now, the association has succeeded in keeping the Avenue above Twenty-Third Street torn up in an impressive manner. All attempts to get the section paved have so far been defeated, and at the present writing, officials say they have every hope of keeping things as they are until Christmas (ibid.).

The wit of the reviewers

Sophistication also animated several of the magazine's critical departments, which over the years expanded to contain reviews on theatre, art, architecture, the press, the world of fashion, art, music, dance and film. Indeed, *New Yorker* criticism helped make it a tome of cleverness and wit. This was especially true for the book reviews by Dorothy Parker (1927-1930) and her successor Robert Coates (1930-1933), Robert Benchley's theatre criticism (1929-1940), and Lois 'Lipstick' Long's debonair-ish reporter series on New York nightlife, 'Tables for Two' (1925-1928) and her much admired fashion criticism, 'On and Off the Avenue' (1925-1970). Here is Long describing a raid on one of New York's many speakeasies which, she complains, lacked all modern subtleties:

> It wasn't one of those refined, modern things, where gentlemen in evening dress arise suavely from ringside tables and depart, arm in arm, with head waiters no less correctly clad, towards the waiting patrol wagons. It was one of those movie affairs, where burly cops kick down doors, and women fall fainting on the tables, and strong men crawl under them and waiters shriek and start throwing bottles out of the windows (Long: 1925: 32).

Dorothy Parker's book reviews, signed 'Constant Reader', attracted a lot of attention during the magazine's first years and in Ross's own estimate, 'did more than anything to put the magazine on its feet' (cited in Lee 2000: 98). Parker was at her most notoriously funny when expressing scorn. Her most successful strategy was to feign a lack of sophistication and worldliness by adopting the persona of the mock innocent figure (Walker 1998: 221). Combined with her predilection for irony and hyperbole, Parker's strategy resulted in such scathing reviews as the one of Elinor Glyn's *It*, a novel on sex appeal that was considered scandalous at the time:

> On this day, there first fell into these trembling hands *The Book, The Ultimate Book*. There is grave doubt that I shall ever be able to talk of anything else. Certainly, I have read my last word. ... I have read but little of Madame Glyn. I did not know that things like 'It' were going on. I have misspent my days. When I think of all those hours I flung away in reading William James and Santayana, when I might have been reading of life, throbbing, beating, perfumed life, I practically break down (1927: 104).

Much less well-known than Dorothy Parker, the journalist and novelist who took over the book section in 1930, Robert M. Coates, continued the *New Yorker* book review as a personal and humorous venture until 1933. Even more than Parker, Coates used the first-person pronoun 'as a means of both personalizing [his] remarks and seeming to speak directly to the individual reader' (Walker 1998: 220). A staunch proponent of such modernist values as sincerity, courage and originality, Coates lamented the commercial interference of the publishing business in the world of creativity. Thus, in a delightful review (of an imaginary author's work), he accused the publishers' marketing machinery that stuffed his mailbox with information of distracting him from the real work at hand, as follows:

> When a publisher spends about eight dollars over a period of six months – sending me bulletins about a Roger Dilworthy: that Mr Dilworthy is resting; that his new book, *Lethargy*, will be about the mountain folk of Tennessee; that he is sailing for Naples; that he always keeps a bowl full of pears on his desk, to munch while he's working; that he's moved up to Villefranche, takes a dip every morning, and is working hard on the novel; that he's fond of whittling and just drives his wife to distraction, the way he strews shavings all over the floors; that the book is half-done, that it's two-thirds done, that it's finished, printed, bound, ready at last for me to read – well, by that time, I've worked myself into a pretty sullen attitude toward Mr Dilworthy and his novel, and I'm all set (and even hoping) to find it lousy (1931: 54).

Little men

During the late 1920s and throughout the 1930s, the *New Yorker* continued to attract major American humorists to its pages as staff writers and prolific contributors: in addition to writers and journalists such as Corey Ford, Robert Benchley, Dorothy Parker, Alexander Woolcott, Arthur Kober, E. B. White, Wolcott Gibbs, Ring Lardner, James Thurber, Robert Coates, Lois Long and Frank Sullivan, the *New Yorker* welcomed Sally Benson, Ogden Nash, Sid Perelman, Clarence Day, Ruth McKenney, and Leo Rosten, among several others.

Indeed, towards the end of the 1930s, the *New Yorker*'s distinctive style began to attract critical attention and was securely placed in the tradition of American humour in a review of Walter Blair's classic anthology *Native American Humor* by Bernard DeVoto. He was largely pessimistic about the state of American humour, lamenting its present-day tameness, its lack of courage and the absence of such talents as Mark Twain (1937: 3-4, 20). Still, DeVoto conceded, 'the true and most flourishing successors of the southwestern school are to be found in the *New Yorker*'. The comic writers whom he singled out as worthy successors were all authors of series – another important feature of the *New Yorker* during the 1930s that served to provide continuity through the development of recognisable characters (Yagoda 2000: 104). These included Ruth McKenney's series about her eccentric sister ('My Sister Eileen'); Richard Lockridge's collection of stories about two amateur detectives ('Mr and Mrs North'); Leo Rosten's series about a Jewish immigrant ('Hyman Kaplan'); and especially Clarence Day's collection of reminiscences about his father ('Life with Father'); and James Thurber's frequently bizarre recollections of his childhood, 'My Life and Hard Times'. These writers, DeVoto wrote, used characters who 'issue from the life immediately at hand [and] speak the living language' and, in so doing, had created successors to such classic characters from the American vernacular tradition as George Harris's Sut Lovingood, Johnson Hooper's Simon Suggs and William Thompson's Major Jones.

Indeed, the 'little man', the neurotic and confused anti-hero confronting a hostile world that became the *New Yorker*'s most famous comic manifestation, provided laughter at the ridiculousness of human life, but also exposed human (especially male) frailty, drawing sympathy rather than scorn as a result. Essentially a strand of self-deprecating humour, little-man humour both ridiculed and celebrated the ineptness and confusion of ordinary men overwhelmed and disempowered by the startling demands of modernity. The comic type first appeared in the work of Robert Benchley who, as Pinsker put it, 'understood that modern humorists fatten on modern trouble' (Pinsker 1984: 192). It immediately met with popular success, as Blair and Hill described it: 'Something of the futility, the hopeless bravado, the glorious confusion and the lurking terror that Benchley embodied in his invention [of the little man] struck universal chords' (1978: 433). The little man could also be found, in very mild form, in the work of E. B. White, as well as in the more extreme delusions, neuroses and paranoia of the misanthropic Ring Lardner who, according to Blair and Hill, brought 'the popularization of abnormal states of behavior' to the magazine (1978: 416).

But it was Thurber, with his major talent at creating 'an indelible image' of certain situations through the focus on certain significant details (Gale 1984: 19) who brought the most memorable associations and images to the trials and tribulations of the common modern man. As a result, James Thurber's often almost clinical variety most memorably came to represent the 'dementia praecox field', as Benchley once characterised this brand of humour (1934: 13). Thus, *New Yorker* readers regularly met strange and harassed men such as Thurber's Mr Bidwell, a man who developed the habit of holding his breath, first at home, but then also at parties. Driving home from one of these, Mrs Bidwell confronts him with his behaviour:

> 'I wasn't hurting anybody,' said Mr Bidwell. 'You looked silly!' said his wife. 'You looked perfectly crazy!' She was driving and she began to speed up, as she always did when excited or angry. 'What do you suppose people thought – you sitting there all swelled up, with your eyes popping out?' 'I wasn't all swelled up,' he said angrily (Thurber 1933: 12).

Appearing in the middle of the Great Depression, these humorous utterances have been read as responses to the widespread 'sense of worthlessness' among men as a result of unemployment and breakdown of status (see, for instance, Gates 1999: 30). Seen in that light, their ineptness and sense of powerlessness can be seen to comment on the impotence of the ordinary man faced by the impersonal anonymous forces of the economic depression. On the other hand, the *New Yorker*'s 'little men' have also been seen to reflect the magazine's flippancy in the face of the major political and economic upheavals of the 1930s and its complacent and blasé attitude in which 'problems of magnitude could be neatly reduced to whimsy' (Hausdorff, 1984: 76). As the magazine moved on towards the Second World War, it radically changed its degree of involvement with the outside world and, with such literary journalists as Joe Liebling, Janet Flanner, Joseph Mitchell, Mollie Panter-Downes and John Hersey, would produce top-rate reportage, making a new name for itself. The *New Yorker*, as Yagoda put it, 'would never again be thought of as primarily a humorous magazine' (1995: 193).

Conclusion

Propelled by the passionate belief of Harold Ross in the feasibility of a local rather than a national humorous magazine, the *New Yorker* established itself as a major cultural force during its first two decades. Sustained by an innovative journalistic formula that set the magazine apart from its competitors, and strengthened by a remarkable wealth of comic talent, the magazine also benefited from the rise of a newly metropolitan audience in the city of New York. Keen to establish an identity of their own, many of these newcomers were attracted to the magazine's humorous and often flippant treatment of questions of class, identity and belonging at a time of social flux.

There was, indeed, something tantalising about the *New Yorker* and the aura it projected. Its formula of humorous sophistication was as recognisably distinct as it was elusive and the magazine thrived on paradox: prone to self-importance, it was equally ready to mock itself; metropolitan in outlook and style, it simultaneously displayed a nostalgia for small-town news and gossip; a champion of modern individualism, it sought to build a community of kindred spirits; committed to bring as many different comic voices to its readers as possible, it actively downplayed the importance of individual talents and, on the editorial level, insisted in speaking in an anonymous and communal voice.

Of the many humorous contributions that the *New Yorker* made to American culture during its first two decades, the phenomenon of 'the little man' met with recognition and success so great as to have rendered it almost synonymous with '*New Yorker* humour'. However, manifestations of a comic worldview took many forms in the magazine's pages: from the mock-oral dialogues and monologues which transplanted and adapted the rural tradition to a metropolitan context, to the urbane criticism of Dorothy Parker or Lois Long; or from the character-driven series of the 1930s like 'My Sister Eileen' and 'Life With Father' to the editorial fillers such as the 'Newsbreaks' and the host of miniature departments like 'Answers-to-hard-Questions Department'. *New Yorker* humour was highly diverse and reflected a greater variety of social and cultural ideas and needs than those experienced by 'little men' alone.

Note

[1] The document was never published. James Thurber reprinted it in his book of memoirs *The Years with Ross*, in 1959

References

Baker, Russell (1993) From Robert Benchley to Andrew Dice Clay, *American Heritage*, Vol. 44, No. 6 pp 105-108

Benchley, Robert (1934) All aboard for dementia praecox, *San Francisco Examiner*, 18 June p. 13

Blair, Walter and Hill, Hamlin (1978) *America's Humor*, Urbana, Chicago, London: University of Illinois Press

Coates, Robert Myron (1931) Book-chat, *New Yorker*, 8 August

Coates, Robert (1961) James Thurber, *Authors Guild Bulletin*, December

Corey, Mary F. (1999) *The World Through a Monocle: The New Yorker at Midcentury*, Cambridge: Harvard University Press

DeVoto, Bernard (1937) Review of *Native American Humor*, by Walter Blair, *Saturday Review of Literature*, 25 September

Doren, Carl van (1923) Day in and day out, *Century*, Vol. 107, December

Douglas, Ann (1995) *Terrible Honesty: Mongrel Manhattan in the 1920s*, New York: Farrar, Straus and Giroux

Douglas, George H. (1993) *The Smart Magazines: 50 Years of Literary Revelry and High Jinks at* Vanity Fair, *the* New Yorker, Life, Esquire *and the* Smart Set, Hamden: Archon Books

Ford, Corey (1922) Laundry art: Study in wash: Further investigation of creative art in New York, *New Yorker*, 16 May

Ford, Corey (1967) *The Time of Laughter*, Boston: Little, Brown

Gale, Steven (1984) Thurber and the *New Yorker*, *Studies in American Humor*. New Series 2. Vol. 3, No. 1 pp 11-23

Gates, Robert A. (1999) *American Literary Humor During the Depression*. Westport and London: Greenwood Press

Hausdorff, Don (1984) Politics and economics: The emergence of a *New Yorker* tone, *Studies in American Humor*. New Series 2. Vol. 3, No. 1 pp 74-82

Hill, Hamlin (1963) Modern American humor: The Janus laugh, *College English*, Vol. 25, No. 3 pp 170-176

Holmes, Charles (1972) *The Clocks of Columbus: The Literary Career of James Thurber*, New York: Atheneum

Hyman, Stanley Edgar (1942) The urban *New Yorker*, *New Republic*, 20 July pp 90-92

Keyser, Catherine (2010) *Playing Smart: New York Women Writers and Modern Magazine Culture*, Piscataway, NJ: Rutgers University Press

Kober, Arthur (1929) The show-off, *New Yorker*, 30 March pp 25-26

Kunkel, Thomas (1995) *Genius in Disguise: Harold Ross of the New Yorker*, New York: Random House

Kunkel, Thomas (ed.) (2000) *Letters from the Editor: The New Yorker's Harold Ross*, New York: The Modern Library

Lee, Judith Yaross (2000) *Defining New Yorker Humor*, Jackson: University Press of Mississippi

Lois, Long (1925) Tables for two, *New Yorker*, 12 September pp 32-33

Mahon, Gigi (1988) *The Last Days of the* New Yorker, New York: McGraw-Hill

McGrath, Charles (1993) Hey Eu!, *New Yorker*, 22 February

O'Hara, John (1928) Spring 3100, *New Yorker*, 8 September

Parker, Dorothy (1927) Reading and writing, *New Yorker*, 26 November

Pinsker, Sanford (1984) On or about December 1919: When American character – and American Humor – Changed, Clark, William Bedford and Turner, Craig W. (eds) *Critical Essays on American Humor*, Boston: Hall pp 184-199

Popkin, Zelda (1926) Reflections of more or less silent New Yorkers, *New Yorker*, 11 December 11 pp 103-104

Remnick, David (2015) Out loud: Ninety years of the *New Yorker*, 16 February. Available online at http://www.newyorker.com/podcasts, accessed on 16 February 2015

Roza, Mathilde (2011) *Following Strangers: The Life and Literary Works of Robert Myron Coates*, Columbia: University of South Carolina Press

Thurber, James (1933) The private life of Mr Bidwell, *New Yorker*, 28 January pp 12-13

Thurber, James (1959) *The Years with Ross*, London: Hamish Hamilton

Tracy, Daniel (2010) Investing in Modernism: Smart Magazines, Parody and Middlebrow Professional Judgement, *Modern Fiction Studies* Vol. 1, No. 1 pp 38-63

Walker, Nancy A. (1997) The remarkable Constant Reader: Dorothy Parker as book reviewer, *Studies in American Humor*, Vols 3 and 4 pp 1-14

Wilson, Edmund (1952) *The Shores of Light: A Literary Chronicle of the Twenties and Thirties*, New York: Vintage Books

Yagoda, Ben (2000) *About Town: The New Yorker and the World it Made*, New York: Scribner

Note on the contributor

Mathilde Roza is Associate Professor of American Literature and American Studies at Radboud University Nijmegen, the Netherlands. She is the author of a critical biography of the largely forgotten American modernist and *New Yorker* staff writer Robert M. Coates, *Following Strangers: The Life and Literary Works of Robert Myron Coates* (2011), which was published by the University of South Carolina Press. Her research interests include American modernism and avant-gardism, magazines and periodicals, as well as contemporary ethnic North American literature.

Leading with Humour: How the Press is Adapting to Market Pressures

Miki Tanikawa

Introducing the new family of leads

In regular news reporting, journalists normally don't make jokes or use flashy language, especially in respectable daily newspapers such as *The New York Times*, *Washington Post* and *Wall Street Journal*. The objective paradigm that mainstream newspaper journalism has held on to dearly repels such journalistic heresy. But journalists actually do sneak humour, hyperbole, and novel-like descriptive writing into their articles, in marginal yet noticeable ways. They are hard to miss, as these techniques have become a common diet in newspaper journalism for the opening, lead paragraphs of feature articles. This chapter will first consider a range of literary devices journalists use to introduce humour into their opening paragraph/s (known as leads in the US, intros in the UK). It will then go on to highlight other 'featury' intro styles. A content analysis of the *International Herald Tribune* (now the *International New York Times*), which drew much of its editorial content from *The New York Times*[1], will then aim to identify in quantitative data the range of soft, featury intros and the percentages of humorous intros.

I argue that much of this 'featurisation' of the news intro is part of an inevitable push to make journalism more engaging, readable and fun for the audience as traditional news outlets struggle to keep their brand of journalism alive and competitive (Tanikawa 2014; see also Usher 2010). I also show that this type of intro is not entirely new – some are, indeed, known as classics, although their application may have changed. As commercial competition intensifies, newspapers are ditching some cherished editorial and stylistic conventions. But they are doing so – at least partly – by drawing on practices that have existed in the margins of journalism. Additionally, I have elicited comments from newspaper and magazine editors for insights and the reasoning behind these lead forms. Further, I will present the well-crafted leads of David Pogue, former technology columnist for *The New York Times*, whom I consider to be one of the foremost practitioners of this technique. His conversational style of lead is especially noteworthy, as it seems to be gaining currency across a range of leading US newspapers. And lastly, I will offer thoughts on what this story opening style means in today's journalism, the language of journalism, and the textual theory of news.

Leads designed for impact and arousal
Consider the following examples for starters:

> After last winter you were ready to pack up and move south. Too much cold, too much snow, too much wretched weather. This winter? So far, not so much. (Halsey III and Samenow 2015: 1).

> It was probably inevitable in a country so obsessed with food and drink that Thailand's political turmoil would spill over into beer (Fuller 2014: 7).

In the first instance, from the front page of the *Washington Post*, very few residents would have actually been ready to pack up and leave the DC area and head for the south, due to one cold winter. The intro is designed for its impact and arousal. In a direct address style, it seeks to grab the audience's attention and create a thinking process in readers' minds about the winter weather in the region. In the second example, from *The New York Times*, the literal transgression may be less obvious – but it is *not* inevitable that Thailand's political crisis will spill over into beer. (The story concerns consumers' revolt against the beer brand whose owner was a force behind the latest anti-government demonstration.) The writer's insertion of the adverb 'probably' indicates his coyness in projecting the sentence literally. The statement is an exaggeration, and the forced connection between the current political turmoil and Thai food and drink, with which readers might be more familiar, is a way to plug the readers into the subject matter.

Here is another example, from the *Los Angeles Times*, where the introductory paragraph does not mean what it says literally:

> Although the Chinese zodiac has designated 2008 as the Year of the Rat, some Belgians might beg to differ. They're celebrating the year of the Smurf, honoring those little blue creatures with white pants and white caps that stand no more than three apples high (Ziemba 2008: E3).

No Belgian really said they disagreed with the Chinese zodiac's designation of 2008 as the Year of the Rat, nor did the journalist mean to say she heard a Belgian say so. The writer simply wanted to tease the reader with a humorous lead. This, readers understand.

There seems to be an inherent understanding between the journalist and the audience that when it comes to lead paragraphs, things are not to be taken literally if the joke or humour is obvious.[2] Journalists exploit this understanding and take liberty with form, style and even literal facts, in ways they rarely do with the rest of the article.[3] The lead actually can be a fiction. Thus my argument that, despite the much vaunted claim of American journalism to convey facts and information, journalists can strain and stretch 'facts' in the lead (and even incorporate humour) because the function of the intro is to attract audience and to give an idea what the story is about (Hart 2006: 47-48; Kensler 2007: 91; Scanlan 2001: 115; Yopp 2007: 113).[4] In this sense, the textual function of the lead shares its main properties with the headline – where playfulness can be even more obvious (Conboy 2007: 15, Develotte and Rechniewski 2001: 2).

Classification

The intros under study here are the kind that include jokes, play with words (including the use of puns and alliteration) or otherwise deviate substantially from the literal meaning of the sentences, with the goal being to tease the reader. Because of their colourful structure or wording, they are much less likely to have appeared in the main body of the article, where 'objective' news values still largely reign. It is possible to group these varieties of leads into several types.

The first type is what I would describe as 'overtly humorous' or 'playful', exemplified by the above mentioned lead from the *LA Times*. Another example of a humorous lead:

> The baking tins and muffin cups lining the countertops in a corner of Ronald Holser's cluttered laboratory were filled with curious substances resembling angel food cakes and loaves of bread. But Mr Holser did not advise eating them. The concoctions were prototypes for biodegradable weed barriers… (Rosner 2007: C1).

This article was part of a series in *The New York Times* on how scientists and engineers are inventing ways to recycle biofuel waste into useful materials such as a weed fighting substance. Crafting humour out of curious-looking substances is a smart journalistic move and often, as this chapter will consistently argue, necessary to captivate audiences, especially when covering issues normally considered complex and intimidating such as science, technology and medicine. Take this intro, for instance:

> Tis the season to be jolly. Translation: Chances are you'll be drinking. A lot. How to survive until the New Year rings in? (Sintumuang 2014: D1).

Following this intro the article, from the *Wall Street Journal*'s 'Off Duty' section, highlights the virtue of champagne cocktails which, apparently, are less intoxicating. The culture and entertainment section of the *Journal* – like similar sections in many other papers – has tended to carry leads that cajole readers in a lighthearted way to indicate that amusing (and often useful) content will follow. More recently, journalists are acting more freely and experimenting with styles that take in contemporary conversational forms and language. The humorous/playful forms are also employed throughout the pages of the newspaper – breaking away from more neutral writing conventions which papers such as *The New York Times* have long adopted.[5]

The second type of lead is what I would call 'hyperbole' or 'use of exaggeration'. For example:

> What celebrity chef worth his lamb chops with pomegranate glaze would risk culinary shame by creating airline food -- the butt of innumerable jokes about reheated hash that always seems to taste like chicken or even a salty tire? Ask Charlie Trotter, a world-renowned chef who owns a five-star restaurant here and has written more than a dozen cookbooks. Trotter recently joined forces with United Airlines…. (Wilber 2008: D1).

This intro comes in the form of a conventional 'question lead', but with a considerable twist. To call making airline food a 'shame' (for celeb chefs) seems too strong, but it is not too strong because the lead sentence is meant as a hook, not to be taken word for word. It is an extravagant question whose hyperbolic intention is obvious. As a form of trope, it does what hyperbole generally does: shock the audience and re-orient their perspective (Ritter 2010: 6). As examples from other categories below will illustrate, it is a kind of 'deviation' (and in some instances, outrageousness) that separates many of the new species of leads from what are known conventionally as feature or soft leads. In news writing textbooks (Hart 2006, Itule and Anderson 2007, Yopp 2007), these go by names such as anecdotal leads, question leads and descriptive leads.

'Wordplay' leads display a certain degree of wit, and are quite common. For instance, the following intro plays on the cigarette brand's classic ad. line: 'I would walk a mile for a Camel.'

> A cigarette maker that once used print advertising to ask smokers to walk a mile for a popular brand is walking away from the medium, at least for next year (Elliott 2007: C1).

The 'staccato' intro also involves a play on words. In the past, this kind of lead (involving short sentences, sometimes even just a succession of single words) was considered appropriate only for a 'soft' story. That staccato is today considered suitable for serious news is surprising and noteworthy. For instance, *The New York Times* carried this intro:

> A loner. A drug addict. A criminal. A drifter. And lately, an Islamic radical. Michael Zehaf-Bibeau, the bearded, 32-year-old gunman who was shot dead Wednesday after killing a soldier and storming Canada's Parliament, aptly fits each of those descriptions. In the tumultuous wake of what Canada's prime minister has called a terrorist act, Mr Zehaf-Bibeau's radicalism has become the defining one (Wines and Yardley 2014: 1).

Another category I would designate is the 'extensive use of rhetoric' – as in the following two examples:

> Atop the globe, the icy surface of the Arctic Ocean has remained relatively peaceful. But its depths have boiled with intrigue, no more so than in the

Cold War. Although the superpowers planned to turn those depths into an inferno of exploding torpedoes and rising missiles, the brotherhood of submariners – the silent service, both Russian and American – has worked hard over the decades to keep the particulars of those plans hush-hush (Broad 2008: F1).

Farid Mesbaah, male belly dancer, hopped on a car in Cairo's Shobra district and strutted his stuff. He clanged metal castanets, magically converted his hips into pistons and twirled his head around like a centrifuge. The crowd at tables lining a dirt alley clapped rhythmically. Young men in jeans jumped up to wiggle along (Williams 2008: 2).

The first story, from the science section of *The New York Times*, brings out details of submarine manoeuvres in the Arctic Sea during the Cold War. Rhetorically dense, the opening paragraph employs a novelistic writing style generally reserved for fiction. Its intended impact here is to raise an expectation that what people are about to read is a *story*. The second intro, which similarly exhibits rhetorical richness, powerfully brings readers to the forefront of the scene, where the actions of the protagonist, the Egyptian male belly dancer, are concisely and vividly described.

The final category is *simplification*. For instance:

Most Cambodians live with two realities: rain and rice. The country that three decades ago abolished money has today embarked on the very long process of adding two new words to the national vocabulary: stocks and bonds (Kinetz 2007:15).

As with other types of leads, hooking and focusing are key in making powerful and impactful leads. The writer mobilises words/expressions and creates a focus by resorting to a parallel or contrast. It is obvious rain and rice are not the only realities Cambodians face, nor are stocks and bonds the only new things confronting the nation. But the over-simplification created by contrasting the two olds and two news carries significant journalistic impact. A common thread in these types of leads is that the literal truth (factuality) is compromised – sometimes flagrantly – but the writer is neither guilty of journalistic heresy nor in violation of ethical standards, as long as the audience broadly shares the understanding.

Content analysis

The following content analysis was designed to show how prevalent these types of leads are in a given newspaper. The analysis (n=772) used the *International Herald Tribune*, which drew approximately 40 to 50 per cent of its content from *The New York Times*, for the sample. Articles were drawn from three randomly chosen one-week periods between November 2007 and March 2008 (one week from late November 2007, one week from early January 2008 and one week from mid-March 2008). The editorial/opinion pages and special sections that did not appear regularly in the newspaper were excluded. Also excluded from the sample were small news briefs on the sides of the news pages. All articles were first grouped into 'straight' news and 'non-straight' news, broadly corresponding to hard news and features. Only 'non-straight' news was searched for 'playful' leads, as it was expected that the event-oriented, fact-filled 'straight' news stories were much less likely to contain such leads.[6] Straight news items are usually rooted in a specific, immediate time and thus often contain a reference to 'yesterday' or the day before the publication of the article. Those articles without a 'yesterday' reference were coded as 'non-straight news'.[7]

Results

Of the 772 articles found in the three-week sample, 267 were categorised as 'straight' news and 505 as 'non-straight' news. The 'non-straight' news stories were content analysed for the types of leads I have identified above. Among the sample, 41 were identified as clearly having one of the five types of leads (Table 1). In other words, 8.1 per cent of the 'non-straight' news stories (n=505) displayed some type of 'deviation' in their leads. This became 5.3 per cent when the entire sample, including straight news stories, was included (n=772). This means only a small portion of the newspaper articles exhibited this literary tendency in their intros. Nevertheless, the use of this kind of intro has grown over the last 15 to 20 years or so, along with newspapers' tendency to decrease straight news and increase non-straight news content (Tanikawa 2014).

Table 1
Result of the Content Analysis / Classification of Humorous/Playful Leads

	Humorous/ Playful	Hyperbole	Wordplay	Rhetorical	Simplification	Total
Number of Articles	10	13	7	8	3	41
As % of Total	24.4	31.7	17	19.5	7.3	100%

* 41 humorous/'playful' leads were identified in 505 non-straight news articles

Comments from editors/journalists

What are the editorial purposes behind these types of story openings? To investigate this, I interviewed editors at three different kinds of news organisations. Interviews were originally conducted in 2008, and the comments were confirmed and updated/expanded in December 2014 and January-February 2015 for the purpose of this chapter. The responses from the three editors follow my question:

> Feature stories in mainstream news media often contain a lead with humorous or exaggerated expressions to lure the readers in. There seems to be greater tolerance for 'playing things up' in the lead more than in other parts of the story because the role of the intro is to hook the audience. Do you agree? If so, how do you account for this?

Mitchell Martin, currently based in New York for Bloomberg, having previously worked with *Forbes* magazine and the *International Herald Tribune* as an editor, commented:

> American journalistic standards of the 1960s and 1970s were very hands-off. The lead, the headline and the story in quality newspapers were meant to be neutral in tone. If you think back to the period, a lot of the news was inherently interesting, be it Vietnam, the space race, the Beatles or drugs – and people still got a lot of their information from newspapers. More recently, there have been a lot of pressures on newspapers. Circulation has declined, and there are many competing sources that seem to be free. Newspapers have to offer something compelling to readers, and leads and headlines are used to lure people into reading their stories (personal communication via email, 31 December 2014).

Anne Bagamery, Paris-based Senior Editor of *International New York Times*, commented:

> Yes, absolutely – on a longer story the lead is the appetiser that, hopefully, gets the reader to stick around for the main course. Although I'd also say that the best leads aren't just a cute anecdote or a few lines of wordplay. They are closely linked to the main theme of the story, and act as a set-up for everything that follows – in tone and in content. You wouldn't put a 'cute' lead on a very serious story; it would look out of place and amateurish (personal communication via email, 5 January 2015).

Tom Leander, Hong-Kong-based Editor-in-Chief, Asia, at *Lloyd's List*, formerly, senior editor of the Economist Group, said:

> I think that's right. Particularly in US journalism, you're encouraged to deploy the common touch in opening sentences. There's sort of a studied informality in writing the opener to a feature article on wind power or advances in seismology, say, that examines and explains some sort of specialty. The idea is to tease the reader into thinking that he or she is reading a fun piece rather than a technical one. That said, doing a good job of writing a light opener to a serious topic is not as easy as it looks. The tone has to respect the topic. A writer might be on the wrong track if he adopted a flip tone to open a story about auto-safety airbag testing, for example. On the other hand, maybe he could pull it off (personal communication via email, 4 February 2015).

Several significant points emerge from these responses. First, the lead is a crucial appetiser and teaser (Bagamery, Leander, Martin) that needs to hook the audience. Also the significance of crafting an enticing lead is growing more important (Martin). There is an ethical responsibility of the writer of the intro to respect the overall tone of the content (Bagamery, Leander).[8] And science and technology articles are a breeding ground for these types of soft leads, because writers take care to ensure their stories are readable to the general audience (Leander).

David Pogue: Master of the humorous lead

David Pogue, for 13 years tech-columnist of *The New York Times*, left the newspaper in 2013 to produce technology content for Yahoo News. The quality of humorous/'playful' leads he produced over the course of his career is staggering. Consider these two for openers.

> Just by looking at it, you'd never guess that Sony's new Alpha A300 digital camera represents a huge technical breakthrough. To discover what it is, you need a tour of its innards. Keep hands and feet inside the tram at all times (Pogue 2008: C1).

> Sony's concept for the new QX100 is among the most brilliant in its history. Unfortunately, the good idea ended with the concept. By the time the poor QX100 reached the production line, it never really had a chance. Oh, wait – you want to know what it is? (Pogue 2013a: B1).

In the first example, the lead raises the expectation that the rest of the story is going to be fun, an adventure. Discussing the technical complexities of a camera poses the risk that the general reader will dart off immediately. Instead, Pogue entices readers with colourful, concise, lively and accessible prose. In the second example, after a potentially off-putting, esoteric-sounding sentence, the familiar 'Oh, wait' is an engaging trick to grab the attention of the reader. Another Pogue lead example:

> Year after year, Steve Jobs used to blow our minds with products we didn't know we wanted. Now, two years after his death, we still expect every new iPhone to clean our gutters, cook our popcorn and levitate. So when hardware revisions are minor each year, we're disappointed (Pogue 2013b: B1).

In referencing gutter cleaning, popcorn and levitating, Pogue's aim is clear: cast a wide net by throwing in ideas that have nothing to do with technology – but have everything to do with everyday life – and thereby show that this article is for everyone.

Conversational style

Exemplified by Pogue's articles, more journalists seem to favour what's known in the news writing lexicon as the 'direct address lead' (Itule and Anderson 2007: 119-120; Friedlander and Lee 2000: 198-199). Dialogic and familiar in its modality, direct address style is enjoying a new mutation in recent years and is no longer limited to feature sections or personal, how-to types of columns and articles. For an illustration, here is a somewhat longer lead which appeared in the metro section of *The New York Times*. Direct address is found in the fourth paragraph.

Carles Guillot, a 42-year-old financial services entrepreneur who lives on Broad Street in Lower Manhattan, was awakened early on a weekend morning by workers wielding a jackhammer to repair the roadway nine floors below.

'I understand the need to work, but it's the timing that's not good,' he said of the noisy pre-breakfast intrusion. 'Jackhammers – I can't think of a worse noise.'

Nobody who lives in New York will ever mistake it for Walden Pond, what with its earsplitting police sirens, screeching subway wheels, beeping backup truck alarms and a cacophony of thunderous mechanical equipment that the city's construction boom has elevated to a peak.

Keep covering your ears, New York, although help may be on the way (Roberts 2014: 31).

Another lead in this style comes from a page one article in *The New York Times*.

Authors are upset with Amazon. Again (Streitfeld 2014: 1).

These conversational/colloquial forms, still used rather sparingly, arouse readers' interest immediately – a very different approach from the impersonal, factual reporting newspapers were known for. They are also valued for efficiency and economy. The above intro on Amazon tells the readers the article is not more of the same. Without the direct address 'again' it would require more gimmickry, using perhaps the combination of a headline and a few sentences, to show that the article contains a significant new development concerning authors' discontent over Amazon's policy. Still, as with the earlier *Times* and *Post* examples, many journalists and editors would have scratched their heads over these leads decades ago. They perhaps would have rejected them as ruining front page decorum.

Discussion and conclusion
Comprehending the new intro trends calls for a broader and contextual understanding of where newspaper journalism finds itself today. A recent content analysis I conducted (Tanikawa 2014) confirmed what seemed like an obvious phenomenon: reflecting powerful commercial imperatives, newspapers have drastically cut down on time sensitive straight news on the front page, from 70 per cent to 35 per cent in the last 25 years, with the biggest decline taking place in the last five to ten years. They have also shrunk the number of articles and increased the size of the photographs on page one, embracing a more magazine-like layout (ibid). The crisis of confidence brought on by falling circulation and collapsing advertising revenues is the biggest driver forcing newspapers to change. In the process, news reports have become more contextual, in-depth and analytical, as well as 'playful'. This is dictated by one overriding consideration: to add value and distinguish the newspaper from

commoditised news on the web. In a world full of free news, editors and journalists sense the acute need to jostle the jaded public. The jazzy story openings are but one manifestation of an overall transformation of the news. Linking the transformation of newspaper front pages and the changing newspaper language, Anne Bagamery of the *International New York Times* offered further thoughts:

> Page One has become less newsy in general as more readers get breaking news from digital. Newspapers like *The New York Times* and the *Washington Post* have always had a feature story on Page One in addition to news, but now the mix has reversed – maybe one news story and the rest features. And the features are written in a folksier tone that would have been considered too flippant before. I think this is the influence of digital, which tends to be lighter in tone. A lot of this writing I recognise from my magazine days at *Forbes* – and that is not surprising to me, since newspapers now want to be more like magazines (personal communication via email, 5 January 2015).

The intro has a dual mission of grabbing readers' attention and demonstrating to them the story's core relevance. And so, leads/intros share their textual properties with headlines (Bell 1991: 149-153, Conboy 2007: 15).[9] While it is well-known that the intro is often written by the sub-editor (in the US known as the copy editor or assignment editor), not the reporter (Bell 2007: 81), it should also be noted that often, the editor's involvement in revising the intro is greater than other parts of the text because of its singular editorial importance (Tanikawa 2013: 76).[10] and.[11]

As demonstrated by many examples in this chapter, the stylised intros give the news text a voice and a perspective that conventional journalism has often shied away from. In just a few words these intros reorient readers and give them perspective in a way that distanced, authoritative journalism is not able to with dry, straightforward, declarative sentences. These changes are part of the larger editorial shift in which newspapers are giving up, at least partially, their cherished objectivity standards and allowing journalists and editors to insert themselves more into both news reporting and personal columns (Sullivan 2015: SR12).

Notes

[1] The study carried out originally was first published in the following publications. Tanikawa, Miki (2008) The use of hyperbole in American journalism, *Current English Studies* (Journal of Japan Association for Current English Studies) Vol. 15 pp 17-34; Tanikawa, Miki (2010) The use of humor and its serious implications, *Literary Journalism Studies* (The newsletter of International Association for Literary Journalism Studies) Fall, Vol. 4, No 4 p. 5

[2] If the understanding is mutual, it does not give rise to ethical concerns. There are, however, problems with leads that are obviously bait and switch, the kind that arouses

but does not live up to the promise in the rest of the article. Interview comments later in the chapter will touch on this issue

3 An exception might be the 'kicker' (final paragraph) of feature articles where, like the lead, it is often fashioned for its emotional impact rather than for its informational content

4 Leading American newswriting textbooks, including by these authors, are nearly unanimous in stating these two purposes of the lead

5 Some literary scholars have noted the general, stylistic changes of *The New York Times* in recent years; see Abrahamson (2006). For a discussion on narrative journalism styles finding their way into mainstream news media see Hartsock (2007)

6 As of 2008, when this content analysis was carried out originally, it was not clear that the 'playful' intros had spread into hard news in leading US newspapers such as *The New York Times* and *Washington Post*. However, hard news itself has diminished to the point that it represented only about a third of the news content in US newspapers such as the *International Herald Tribune*, which drew almost half of its content from original *Times* articles (Tanikawa 2014)

7 See Tanikawa (2014) for details of the definitions

8 Since the editors pointed this out it does suggest that some writers do violate this principle

9 While comprehensive cross-cultural comparisons are yet to be conducted, some studies resonate with this perspective. For example, a study shows that in Thai newspaper language, the lead occupies a linguistic middle ground between the headline, which uses low Thai (an informal and vernacular form of the language) and the body of the text, which must use high Thai, a more formal version of the language (Khanittanan 2007)

10 Editors I have interviewed indicated, for example, that they sometimes change the lead to fit the headline they have come up with (Tanikawa 2013: 76)

11 While giving this chapter several tasks, it neglected others. Like headlines, leads are a rich source of cultural references as they rely on widely disseminated cultural and linguistic knowledge so as to be understood (Develotte and Rechniewski 2001:3). They thus offer great potential for cultural, linguistic and literal analysis. As noted, emergence of the playful and literary intro is associated, at least loosely, with the growing adoption of literary styles in newspaper journalism (see Abrahamson 2006; Hartsock 2007 and Sims 2007)

References

Abrahamson, David (2006) Teaching literary journalism: A diverted pyramid? *Journalism & Mass Communication Educator*, Vol. 60, No. 4 p. 430

Bell, Allan (1991) *The Language of News Media*. Oxford: Blackwell

Bell, Allan (2007) Text, time and technology in news English, Graddol, David, Goodman, Sharon and Lillis, Teresa M. (eds) *Redesigning English*, Abingdon: Routledge pp 78-112

Develotte, Christine and Rechniewski, Elizabeth (2001) Discourse analysis of newspaper headlines: A methodological framework for research into national representations, *The Web Journal of French Media Studies*, Vol. 4, No. 1. Available online at http://wjfms.ncl.ac.uk/titles.htm, accessed on 5 January 2014

Friedlander, Edward Jay and Lee, John (2000) *Feature Writing for Newspapers and Magazines: The Pursuit of Excellence*, New York: HarperCollins College Publishers, fourth edition

Hartsock, John. C. (2007) 'It was a dark and stormy night': Newspaper reporters rediscover the art of narrative literary journalism and their own epistemological heritage, *Prose Studies*, Vol. 29, No. 2 pp 257-284

Khanittanan, Wilaiwan (2007) Language of the news media in Thailand, *International Journal of the Sociology of Language*, Vol. 186 pp 29-41

Ritter, Joshua R. (2010) *Recovering Hyperbole: Re-imagining the Limits of Rhetoric for an Age of Excess*, PhD thesis, Georgia State University

Scanlan, Christopher (2000) *Reporting and Writing: Basics for the 21st century*, New York: Harcourt College Publishers

Sims, Norman (2007) *True Stories: A Century of Literary Journalism*, Chicago: Northwestern University Press

Tanikawa, Miki (2013) Midashi nadono kiji shoukai bubun no sakuseishutai to nyu-su gengo no taiyo. Bei jya-narizumu wo jirei to shite ['Who writes the headlines?' A multi-dimensional analysis of the language-forming processes of news headlines, subheads, and captions in American newspapers]. *JASEC Bulletin* (The Japanese Association for Studies in English Communication), Vol. 22 pp 67-81

Tanikawa, Miki (2014) Transformation of the print: Analyzing the diminishing news orientation of leading American newspapers. Paper presented at AEJMC Conference, Montreal, August

Usher, Nikki (2010) In a hamster-wheel world, is there room for journalistic creativity? Evidence from *The New York Times*, 20 September. Available online at http://www.niemanlab.org/2010/09/in-a-hamster-wheel-world-is-there-room-for-journalistic-creativity-evidence-from-the-new-york-times, accessed on 12 January 2015

Newspaper References

Broad, William J. (2008) Queenfish: A Cold War tale, *New York Times*, 18 March p. F1

Elliott, Stuart (2007) Once a mainstay of magazines, cigarette makers are dropping print ads, *New York Times*, 29 November p. C1

Fuller, Thomas (2014) Thai beer loses esteem after heiress's remarks, *New York Times*, 11 January p. 7

Halsey III, Ashley and Samenow, Jason (2015) Few flakes after no-snow Decembers just a fluke? *Washington Post*, 2 January, Section 2 p. A1

Kinetz, Erika (2007) A mouse in Asia gets ready to roar: Investors are giving Cambodia a second look, as its economy stays stable and grows, *International Herald Tribune*, 28 July p. 15

Pogue, David (2008) A camera that frees your face, *New York Times*, 6 March p. C1

Pogue, David (2013a) A whole new idea: Half a camera, *New York Times* 26 September p. B1

Pogue, David (2013b) In arrival of 2 iPhones, 3 lessons, *New York Times* 18 September, p. B1

Roberts, Sam (2014) With electric jackhammers, plans to quiet an earsplitting city sound, *New York Times*, 18 December p. 31

Rosner, Hillary (2007) Cooking up more uses for the leftovers of biofuel production, *New York Times*, 8 August p. C1

Sintumuang, Kevin (2014) The tipping point, *Wall Street Journal*, 13 December p. D1

Streitfeld, David (2014) Amazon offers all-you-can-eat books: Authors turn up noses, *New York Times*, 28 December p. 1

Sullivan, Margaret (2015) An uneasy mix of news and opinion, *New York Times*, 11 January p. SR12

Wilber, Del Quentin (2008) Celebrity chefs bring plane food to new heights: Airlines upgrading menus for premium passengers, *Washington Post*, 1 January p. D1

Williams, Daniel (2008) An old custom is back: Belly dancing by men, *International Herald Tribune*, 3 January p. 2 (original source: Bloomberg News)

Wines, Michael, and Yardley, William (2014) Ottawa gunman's radicalism deepened as life crumbled, *New York Times*, 25 October p. 1

Ziemba, Christine N. (2008) A happy case of the blue, *Los Angeles Times*, 27 January p. E3. Available online at http://articles.latimes.com/2008/jan/27/entertainment/ca-smurf27, accessed on 7 January 2015

Note on the contributor

Miki Tanikawa is a long-time feature writer on *The New York Times* for its international (formerly *International Herald Tribune*) and domestic editions. As contributing editor for the Economist Intelligence Unit, he authored business reports on Japanese business, economy and industry. Currently, he is pursuing a doctoral degree at the University of Texas, Austin. While teaching at Japanese universities such as Sophia and Waseda Universities, he researched and published extensively on the language of the news in Japanese language journals.

Swimming in a Sea of Death: Reviewers Respond to a Journalist's Work of Mourning With Humour

Carolyn Rickett

In an article for the *New York Review of Books* entitled 'For sorrow there is no remedy', author and critic Julian Barnes (2011) makes this astute observation: 'In some ways, autobiographical accounts of grief are unfalsifiable, and therefore unreviewable by any normal criteria.' While Barnes is largely referring to Joyce Carol Oates's *A Widow's Story: A Memoir* (2011), his statement highlights a reticence that can inhibit critical reviews of works of mourning. Other texts exploring less personal and poignant themes are subjected to analytical and exacting commentary; the burgeoning field of memoir recounting the death of a family member is publicly quarantined from this.

After his mother, the American writer and film maker, Susan Sontag (1933-2004), died, David Rieff – an acclaimed investigative journalist, author and literary editor – turned to memoir to reflect on the final months of her life. Rieff, whose literary reputation had long been established through polemical prose on humanitarian issues, war and politics appearing in high profile publications such as *The New York Times*, *Le Monde*, *The Atlantic*, and *Harper's*, typically received reverential regard for his autobiographical work, *Swimming in a Sea of Death: A Son's Memoir* (2008).

This chapter draws attention to a range of dissenting critiques featured in selected newspapers and online publications that refused to be constrained by either Rieff's literary lineage or the pathos of his prose. Instead, these selected reviews employed unanticipated humour and wit to appraise and question the motivation and merit of his memoir.

A puzzling choice?

There are few, if any, funny lines or anecdotes recorded in journalist David Rieff's memoir *Swimming in a Sea of Death: A Son's Memoir*. Perhaps the wittiest observation about death comes from his sourcing of quotes:

There was an eighteenth century French writer who wrote to a friend asking 'Why, hating life as I do, do I fear death so much?' That was Larkin's perspective, too. It was even Canetti's when he wrote, 'One should not confuse the craving for life with endorsement of it' (Rieff 2008: 14-15).

Despite these wry observations attributed to other writers, his memoir is largely freighted with anxieties around the way in which his mother, Susan Sontag, died. It is a text given over to him working through feelings of guilt and complicity in not engaging in honest conversations about her health status, thereby partly facilitating her avoidant responses to a terminal illness.

Naturally, Rieff reserves the right to treat such matters with deep solemnity and regret without a hovering readerly expectation demanding moments of light relief or witty rejoinders. So, respecting his right to choose a style and tone fit for the memoir's purpose, it may seem a puzzling choice to select Rieff's autobiographical writing as a focal point for a chapter exploring humour in journalism. However, my interest lies not in analysing the humour (or absence thereof) contained within Rieff's recount, but exploring the way in which works of mourning can constrain journalists who might wish to draw on humour to write unfavourable reviews of texts that deal with the pathos of death. And importantly here, to draw attention to those rare reviewers who, despite the solemnity of Rieff's content, refuse to quarantine the memoir from the practices of witty and dissenting critique.

'Discussing the undiscussable'

In the December 1994 edition of the *New Yorker*, dance critic Arlene Croce offers this riposte to a performance premiering at the Brooklyn Academy of Music: 'I have not seen Bill T. Jones's "Still/Here" and have no plans to review it' (Croce 1994: 54). She titles her provocative essay 'Discussing the undiscussable' and proceeds to outline her aversion to assessing a work incorporating video footage of ill people who had participated in workshops that Jones had led. During the mixed media choreographed performance of 'Still/Here' the audience functions as witnesses for people with a life-threatening illness. Croce's chief complaint is that 'by working dying people into his act Jones is putting himself beyond the reach of criticism' (ibid). Her critique of Jones and his choice of subject matter is founded on her assertion that 'victim' art is being popularised and valorised, particularly works relating to AIDS. In Croce's estimation:

> Instead of compassion, these performers induce, and even invite, a cozy kind of complicity. When a victim artist finds his or her public, a perfect, mutually exclusive union is formed which no critic may put asunder (ibid: 55).

With the seriousness of the subject matter dominating such performances, she trenchantly protests over what she considers the marginalisation of the critic, and highlights examples of artists such as Jones who are seen to 'have effectively disarmed criticism' (ibid: 58). The disarming of criticism, as Croce contends, is due to the privileging of the performer and their work above artistic standards because of the vulnerable state of their corporeality. They become, she suggests, off-limits because to critique the work is to pass judgement directly and inextricably on their embodied selves. With this conflation, and following Croce's line of argument, such artists are not then purely performing an aesthetic work, but are inherently performing *themselves*. For Croce, narrative performances in these contexts elide the purview of criticism because she can only consider the participants as victims. As people narrate their real-life illnesses on stage (or use other creative modalities), Croce sees the critic as no longer being able to judge such work using objective measures. This, in part, could be seen as a refusal to challenge core readings about identity, instead favouring the argument that 'When it comes to our identities, narrative is not merely *about* self, but is rather in some profound way a constituent part *of* self' (Eakin 2008: 2, emphasis in the original).

While Croce's essay cogently outlines reasons for not writing a review of Jones's work, her treatise invited criticism about a perceived failure to do her job. For example, Bordwell offers this strong rebuttal: 'How, I wondered upon reading "Discussing the undiscussable", could such a reputable dance critic summarily dismiss this work, sight unseen?' (1998: 369). Bordwell's concern typifies the standard view that to be eligible to critique a work of any kind one must have *personally* engaged with it first.

Whilst I am sympathetic towards Bordwell's view on what should constitute one's eligibility for writing critiques, Croce's essay, nonetheless, pertinently raises the notion that some works, due to their sombre and personal subject matter, evade the exacting criteria of criticism. The trademark wit, humour and irony often drawn on by a reviewer, and then unsparingly applied to texts under review, is often conspicuously avoided when the work is about a terminal illness or serves as an emotional testament to a mourning process. As Carroll argues in relation to humour: 'Emotions are appraisals directed at particular objects that are assessed in light of certain criteria or appropriateness and which cause certain phenomenological and/or physiological states in the subject undergoing the emotion' (2014: 5). This idea of 'certain criteria or appropriateness' might also be referenced to a reviewer's wit and humour not being seen as acceptable modes of address when assessing certain texts. Hence, with this kind of censoring or self-regulation in play, a text with sombre and melancholy content related to terminal illnesses could easily become artificially elevated and revered because of a reluctance to judge it primarily on artistic values.

'Confessions of a book reviewer'

While Croce registers particular views on her role as a dance critic, George Orwell, writing in 1946, offered his own witty perspective on the book reviewer:

> Until one has some kind of professional relationship with books one does not discover how bad the majority of them are. In much more than nine cases out of ten the only objectively truthful criticism would be 'This book is worthless', while the truth about the reviewer's own reaction would probably be 'This book does not interest me in any way, and I would not write about it unless I were paid to.' But the public will not pay to read that kind of thing. Why should they? They want some kind of guide to the books they are asked to read, and they want some kind of evaluation (Orwell 1970 [1946]: 217-218).

Depicted here is the portrait of a jaded 'hack' whose truthful and objective criticism is curtailed by the pragmatism of serving the reading public what it wants to hear. Orwell's portrait of the book reviewer is that of a professional writer/journalist who is paid by a newspaper editor to produce copy that will ultimately satisfy consumers. However, in more contemporary times, the specialised or professionalised nature of the review is being challenged for primacy, as literary scholar and critic Morris Dickstein highlights:

> The professional reviewer, who has a literary identity, who had to meet some editor's exacting standard, has effectively been replaced by the Amazon reviewer, the paying customer, at times ingenious, assiduous, and highly motivated, more often banal, obtuse, and blankly opinionated (Ciabattari 2011).

While the role of the professional reviewer now co-exists with amateur World Wide Web posts found on commercial book sites and blogs, there are still nonetheless important and ongoing conversations about the role of literary reviewers. In a newspaper article entitled 'The role of the book critic', Tom Payne begins his piece with this humorous reference:

> 'Don't write crap.' That is was what Julia Gillard, the Australian Prime Minister, offered recently as a contribution to the debate on the responsibilities of journalism. Since all pages of newspapers are under scrutiny these days, it's worth remembering what the duties of literary critics are (2011).

While it is seen as paramount for journalists (and book critics) not to 'write crap', this duty of fearless honesty may be compromised, as Croce would suggest, when the work under review seems to be beyond criticism. However, I would argue that books cannot put themselves *beyond* a reviewer's critique. Rather, it is the reviewer who deliberately, or inadvertently, chooses to sanction or frame work in particular ways, and who decides when and where to draw on humour and wit as critical tools in responding to specific texts, even ones mediating the seriousness of death.

Reviewing the unreviewable

In his timely review 'For sorrow there is no remedy' (2011), Julian Barnes provides an insight into the impact of a heightened sense of mortality:

> Of course, at one level we know that we shall die, but death has come to be looked upon more as a medical failure than a human norm. It increasingly happens away from the home, in hospital, and is handled by a series of outside specialists – a matter for the professionals. But afterwards we, the amateurs, the grief-struck, are left to deal with it this unique banal thing as best we can (2011).

Because it is often 'the grief-struck' who reactively write memoirs as a meaning-making exercise for the loss of their loved one, critics can be disarmed by the sincere nature of such testimonial enterprises. The representation of death, and subsequent mourning, can serve as inhibitors to the assiduous analysis and witty critique that might normally mark a book review in other circumstances. As Barnes suggests: 'In some ways, autobiographical accounts of grief are unfalsifiable, and therefore unreviewable by any normal criteria' (ibid). The well-established criteria of 'all gloves off' can be superseded by a reviewer's impulse to protect such accounts of grief from an ironic or witty gaze or retort. This can be evidenced by the way in which memoirs dealing with terminal illnesses are frequently quarantined from scathing or humorous criticism; their virtues are argued in psycho-social terms rather than literary ones.

Interestingly, in her scholarship on illness narratives and their relationship to the academy, Ann Jerecic notes that 'since their ascendance, these narratives have shifted the boundaries of literary study' (2012: 2). By this she means 'the medical humanists who teach literature in medical schools and centers have drawn attention to how narratives about suffering sustain individuals and communities' (2012: 2-3).

Importantly, she makes the distinction that while medical practitioners are encouraged to respond to patient or family stories with 'respect and understanding' (ibid: 3), this dignified approach does not always describe the ways such texts are treated by academics skilled in the field of literary criticism. However, from my general observation, the kind of literary critique carried out by industry practitioners such as professional journalists or reviewers tends not to ascribe automatically the same hermeneutics of suspicion to illness narratives that those working in academe might. Instead, they look for ways to affirm the writer's bravery, and dutifully assign the autobiographical text an added personal, social or political value. As Couser notes '… memoir now rivals fiction in popularity and critical esteem and exceeds it in cultural currency' (2012: 3). In professionalised book review columns, illness memoir, more often than not, is typically read and circulated as offering an invaluable personal and cultural contribution.

Our last great taboo

Returning to the example of *Swimming in a Sea of Death: A Son's Memoir*, one can see the particular ways in which reviewers choose to ennoble the work rather than lampoon it. For example, Penelope Lively's review for the *Financial Times* dignifies Rieff's efforts:

> In this fiercely honest and beautifully written memoir, her son David Rieff chronicles the last months of Sontag's life.... He writes with elegance and high intelligence; this book is a fine epitaph to his mother (2008).

Naturally, the original publisher of the memoir, Simon & Schuster, frames the memoir in this partisan way:

> Both a memoir and an investigation, *Swimming in a Sea of Death* is David Rieff's loving tribute to his mother, the writer Susan Sontag, and her final battle with cancer. Rieff's brave, passionate, and unsparing witness of the last nine months of her life, from her initial diagnosis to her death, is both an intensely personal portrait of the relationship between a mother and a son, and a reflection on what it is like to try to help someone gravely ill in her fight to go on living and, when the time comes, to die with dignity (Simon & Schuster 2008).

The original publishers also position the memoir as having currency beyond the private and argue for its wider utilitarian value:

> Drawing on his mother's heroic struggle, paying tribute to her doctors' ingenuity and faithfulness and determined to tell what happened to them all, *Swimming in a Sea of Death* subtly draws wider lessons that will be of value to others when they find themselves in the same situation (ibid).

The atmospherics of the publisher's review are replete with notions of heroism and pedagogical purpose. And other reviewers typically follow the Simon & Schuster lead, ably supported by Janet Malcolm's reverential endorsement that appears on the book's front cover: 'The delicacy and restraint of this book give it its painful force. It is a work of the highest originality and artistry – and truthfulness' (Rieff 2008).

Also positioning the book as a work of high seriousness are the paratextual interviews with Rieff, who establishes his literary pedigree. This strategically affords him protection from rigorous literary scrutiny with some reviewers:

> It's complicated to talk about the influence on one's work. In my family it's a bit like in the *Godfather*; I was born into a family that was involved in a certain business, the business of writing, and I also always wanted to be a writer. My mother was a famous writer, my father was also a writer – at the time he wrote some important books in his field – and when you come from a family like that and you want to be a writer, you know that you need to write about things which they don't write about; so I suppose

there's a kind of negative effect, in the sense that I became a war correspondent because that was something they didn't write about. I'm sure that my mother influenced me, in the same way that I hope that I might also have influenced her (Alba 2009).

By establishing and authorising his writerly credentials, Rieff's comments can work to curtail critique on the literary qualities of the text. While his comments are at times self-effacing in relation to his own craft compared to that of his mother's, it is his references to death that offer potential reviewers a sense of anticipated (and expected) gravitas:

But the book is about those nine months. It's also about death to some extent. I'm not an idiot and I'm very well aware that if people are interested in this memoir it has mostly to do with my mother's celebrity and maybe a little bit to do with my reputation, but I don't think it's either a book only about the two people we happened and happen to be, but it's a book trying to think through what it is to be reconciled or unreconciled to death, which I don't think is the purview of one dead and one middle-aged American writer (Koval 2008).

With such framings of high seriousness, there is little scope in a reviewer's repertoire for the deploying of wit or irony when deconstructing the memoir. In an interview with Susan Wyndham at the Sydney Writers' Festival, Rieff represents the act of constructing his memoir as some kind of herculean task:

As a hard-nosed journalist and author, David Rieff has covered politics and wars in Cuba, Bosnia and the Middle East. Yet *Swimming in a Sea of Death*, a memoir about the death of his mother, Susan Sontag, is 'certainly the hardest thing I ever did as a writer' (2008).

When arguing the confessional value of his work in relation to his mother's death and the way in which she died, he notes that up until the act of writing the memoir '… I found I hadn't had my say' (ibid). In this sense, he cites his work as a formative right of reply:

Had my mother not involved me in telling her she was going to make it, or had there been any way of talking about the past that did not make her angry or sad, I suspect I wouldn't have written it. I don't have an Oprah-oriented bone in my body (ibid).

The memoir, while responding to (and correcting) his complicit and false affirmations during the last months of Sontag's illness, forms a therapeutic space in which Rieff narrates and expiates his guilt. When asked the question by Steve Paulson: 'Did not telling her the truth about her condition take a toll on you?' (2008) Rieff replies:

It exacted a tremendous price. I never got to say goodbye. I don't want to romanticize the end of life, but we never had the kinds of conversations I

> would've liked to have had with her. Conversations about the past. I would've liked to have said certain things to her. We had a complicated relationship. There were very good times and very bad times between us. I would have liked to have gone beyond those before she left us. But that's impossible if you decide not to acknowledge the fact of dying. So that's the price I paid. But she made it very clear what she wanted. I didn't feel that my interests could be put ahead of that (ibid).

The positioning of his memoir, and in some ways himself as a victim engaged in a reparative act, makes it increasingly difficult to review the work in any other way than as an important *personal* intervention on his part. In the same interview he notes: 'I'm not a confessional person. This is all very new territory to me' (ibid). This claim of traversing emotionally 'new territory' can also work to engender empathy and potentially preserve him from reviews that might seek to negatively assess his writing ability.

In fact, the kinds of reviews that classically constellate around his memoir tend to identify with his diminished sense of self, and valorise his confessional efforts. Blake Morrison's review for the *Guardian* enshrines the solemn tenor of his memoir:

> But the palace of guilt has many pavilions, and as well as suffering from survivor's guilt and filial guilt he's haunted by a sense of failure: 'I still cannot believe that there was nothing I could do to help.'… This is a sad and sombre book, but it's leavened with wise quotations. And, like Joan Didion's *The Year of Magical Thinking*, its story of an embattled death-refusenik is the more affecting because it sheds no tears (2008).

Diane Johnson's and John Murray's particular representation of the memoir for the *New York Review of Books* imbues Rieff's work with the kind of seriousness that could work to place it outside witty critical redress:

> Few of us lose a parent without regret and some self-reproach, some sense of things undone or injustices unredressed; it is a natural component of grief. The literature of memoirs by children of their parents, from Father and Son to Mommie Dearest – whether by Edmund Gosse or John Stuart Mill, Sean Wilsey or Francine du Plessix Gray – may be affectionate, angry, or ambivalent, but such works inevitably contain conscious or unconscious expressions of the reservations and differences essential in a parent-child relation if the child isn't to be submerged in the parent's tremendous identity. David Rieff's memoir of his mother, Susan Sontag, has all of these qualities, which perhaps accounts for its power beyond mere eulogy, elegy, or complaint (2008).

For a reviewer, it would be somewhat difficult to respond oppositionally (and humorously) to a text that is *singularly* and deliberately read as primarily contributing to, and advancing, social attitudes: 'Besides being an eloquent record of grief, it raises a number of issues pertaining to cancer, its treatment, and our attitudes toward the language of illness and dying – subjects long of interest to Sontag herself' (ibid). In other quarters, the memoir's merit is further argued on the grounds of its consciousness-raising:

> Few of us weather the death of a loved one without second thoughts. Rieff's book is a moving account of his own situation, and might serve a larger cause by encouraging conversations about the complicated art of dying. Now that we're beyond shame in talking about sex and money, candor about dying could be our last great taboo (Benedict 2011).

Accordingly, texts that are largely positioned as breaking such taboos, can, at times, be afforded a type of exemption from stringent literary standards and subsequent ridicule.

'Rebellious humour mocks the social rules'

There are prevailing social etiquettes around the taboo of dying, and humour used in these contexts can often be interpreted as transgressive. As Billig points out: 'Rebellious humour mocks the social rules, and, in its turn, can be seen to challenge, or rebel against, the rules' (2005: 202). However, there are a minority of critics and journalists who, while noting the serious import of Rieff's work, offer 'rebellious' critiques by drawing on wit and irony as ways of assessing the merits of *Swimming in a Sea of Death: A Son's Memoir*.

Adam Mars-Jones, in a column for the *Guardian* questioning Rieff's motivation and skill in writing the memoir, notes: 'Something graver than disillusionment emerges from these pages, though – the sense of a large figure being cut down to size by someone who resents his dependence and a competition that he can't win, even after her death' (2008). While, as Mars-Jones argues, 'Death disinhibits the survivors' (ibid), what is refreshing about his review is that death has not inhibited his commentary. Beyond the opening paragraphs, he displays a freedom to reflect colloquially and draw on witty analogy to accentuate his assessment of the memoir's literary value:

> Being a mediocre writer isn't a crime, but it's certainly a crying shame on a project like this. If Sontag was still plying her peremptory pencil, any number of sentences here would have been underlined or simply crossed out: 'His silence was, as the cliché goes, eloquent'; 'Hard cases make bad law, as the cliché goes'; 'Feeling special is part of what makes us human.' She would have demanded a proper source for the 'old Oxbridge joke' that 'what's true is obvious and what isn't obvious isn't true', over which even the great god Google shrugs its shoulders helplessly. She would have queried his attribution of the 'gnomic aphorism "Less is more"' to Buckminster Fuller rather than Mies van der Rohe. As a young man, Rieff may have thought of writing as being the equivalent of a 'family olive oil business', but his pressing produces an off flavour (ibid).

Having cleverly undercut assumptions about Rieff's lineage and refused to offer the work a status not earned by its own compositional excellence, Mars-Jones uses wry comparison to validate his point. The 'off flavour' of the memoir is cogently summarised by Mars-Jones's chief complaint relating to the way Rieff handles Sontag's death: 'He places emphasis on his mother's loss of dignity in her last illness, and there is much about modern medicine which can dehumanise the patient, but he chips away at what is left' (ibid).

While Mars-Jones, like other reviewers, concedes that 'the terrain of *Swimming in a Sea of Death* is necessarily bleak' (ibid), he draws on irony to register the other concerns he has with the text:

> Even the professional world mentioned at the beginning of the book soon disappears, although in the short term, he [Rieff] found himself discussing Middle East affairs with his mother, 'as if that mattered anymore'. Elsewhere he quotes, apparently with approval, her standard response to accusations of excessive seriousness ('If I don't believe in my own work, why should anyone else?'), but isn't tempted to imitate her (ibid).

Again, instead of the praise-worthy treatment of the memoir found in so many other reviews, Mars-Jones continues to use irony as a way of interrogating the complexity of the author's motivation for writing the book: 'Rieff is hard on himself, lamenting his tendency to be inhibited, withholding, morose, clumsy, cold, except that in this specialised context, every confession masks an accusation' (ibid). But, unlike a number of other reviews that interpret the text as a moving epitaph to Sontag, Mars-Jones makes reference to the concerns that Rieff raises about his mother's one-time companion Annie Leibovitz and the photographs she took and circulated of Sontag's ill and deceased body. In the memoir Rieff reflects: 'She would not have had time to mourn herself and to be become physically unrecognizable at the end even to herself, let alone humiliated posthumously by being "memorialized" that way in those carnival images taken by Annie Leibovitz' (2008: 150). In a witty critique of this treatment of Leibovitz, Mars-Jones responds:

> He doesn't claim a symmetrical isolation for his mother but he edits her dance card. There are just two references to Annie Leibovitz. The first describes her as Sontag's 'on-again, off-again companion of many years', which makes her sound like an unsatisfactory family retainer (2008).

The tone and 'rebellious' use of Mars-Jones's wit stands in direct contrast to the frequently standardised and rarefied descriptions of the memoir, of which Diane Leach's partially serves as an exemplar:

> Rieff is Susan Sontag's son. His memoir of her final battle with the cancer is eloquent, elegant and pained. Three years after the death of one of our great intellectuals, her son remains in a state of deep, guilty grief. His is not

a year of magical thinking; it is a lifetime ration, and we can only hope writing this book gave him some solace (2008).

Interestingly though, despite Leach's desire for Rieff to have experienced the consolation of mourning via the production of his text, she is still capable of deftly raising her own observational irony:

> It's certain the cognoscenti will jump on this, a sort of Britney debacle for the intellectual set, but these same cognoscenti weren't there, rendering them unqualified judges. As a member of the unqualified party, I cannot help but notice Rieff's own set of posthumous carnival images that, if anything, expose his mother even more than her lover's photographs. It is Rieff who tells us what Sontag thought and felt during her last days and in quotes from earlier diaries. He describes her decline – this once brightest of intellectual lights, equally celebrated for her cerebral beauty – suffering from 'chemo brain', too weak to roll over in bed, 'covered in sores, incontinent, and half delirious...' carrying on to her final moments of life, which were blessedly peaceful (ibid).

In this isolated instance, Leach's critique is aligned more with her concern around the literary preservation of the patient's dignity than any protest about the actual quality of Rieff's writing. Conversely for Philip Hensher, like Mars-Jones, the matter of literary distinction proves vital. In his scrupulous review for the London-based *Daily Telegraph*, Hensher discerns:

> A further justification that is often raised in these cases, however – that of the quality of the book – is sadly lacking here. In the end, you feel that, despite the best intentions, the most private of experiences has been described without producing something good enough (2008).

Again, adopting a colloquial and witty tone that declines to be disarmed by the serious themes of the book, he writes:

> When one reads, early on in the book, the expression 'I thought to myself' one has to conclude at a stroke that Rieff can't be the author of 'the highest originality and artistry' proclaimed by Janet Malcolm on the back cover (ibid).

For Hensher, the responsibility of the book critic remains governed by literary standards. He boldly asserts that: 'Clearly, Rieff wants to be a great writer, not just a peddler of reportage. Signs of this anxiety are everywhere' (ibid). Hensher refuses to provide Rieff with a free literary pass on the basis that the book deals with disease and dying. While Hensher does not overtly delight in pointing out the stylistic concerns he has with the text, as a diligent reviewer he continues to hold Rieff to ethical account:

> There is no pleasure in dismissing a book that is, after all, the product of an appalling human experience, but it seems like bad taste to ask of the

medical profession and, indeed, of the terminal disease itself: 'Do you know who my mother is?'... This bad taste is epitomised in a final description of Montparnasse Cemetery, where Sontag is buried: Beckett, we are told, Emil Cioran, Jean-Paul Sartre, Raymond Aron and Charles Baudelaire are all buried nearby. One wants to suggest, politely, that a cemetery is not the same thing as a cocktail party (ibid).

Again, Hensher's wit and clever analogy adeptly point to and gently ridicule the vanity of celebrity, leaving the reader with a haunting reminder he sees as somewhat overlooked in Rieff's rendering: 'Between those graves, too, are the graves of people no one has ever heard of. Their lives might have been less distinguished than Sontag's; but their deaths were probably very much the same' (ibid). Clearly evident in Hensher's treatment of the memoir is Billig's conception that 'humour and seriousness remain inextricably linked' (2005: 243). Here the reviewer has an opportunity to use one in service of the other.

Who am I to pass judgement?

For many reviewers, however, there is an initial reticence to use humour to critique a grave autobiographical account of the disease and death of a loved one. This hesitancy is gestured by Adam Begley's opening remarks in his book review for the *New York Observer*:

> There's something obscene about sitting at a desk, in a chair that corrects the posture, sipping warm, sugary tea, yawning or scratching, barely aware of the fug of felt life, all the while getting ready to give the thumbs-up or thumbs-down to a book that records a mother's desperate losing battle against disease and her son's numb grief when she dies. I am in the realm of the living, foolishly taking it for granted as most of us do; David Rieff has been immersed in death ever since the day nearly four years ago when his mother, Susan Sontag, was diagnosed with a rare, particularly lethal cancer of the blood. Who am I to pass judgement on her mortal struggle, on his howl of pain? (2008).

Begley's question 'Who am I to pass judgement on her mortal struggle, on his howl of pain?' in some ways offers a temporary return to Croce's reluctance to discuss the undiscussable. Begley, however, is ultimately able to justify critiquing Rieff's work providing the following rationale:

> But here it is, a book, a memoir: *Swimming in a Sea of Death* – it's out in the world now. No longer just an oozing wound Mr Rieff felt compelled to poke at in the privacy of his office (imagine him sitting there day after day, reliving the anguished stages of an unquiet death), it has become a cultural artefact, a document that tells us something about Susan Sontag, about David Rieff – and, of course, about ourselves (ibid).

Evident in his reflection is a cogent resolution of potential disparate resistances or instinctive (over)privileging when it comes to reviewing 'oozing wounds'. For Begley, despite personal preferences to protect the feelings of the grieving, the duty of the reviewer/journalist necessarily comes to the fore when there is a 'cultural artefact' to be professionally assessed. In Begley's reckoning, once a writer has publicly circulated their work (and commercially profited from it) then the reviewer is entitled to apply some kind of rigorous criteria to the work.

Despite his initial reluctance, Begley soon enforces similar literary expectations to those of Mars-Jones and Hensher. He writes: 'Though in some ways profoundly intimate, it's a portrait curiously lacking in detail. We never get a good look at her. That could be because Mr Rieff has no talent for description, and it could also be a matter of scruple' (ibid). Adopting a similar tenor as Mars-Jones and Hensher, he casually uses ironic asides to clever effect: 'We learn nothing about Sontag the thinker and very little about Sontag the writer. (Very occasionally, Mr Rieff quotes from her journals to dazzling effect: Her brilliance is immediately apparent.)' (ibid).

And again, this longer passage demonstrates Begley's sustained commitment to using the clever parenthetical aside and rhetorical questions as modes for further interrogating Rieff's motives:

> He writes, 'Had I been a better person, doubtless I would have had at least a somewhat more intelligent apprehension about what I should have done [i.e. for his mother]. But even to put my own failings at the center of this is a species of vanity.' It's hard not to supply an addendum: And what if Susan Sontag had been a 'better person'? Would she perhaps have made it easier for her son to be helpful? (ibid).

Most importantly here, Begley also performs the important task of inviting readers to fill in lacunae and actively locate the subtext in any text purporting to be, or positioning itself as, a work of memorialisation.

Books (and reviews) are not made out of emotions

In briefly looking at the registers of Mars-Jones, Hensher and Begley in particular, one finds that these reviewers are able to hold in creative tension the seeming polar opposites of the memoir's memorialising and grim content with their own honed and reflexive journalistic wit. In this way their work (and readers' responses to their critiques) become illustrative of Billig's more general observation: 'Philosophers have called humans "the laughing animal". But we are the laughing animal only because we are also the unlaughing one' (2005: 7). In this sense, a reader may find that they are not invited to laugh at Rieff's personal circumstances, but perhaps smile wryly at the reviewers' clever assessments of his literary presentation of those circumstances.

In returning to Croce's notion of discussing the undiscussable, and by extension, reviewing the unreviewable, the contributions of Mars-Jones, Hensher and Begley offer an intervention of sorts. That is, they demonstrate the potential complex dichotomous unlaughing/laughing response to works of mourning, and the staunch refusal to rarefy Rieff's memoir or place it beyond the normal bounds of criticism. Hensher astutely, and summarily, offers a template for this kind of reviewing praxis:

> Degas once told Mallarmé that he had had an idea, and wanted to write a sonnet. Mallarmé replied, truthfully: 'Ce n'est point avec des idées que l'on fait des vers: c'est avec des mots.' No one will doubt the intensely felt emotions that drive this book. The trouble is that books are not made out of emotions; they are made, as Mallarmé said, out of words (2008).

Or as Begley so finally, simply (and sympathetically) puts it: 'To his credit, David Rieff is more of a son than a writer' (2008).

References

Alba, Ana (2009) Interview with David Rieff. Available online at http://w2.bcn.cat/bcnmetropolis/arxiu/en/page86a6.html?id=22&ui=254, accessed on 17 January 2015

Barnes, Julian (2011) For sorrow there is no remedy, *New York Review of Books*, 7 April. Available online at http://www.nybooks.com/articles/archives/2011/apr/07/sorrow-there-no-remedy/, accessed on 17 December 2014

Begley, Adam (2008) Rieff's grief: Sontag's son on her death, *Observer*, 1 August. Available online at http://observer.com/2008/01/rieffs-grief-sontags-son-on-her-death/, accessed on 17 January 2015

Benedict, Elizabeth (2011) Can we talk about Susan Sontag's death and then maybe our own? *Huffington Post*, 25 May. Available online at http://www.huffingtonpost.com/elizabeth-benedict/can-we-talk-about-susan-s_b_81386.html, accessed on 21 January 2015

Billig, Michael (2005) *Laughter and Ridicule: Towards a Social Critique of Humour*, London: Sage

Bordwell, Marilyn (1998) Dancing with death: Performativity and 'undiscussable' bodies, *Still/Here*, *Text and Performance Quarterly*, Vol. 18, No. 4 pp 369-379

Carroll, Noël (2014) *Humour: A Very Short Introduction*, Oxford: Oxford University Press

Ciabattari, Jane (2011) The future of book reviewers: Critics vs. Amazon reviewing, *Daily Beast*, 5 December. Available online at http://www.thedailybeast.com/articles/2011/05/12/the-future-of-book-reviews-critics-versus-amazon-reviewers.html, accessed on 21 January 2015

Couser, Thomas (2012) *Memoir*, Oxford: Oxford University Press

Croce, Arlene (1994) Discussing the undiscussable, *New Yorker*, 26 December-2 January pp 54-60

Eakin, John Paul (2008) *Living Autobiographically: How to Create Identity in Narrative*, New York: Cornell University Press

Hensher, Philip (2008) Susan Sontag: A cemetery is not a party, *Telegraph*, 21 June. Available online at http://www.telegraph.co.uk/culture/books/non_fictionreviews/3554852/Susan-Sontag-a-cemetery-is-not-a-party.html, accessed on 21 January 2015

Johnson, Diane, and Murray, John F. (2008) Will to live, *New York Review of Books*, 14 February. Available online at http://www.nybooks.com/articles/archives/2008/feb/14/will-to-live/, accessed on 21 January 2015

Jurecic, Ann (2012) *Illness as Narrative*, Pittsburgh: University of Pittsburgh Press

Koval, Ramona (2008) David Rieff live at the Sydney Writers' Festival, 23 May. Available online at http://www.abc.net.au/radionational/programs/bookshow/david-rieff-live-at-the-sydney-writers-festival/3266684#transcript, accessed on 22 January 2015

Leach, Diane (2008) Both sides now, *January Magazine*, January. Available online at http://www.januarymagazine.com/biography/finalswim.html, accessed on 21 January 2015

Lively, Penelope (2008) Review of *Swimming in a Sea of Death*, *Financial Times*, 9 June. Available online at http://www.ft.com/cms/s/0/46b86baa-3365-11dd-8a25-0000779fd2ac.html#axzz3Uv48YcM7, accessed on 20 January 2015

Mars-Jones, Adam (2008) Don't look here if you're seeking Susan, *Guardian*, 15 June. Available online at http://www.theguardian.com/books/2008/jun/15/biography.features7, accessed on 19 January 2015

Morrison, Blake (2008) Sons and mothers, *Guardian*, 31 May. Available online at http://www.theguardian.com/books/2008/may/31/biography2, accessed on 19 January 2015

Orwell, George (1970 [1946]) Confessions of a book reviewer, Orwell, Sonia and Angus, Ian (eds) *The Collected Essays, Journalism and Letters of George Orwell*, Vol. 4, London: Penguin Books pp 215-218. Originally published in *Tribune*, 3 May 1946

Paulson, Steve (2008) Susan Sontag's final wish, *Salon*, 13 February. Available online at http://www.salon.com/2008/02/13/david_rieff/, accessed on 19 January 2015

Payne, Tom (2011) The role of the book critic, *Telegraph*, 10 August. Available online at http://www.telegraph.co.uk/culture/books/8682006/The-role-of-the-book-critic.html, accessed on 19 January 2015

Rieff, David (2008) *Swimming in a Sea of Death: A Son's Memoir*, New York: Simon & Schuster

Simon & Schuster (2015) Promotional web page on *Swimming in a Sea of Death: A Son's Memoir*. Available online at http://books.simonandschuster.com/Swimming-in-a-Sea-of-Death/David-Rieff/9780743299473, accessed on 21 January 2015

Wyndham, Susan (2008) Difficult work in the name of the mother, *Sydney Morning Herald*, 20 May. Available online at http://www.smh.com.au/news/books/difficult-work-in-the-name-of-the-mother/2008/05/19/1211182699977.html, accessed on 17 January 2015

Acknowledgements

I wish to acknowledge trauma scholar Dr Victoria Burrows and Associate Professor Jill Gordon for their mentoring of my academic journey, and Dr Robyn Priestley for her generous engagement with this chapter. It is a chapter dedicated to my magnanimous mother and my four-footed soul mates Eliot, Audrey, Lily, Isabel-Sadie, Angel, Nikita and Scout. And, my abiding thanks go to my father for the inspiration he was in life, and continues to be after his death.

Note on the contributor
Carolyn Rickett is an Assistant Dean of Research, Senior Lecturer in Communication and creative arts practitioner at Avondale College of Higher Education, Australia. She is co-ordinator of *The New Leaves* writing project, an initiative for people who have experienced or are experiencing the trauma of a life-threatening illness. Together with Judith Beveridge, she is co-editor of the *New Leaves Poetry Anthology*. Other anthologies she has co-edited with Judith include: *Wording the Word; Here, Not There;* and *A Way of Happening*. Carolyn's research publications include the areas of: trauma studies, writing as therapeutic intervention, cancer narratives, journalism, literary studies, poetry praxis and professional ethics.

Russell Brand: The Compassionate Humorist

Sarah Niblock

He's been damned as a 'chest hair-obsessed Hollywood type' by UK Independence Party leader Nigel Farage, cursed as a 'vacuous soundbite on legs' by tabloid newspaper the *Sun* and pilloried as 'part of the problem' by *Channel 4 News*. One could be forgiven for thinking the 'he' in question is the despotic leader of a rogue state or some terrorist organisation. Rather, they are describing the edgy English comedian and actor-turned-revolutionary Russell Brand.

Brand is known on both sides of the Atlantic for his stand-up routines, radio and TV shows, and character acting in Hollywood movies such as *Forgetting Sarah Marshall* (2008) and the remake of *Arthur* (2011). With his dandyesque appearance and idiosyncratic articulacy, he has made a striking intervention on comedy and journalism. Visually and in writing, Brand resides on the margins of class and gender, offering himself as a fascinating point of contemplation. His self-referential, soul-bearing humour in which he describes his exploits in excruciating detail beckon identification with him. His rock star looks and disarmingly camp manner have attracted legions of female fans and he even recounts his womanising with unflinching, self-deprecating honesty.

Latterly, Brand has been using his fame and, most effectively, his irreverent, articulate and quirky humour, to shine light on causes and injustices overlooked by everyday mainstream news agendas. This strategy has attracted criticism, such as from former tabloid editor Piers Morgan who has likened Brand to the US comedian Bill Cosby, currently under investigation following allegations of a series of serious sexual offences (Morgan 2014). Morgan wrote:

> Of all the famous hypocrites, it's hypocritical comedians who can often provoke the most intense irritation ... and they are also the ones who usually erupt with the most comically indignant fury when their own rank hypocrisy is exposed (ibid).

Morgan was referring to an interview of Brand by *Channel 4 News* reporter Paraic O'Brien on 1 December 2014 as the former stood with campaigners petitioning against US investment company Westbrook Partners. Westbrook was planning to increase massively the rents of tenants on its New Era estate in East London. The estate is located in a once-deprived area, which has undergone significant gentrification with a resultant upswing in property values. O'Brien pointed out that Brand's own East London residence must be highly valuable, and suggested Brand was thereby complicit in the tenants' fate. Angered, Brand responded that the story was not about him and accused the journalist of being 'a snide' (see Press Association 2014). Brand's intervention may have worked though, since instead of evicting families to build expensive properties, the company sold the development to an affordable housing association.

This was a rare glimpse of Brand in a more serious mood; his public demeanour particularly when writing is to use humour to undercut revered institutions, behaviours and rituals. Or as he puts it: 'Have you been out in society recently? 'Cause it's SHIT.'

A prolific writer, Brand has donated fees and profits from his various articles and books – as well as pledging libel damages – to causes such as the Justice for the 96 campaign for families who lost loved ones at the Hillsborough football stadium disaster in 1989. His print journalism, which expounds on topics ranging from drugs policy, celebrity, politics and football, is mainly published by the UK 'quality' the *Guardian*, though he has contributed occasionally to other outlets and guest-edited the UK politics and current affairs magazine, *New Statesman*, in October 2013. He posts daily video podcasts to his YouTube channel, *The Trews*, of which he writes: 'I give you the true news so you don't have to invest any money in buying newspapers that charge you for the privilege of keeping your consciousness imprisoned in a tiny box of ignorance and lies' (YouTube 2014). Some of his recent work has been produced with the assistance of Johann Hari, a former writer for the *Independent* newspaper who lost his job in 2011 for fabricating interviews (Urquhart 2012). Brand is the author of five books – two are autobiographical, one a collection of his football journalism, and another his political manifesto *Revolution* (Brand 2014a). He has now branched out into writing for children, a reworking of the Pied Piper depicting an anarchic rat collective. 'My hope,' he told the *New Yorker*, 'is that children will put down this book and pick up *Manufacturing Consent* [the seminal text about the propaganda role of the corporate media by Edward Herman and Noam Chomsky]' (Schulman 2014).

Brand's editorial *modus operandi* is to subvert his celebrity status to beckon network news crews to protest marches, petition hand-ins and even seedier, unphotogenic spaces such as drug dens rarely entered by reporters. As he wrote in the *Guardian*: 'The greater the power the greater the obligation to be decent. Or as Stan Lee put it – in the mouth of Spider-Man's uncle – "with great power comes great responsibility", a maxim so irrefutably neat that I'd prefer it were

Socrates' (Brand 2013a). Indeed, Brand is a very successful media strategist, exploiting several current trends: the fixation with celebrity culture, his social media jamming savvy and the widespread mistrust in politicians, not least since the MPs' expenses scandal erupted in 2010. For example, he wrote in the *New Statesman*: 'I shook George Osborne's hand once, by accident, it was like sliding my hand into a dilated cow' (2013f).

His writing and often witty commentary explores political and social issues from a compassionate and empathetic perspective to engage and excite young people in politics, something mainstream news struggles to do. Academic Barbie Zelizer has noted that the young and marginalised 'demand opinion and critique as a necessary journalistic engagement' (2008: 90). A poll by the Pew Research Center for the People and the Press (2012) reported that fewer than 5 per cent of 18 to 30-year-olds are interested in political news. The same research centre found that 21 per cent of 18 to 34-year-olds regularly learned about the 2004 US presidential campaign from comedy television programmes such as *Saturday Night Live* or the *Daily Show with Jon Stewart*. The figure was only 2 per cent lower than respondents who said they received campaign information via network news. The teenagers Mindich (2005) interviewed for his survey referred to the apparent detachment of journalists as a cause of their lack of engagement.

Brand now wields considerable power. As he is taken ever more seriously, not only by audiences but also by political figures and policy-makers in the UK and further afield – especially for his campaigning work on drug law reform – he has become something of a problem for journalism. At one time easy to categorise as an accessible celebrity subject replete with easy copy opportunities, he is now journalism's rival and critic. Whereas the *Sun* sells 1.9 million copies per day (see Audit Bureau of Circulations website at http://www.abc.org.uk/), considerably more than Brand's latest book has to date, the comedian's social media following eclipses that of the newspaper. He has nearly 9 million Twitter followers, compared with the *Sun*'s 691,000.

Brand is an important journalistic figure, disruptive at its margins. His disdain for his former media employers is comically expressed; he described MTV as 'perhaps the planet's most obvious purveyor of neurodross and pop-cultural claptrap – like a glistening pink pony trotting through your mind shitting glitter' (2013f). In Brand's hands, journalism is a set of practices geared towards a particular social goal, rather than a set of outlets or institutions that validate its practitioners' authority. When viewed in this way, we can think of journalistic practices outside the frame of mainstream news organisations, profit and professional mores and assess its potential to work much more deeply in the public interest. Barbie Zelizer has pointed out that we must think of journalism as more than some kind of 'shared repertoire of public events' (2008: 86) but as a melding of communication culture and critique.

The academic study and the education of future practitioners have foregrounded journalism as an act of communication, downplaying its role beyond information relay as a site for reflection and negotiation. There is a focus on accuracy, impartiality, law, sourcing, beats, accountability, regulating and reproducing the dispassionately effective inverted triangle. These professional principles and practices are, it is oft relayed in lecture rooms and abiding texts, to ensure journalism informs and supports a living, breathing public sphere. Scholarship looks for empirical evidence to demonstrate when journalism does not fulfil those principles and practices and fails, wittingly or unwittingly, in its watchdog function. However, Brand uses journalism as a reflexive dynamic space rather than a unidirectional journalist-to-reader transaction to political end. For, as Zelizer observes, by…

> … providing information regarded as important and topical, journalism's communicative acts thereby have helped to reinforce the notion that the much heralded triumvirate of polity, public and journalism works; each arm supports the others in a fashion that is continuous, integral, and indispensable (op cit: 86).

As such, media scholarship has tended to favour distant rather than intimate modes of presentation, and valorised authoritative fact-rich, multi-sourced outputs as 'proper' journalism. Where it takes issue is with the messy, immersive, personal or critiquing pieces that appear to subvert the valorised formats. One only has to look at university assessment models that favour long, multi-sourced news broadcast packages over lifestyle features or op-eds. There is little space within the curriculum or scholarship for alternative forms and practices or journalism's liminal intersections with its audiences or with other forms such as the subjective scrutiny comedy places on events and issues. For journalism to function both as an industry and as a quantifiable site for scholarship, education and training it has to have clear professional boundaries.

Brand's oeuvre does not incorporate the normative binary approach of facts versus fictions but is one of interpretation and active negotiation with sources: he does not patronise his audience but properly reflects their own experience of being 'dumbed down' by the corporate media. And it is deliberately humorous, not just for self-aggrandising laughs but because Brand sees humour as a revolutionary force: 'Serious causes can and must be approached with good humour, otherwise they're boring and can't compete with the Premier League and *Grand Theft Auto*. Social movements needn't lack razzmatazz' (2013f).

From suburbia to stardom
Brand's origins were not auspicious, though his early experiences may have framed his mission to align himself journalistically with the marginalised and misrepresented. Born in 1975, Brand grew up in Essex with a single mother, Barbara, a secretary, who suffered three bouts of cancer when he was growing up. His father, Ron, was mostly absent, and Brand did not really get on with his stepfather. Brand's fragility and vulnerability became evident at a young age, expressed initially through depression and an eating disorder, then through addition to heroin, crack cocaine and alcohol from his teens to his twenties. His

potential as a performer gained him a place at a top theatre school, but he was expelled for drug taking. He was arrested many times for drug offences, and for climbing onto a police van and stripping off at an anti-globalisation protest in 2001 (see Sawyer 2008).

Hilariously but excruciatingly confessional, his stand-up comedy invocates his inner demons, which are described unflinchingly in his first autobiography *My Book Wook* (2008). He lays bare his past – his drug taking, cheating the benefits system, using prostitutes. His early stand-up comedy was haphazard due to his chaotic lifestyle, but his intelligence and authenticity quickly attracted agents, awards and media work. In 2000-2001 he hosted the MTV Europe show *Dancefloor Chart*, which involved interviewing intoxicated clubbers acting erratically in Ibiza. The irony was not lost on Brand, who later recalled he was on far stronger substances than his interview subjects, while retaining professional on-screen composure.

Dancefloor Chart may have been something of a blur in Brand's memory but out of it came a much sharper mission to subvert the supposed virtues of journalistic objectivity. His next television project, seven immersive documentaries under the title *Re:Brand*, aimed to take a challenging look at cultural taboos ranging from homelessness to racism. The two *Homeless James* episodes would not endear media ethicists, as Brand gently cajoles and exposes his temporary, pliant adoptee to the point of humiliation. He exposes his own frailties even more, especially the fragility of his and by extension the viewers' potential for finding ourselves on the streets. Russell identifies with Homeless James and implores his viewers to look on with empathy rather than distance or objectification. Journalists' mission and skill in looking at an issue from another perspective other than the received official wisdom is at the basis of muckraking, investigations, cartoons and opinion columns, formats which have always offered reporters a space away from conventional news 'values' and the myths of 'objectivity' and 'neutrality'.

'It's only language'

Brand's reflexive candour and his disarmingly camp, cosmeticised rock'n'roll dandy photogenics led to successful stand-up comedy tours and television appearances. Now clean after a three-month spell in rehab, what emerged most evidently was his remarkable articulacy and talent as a writer, through which he unpacked the machinations and implications of his growing fame. Brand's use of language has been lauded and lambasted in equal measure. He exploits his rich vocabulary, tinged with high Victorian excess, in opposition to the journalistic mantra to use one word when five would do. Instead, he typically sounds quite old-fashioned using terms such as 'loquacious' and 'crepuscular', but disrupts their flow by juxtaposing them seamlessly with terms such as 'wanker' and 'bird' in a high-pitched Estuary screech. For example, describing the vitriolic, right-wing *Daily Mail* columnist Melanie Phillips to his *Guardian* readers, after appearing on the BBC's *Question Time* alongside her, Brand writes:

> In person, inconveniently, she is beautiful. Deep brown, soulful eyes, elegant features and a truthful, caring sensitivity in her tone. It is surprising and bizarre, then, to see her contort on air into a taut, jabbing Gollum figure, untutored index finger fucking the audience in the face when they pipe up about Syria or whatever. Oddly, I still like her, regarding her opinions as an arbitrary appurtenance that she pops on in public, like a daft hat that says 'Immigrants Out' on the brim … Like most of us, Melanie just needs a cuddle (Brand 2013b).

His labelling of the Deputy Prime Minister Nick Clegg as 'Renegey Cleggy' makes a mockery of 'genuine' political journalism. He can also be witheringly brief, writing that Kyoto's climate change agreements are simply 'not worth a wank in a windsock', thus agreeing with Naomi Klein's more conventionally expressed thesis in her book *This Changes Everything* (2014). He upturns the notion that communicating politics via the media must be deferential, formal and unquestioning of authoritative voices. Brand's editorial strategy, both in form and content, is a direct assault on the mainstream journalism that only speaks to white, middle-class men – a very small yet powerful percentage of the population. Instead, he aligns himself with the oppressed and marginalised, to the extent of immersive empathy, and uses his celebrity status to voice their questions and promote their predicaments to those in power. As he recognises himself:

> I think these columnist fellas who give me aggro for not devising a solution or for using long words are just being territorial. When they say 'long words' they mean 'their words' like I'm a monkey who got in their Mum's dressing up box or a hooligan in a policeman's helmet (Brand 2013c).

Despite his command of written English, his rise to fame was interconnected with niche programming and reality TV such as *Big Brother*, for which he presented spin-off shows from 2004-2006, and BBC 6 Music, for whom he had a Sunday lunchtime show from 2006-2007 before it moved to Saturday evenings on BBC Radio 2. His rock and roll persona led to a fascinating feature in *Observer Music Monthly* in 2006. Brand's 3,000 words on meeting Rolling Stone Keith Richards is much less a rock interview and review and much more a reflexive semiotic analysis of the elaborate, symbolic rituals involved in gaining momentary access to a rock legend. Fewer than 30 words of the text are direct interview quotes.

On arrival at the concert venue, Brand is festooned with security permits and wristbands. He wrote: 'Reaching Keith, it transpires, is like attaining enlightenment: you must pass through many levels and exercise great patience and detachment.' He witnesses first-hand the band's control over its visual signification, as they avoid audience shots that lay bare the ageing demographic of their fans. Brand struggles with the incongruence of marketing strategy and creative authenticity:

It's the Rolling Stones, for christ's sake. As omnipresent as the sky, worshipped across the globe for almost half a century. Surely they can afford to relax about their image? They are what they are, one would think. The objective truth, their continued brilliance, their catalogue of work, their longevity all suggests an established immovable force, above harmful critique (Brand 2006).

Despite Brand's swagger, he is intimidated by Richards' imminent presence, writing:

'Keith is coming,' someone said. I realised I simply had to go to the toilet. Before every performance, I ritually evacuate. It makes me feel cleansed, light, literally unblocked; the thought, the very idea, of meeting him with full bowels seemed absurd and someone took me, like a toddler, to the lavvy. ... It's not just the defecation; I like to have a moment alone to gather my thoughts, to focus. It's a hangover from my time as a junkie, when every challenging encounter was preceded by a trip to a cubicle to heighten, or numb, my unreliable senses (ibid).

This contrasts with his own earlier attempts at rock star behaviour when he describes checking into his hotel:

'I should like Mr Beckham's suite,' I requested.

'He had a standard room.'

I paused.

'I shall take the suite regardless' (ibid).

Despite their very brief encounter, Brand defers to Richards: 'I sense the reason he's become an icon is because of an essential quality. Rock'n'roll, it seems, is not borrowed or learned or slung about his shoulders like his guitar but emanating from his core.'

Ethics

While Brand began to craft more and more copy, he also became the subject of copious column inches. Lovers recounted their trysts via kiss-and-tell tabloid tales. When approached by journalists Brand would, instead of speed-dialling his lawyer to raise a super-injunction, provide a balancing direct quote for the reporter to add to the story, along the lines of 'I'd like to thank that woman publicly for assisting me in my hour of need' as if to subvert their shaming, moralistic tone.

Rather than subject himself to formal training, Brand's education in media law and ethics was typically experiential and he tested the regulations to their farthest extremes. When dismissed as a 'c**t' by humanitarian activist Sir Bob Geldof at a 2006 awards ceremony, a visibly-shocked Brand retorted: 'No wonder Bob

Geldof is such an expert on famine. He's been feeding off *I Don't Like Mondays* for 30 years.'

His most publicised ethical *faux pas* occurred while presenting his live BBC Radio 2 show with a celebrity co-host, Jonathan Ross, in October 2008. Andrew Sachs, much loved in Britain for his role as Spanish waiter Manuel in the long-running comedy *Fawlty Towers*, had been booked for a telephone interview on the show, but the hosts made repeated calls to no avail, resulting in them telling Sachs's answerphone that Brand had once had an affair with his granddaughter. The BBC received a handful of concerned calls about the incident in the immediate aftermath, but they were unprepared for the ensuing crisis when a few days later the *Daily Mail* ran headlines calling on the BBC to fire Brand and Ross (Clements 2009). Though the popular press enjoyed taking the high ground at Brand's expense, as an ethical lapse it paled in comparison with the soon-to-emerge Hackgate revelations of widespread 'phone hacking' by journalists (Davies 2014). Clearly very shaken by the episode, Brand departed for the US, briefly marrying pop star Katy Perry, starring in a series of film roles and, as is par for the course, gaining media notoriety and death threats having earlier described the former President, George W. Bush, as a 'retarded cowboy' while presenting the MTV Music Awards on 7 September 2008.

Brand's stateside period was short-lived and he returned to the UK in the wake of the publication of his second autobiography, *Booky Wook 2: This Time It's Personal* (2010) in which he expressed his dissatisfaction with working in Hollywood. As if wishing to forge a more cerebral identity post-Sachsgate, he popped up at protest marches and then, due to his journalistic interventions into UK drugs policy, made notable appearances on flagship news and political programmes. He was interviewed on memorable editions of BBC's *Newsnight* by Jeremy Paxman (see, for example, YouTube 2013) and Evan Davies, and has expounded on his political perspectives on BBC Radio 4's *Start the Week* – all entertaining, but this time none of it delivered to raise laughs.

Brand's journalism illuminates the disjuncture between British media and politics and his own warmth. As media consumers feasting on a 24/7 continuing feed of human suffering, we have become inured to the problems in our society. In newsrooms, earnestness and passion are treated with suspicion, as a reckless route to accusations of bias, the official term being a 'conflict of interest'. Editorial teams respond slickly to disasters, terror attacks, VIP deaths and recessions in time-honoured fashion by regularly rehearsing for them and having minute-by-minute action plans in place for their coverage. When former UK Prime Minister Margaret Thatcher died in 2013, newsrooms had a vast 'arsenal' of prepared material for broadcast, print and upload. Headlines had been written years before. The scenes we tend to associate with newsrooms in our mind's eye when big stories break – noisy panic on the editorial floor, frenzied clacking on keyboards to cries of 'hold the front page' – exist only in the movies these days. Deadlines come and go with barely an audible flicker bar the fizz of a mineral water bottle lid. While editorial chiefs patted their own backs for their seamless ultramarathon coverage of Thatcher's demise, which seemed to go on for many weeks unabated, one of the best-received pieces was penned by Brand. He expressed a tragic disjunction between the Iron Lady and the solemn figure of an old lady with degenerative mental illness (Brand 2013d). He recalled a bizarre encounter with her, which prompted him to recall growing up under the most unlikely matriarch imaginable. While walking in central London he encountered Mrs Thatcher quietly tending to some roses, guarded by police.

> In this moment she inspired only curiosity, a pale phantom, dumbly filling her day. None present eyed her meanly or spoke with vitriol and it wasn't until an hour later that I dreamt up an Ealing comedy-style caper in which two inept crooks kidnap Thatcher from the garden but are unable to cope with the demands of dealing with her, and finally give her back (Brand 2013d).

He then casts his mind back, amusingly, to his experiences of her mediated image in his youth:

> As I scan the statements of my memory bank for early deposits (it'd be a kid's memory bank account at a neurological NatWest where you're encouraged to become a greedy little capitalist with an escalating family of porcelain pigs), I see her in her hairy helmet, condescending on *Nationwide*, eviscerating eunuch MPs and baffled BBC fuddy duddies with her General Zodd stare and coldly condemning the IRA. And the miners. And the single mums. The dockers. The poll-tax rioters. The Brixton rioters, the Argentinians, teachers; everyone actually (ibid).

His recollection of news broadcasters at the time, such as Sue Lawley, Jan Leeming and Moira Stewart, was of their unwavering complicity in Thatcher's ideological war: 'If Thatcher was the headmistress, they were junior teachers, authoritative but warm enough that you could call them "mum" by accident.' The unexpected melancholic reaction of a 'Leftie' friend ('in his heyday all Red Wedge and right-on punch-ups') reveals empathy to be symbolic of humanity, in sharp contrast to the tenets of Thatcherism:

> This demonstrates, I suppose, that if you opposed Thatcher's ideas it was likely because of their lack of compassion, which is really just a word for love. If love is something you cherish, it is hard to glean much joy from death, even in one's enemies (ibid).

The article is distinctive for its personal, touching candour over the impact Thatcherism has had on his identity and subjectivity, as a boy who grew to maturity during her 'reign', to become a young man with a self-avowedly ruthless streak: 'There are pangs of nostalgia, yes, because for me she's all tied up with *Hi-De-Hi* and *Speak and Spell* and *Blockbusters* and "follow the bear". What is more troubling is my inability to ascertain where my own selfishness ends and her neo-liberal inculcation begins.'

He is unafraid to use humour in the context of her death, not disrespectfully but in such a way as to induce identification and recollection on the part of readers who may be familiar or unfamiliar with Thatcherism. Reading this, it is interesting how the mainstream press choose to decry his compassionate work through a process of othering. Brand, they claim repeatedly, is simply not like us because he is wealthy, outrageous, outspoken and employs a bizarre lexical range.

His emotional honesty means he is especially appealing and convincing when tackling drugs policy.

Drugs – and Brand's self-deprecatory and revelatory wit

As student journalists are instructed, if you want to get a news desk interested in your social affairs coverage, you need to make sure you have a human case study such as a child (or other some-such photogenic sufferer), who will conjure the sympathy of even the hardest-hearted in your target demographic. So it comes as some surprise that a 6ft 2ins tall comedian has managed to secure copious column inches on the seemingly dry subject of drugs law reforms. Perhaps it stems from Brand's excruciatingly funny written revelations from his own 'drugbrella' days about the time he was sacked by MTV for going to work dressed as Osama Bin Laden the day after the 9/11 attacks. It was also the day he introduced his drug dealer to pop star Kylie Minogue: 'Before I knew it, I'd walked across that foyer, made a kind of "Woo-ooh" noise – in a mum-across-a-neighbour's-fence sort of way – and said: "Kylie, meet Gritty." Then I just stood back to watch it unfold' (2007).

Despite the bravado, Brand makes no attempt to conceal his own fragility and vulnerability as an ex-heroin and crack user. But his self-deprecatory and revelatory wit has been a highly knowing and effective strategy in making the media willing to run stories about society's folk devils who have, to date, attracted disdain and blame from the mainstream for their own situation. Drug addicts, these messy souls invisible to journalists, do not make sympathetic copy, Brand observes:

> Can there be any other disease that renders its victims so unappealing? Would Great Ormond Street be so attractive a cause if its beds were riddled with obnoxious little criminals that had 'brought it on themselves'? ... I share my brain with one and I can tell you first hand they are total fucking wankers (Brand 2013e).

Brand campaigns for the legalisation of hard drugs and the decriminalisation of addicts. His belief is that substance abuse is an illness and that the only solution is abstinence-based recovery, not the prescription of methadone. Spurred in part by the death of his distant friend, the singer Amy Winehouse, in July 2011, Brand has committed thousands of words to confessional descriptions of his own addictive behaviour, whether drugs, alcohol, sex or fame. 'I cannot accurately convey to you the efficiency of heroin in neutralising pain,' he wrote (ibid). 'From my first inhalation 15 years ago,' he continues, 'it fumigated my private hell and lay me down in its hazy pastures and a bathroom floor in Hackney embraced me like a womb.' A decade clean and a successful life unfolded, but the battle is lifelong, he writes in customary empathy with users. 'The price of this is constant vigilance because the disease of addiction is not rational' (ibid). There's no politically-correct politeness for Brand when referring to addicts – he refers to them as 'junkies' and makes constant jokes about their ineptitude. He crafts quirky, attention-grabbing Tweets – 'Read this about rat junkies and how they get clean if you're nice to them.'

In April 2012, he gave evidence to the Home Affairs select committee looking into drugs policy at Portcullis House, Westminster. His televised appearance was notable for his entertaining appearance: sporting long wavy hair, necklaces and tattoos covering his bare arms, he bore little resemblance to his interlocutors, the drugs policy-makers meant to be representing the interests and wishes of the British electorate. Reflecting in the *Guardian*, he described how even the visual iconography of parliament, with its statues and paintings of the great and the good, place the ordinary citizen at the very bottom rung of the ladder of value. 'When most of us are in these rooms we feel daunted and belittled, remember [citing Sex Pistols' John Lydon] "they're great and you're not", but the bloke up the front near the mace has spent his whole life in rooms like that, schools like that' (Brand 2013a). The power of Brand's humour here, as in so many of his interventions into public life, comes from his sending up of all that is revered.

'The revolution cannot be boring'

In a column for the *Guardian* written after an interview with the then-*Newsnight* anchor Jeremy Paxman in October 2013, which he credits with launching his journey from comedian to revolutionary, Brand makes clear he is planting the seeds rather than offering the solutions:

> As I said to Paxman at the time 'I can't conjure up a global Utopia right now in this hotel room.' Obviously that's not my job and it doesn't need to be, we have brilliant thinkers and organisations and no-one needs to cook up an egalitarian Shangri-La on their own; we can all do it together (Brand 2013c).

In his book-length polemic, *Revolution*, Brand envisions a world where our 'ultimate aim is to live in self-governing, fully autonomous, ecologically responsible, egalitarian communities. Where like-minded people, or people with compatible cultures (because all our minds are ultimately alike), can live together without fucking around with what other people are up to …. All we have to do is disband the corruption that skews them for the advancement of the elite.' Accusations of hypocrisy from newspaper columnists flared up again: the book is published by Bertelsmann-owned Random House, and Brand's only motive in writing it is to boost his career. Leaping to his defence, fellow politicised UK comedian Mark Steel wrote in the *Belfast Telegraph* that 'if you want to become accepted in Hollywood and creep around the people who run the media in America, everyone knows the first thing to do is write a book called *Revolution* and support strikes by the staff of Walmart. Doris Day was exactly the same' (Steel 2014).

Brand is staunchly reluctant to stand for parliament, despite his evident leadership qualities. His politics is a vehement rejection of parliamentary democracy, calling on the electorate not to vote so as to commit an *en masse* symbolic veto of traditional political structures. In a memorable exchange on BBC's *Question Time* in December 2014, Brand answered a man urging him join Westminster with: 'I'm scared I'd become one of them' (Brand 2014b). After *Newsnight*, Brand hurriedly turned to his preferred medium of text to expound on what he felt were the limitations of the broadcast format. In his blog, he told readers that time and format prevented him from presenting his vision (ibid). Whenever Brand appears in the media he produces copy such as this on what happened behind the scenes, as if to lay bare for the general public the workings of journalism that are ostensibly meant to be in the public interest, yet shrouded from public view. For the vast majority of people, even including students and scholars, it is very hard to gain access to newsrooms and witness everyday news production first hand. After appearing on the MSNBC mid-morning news analysis show *Morning Joe*, Brand wrote in depth about the machinations of editorial working.

> There is usually a detachment from the content. 'Coming up after the break we'll be slicing my belly open and watching while smooth black eels loll out in a sinewy cascade of demented horror.' This abstraction, I think, occurs through institutionalisation. If your function is to robotically report a pre-existing agenda, you needn't directly interface with the content (Brand 2013b).

He goes on to describe television as disturbing to watch or be on: 'The Lynchian subjugation of our humanity; warmth and humour, usurped by a sterile, pastel-coloured steel blade benignly thrust again and again into a grey brain' (ibid).

Earnest and soul searching, Brand's political commentary has prompted complaint that he is no longer injecting enough fun into serious issues, as if his portentous message about the dangers of becoming involved with Westminster could have some basis in truth. He wrote: 'The reality is there are alternatives. That is a terrifying truth that the media, government and big business work so hard to conceal. Even the outlet that printed this will tomorrow print a couple of columns saying what a naïve wanker I am, or try to find ways that I've fucked up' (Brand 2013c).

Conclusions: Satirically undercutting politics

What Brand's emotive work highlights so acutely is the way journalists have used the professional notion of objectivity to mean more than avoiding bias. It is used as a defence to injecting any passion in their reportage. While Brand's work cannot be likened to 'critical incidents' such as Watergate (which played its part in dislodging President Richard Nixon in 1973) and the Gulf War of 1991, which caused journalists to reflect and refine their own professional practices (Schudson 1992: Zelizer 1992), he has opened a critical space for journalists and their audiences to review current industry assumptions and approaches.

Subjective and self-deprecatingly flawed as he is, the public may be more trusting of Brand's quirky, edgy wit than of the media or mainstream political figures. His comedic, liminal position on the border of class and gender identities ensures he facilitates an emotional connection to current affairs as opposed to the distanced formality of authority figures. His reflexive approach whereby he unpacks not only the message but also the means of its mediation exposes the ideological meaning-making inherent in government/journalist relations. Mainstream, corporation-produced journalism is more about news management and packaging than inquiry and questioning, and Brand, like many of his comedy heroes, has sought to fill that glaring, screaming gap with compassion and warmth.

Russell Brand's satirical undercutting of politics helps us to see journalism as an act or a verb, rather than as a job or an institution. It helps us to realise the potential – for the betterment of both practice and scholarship – of viewing journalism as a space to engage people, despite and across the distinctions that separate people from one another. His sheer array of comedic writing across traditional and converged media platforms elicits reaction across social categories. The risk, of course, is that too much deviation from institutions and established practices may further dilute journalism's validity at a time when its professional integrity has waned. Brand's engaging, immersive style highlights to journalists that their industry's relationship with its audiences has changed, even if their professional notions of what it is have not. He challenges journalists – if they are to transmit journalism's relevance to younger audiences – to revisit the standards and assumptions of their professional practice. Perhaps instead of attacking him, they might start to think about what he is saying.

References

Brand, Russell (2006) I'm with the band, *Observer Music Monthly*, 13 August 2006 Available online at http://www.theguardian.com/music/2006/aug/13/shopping.popandrock, accessed on 2 February 2015

Brand, Russell (2007) And then I became a junkie, *Guardian*, 13 November. Available online at http://www.theguardian.com/books/2007/nov/13/biography.drugsandalcohol, accessed on 25 March 2015

Brand, Russell (2008) *My Booky Wook*, London: Hodder

Brand, Russell (2010) *Booky Wook 2: This Time It's Personal*, London: Harper

Brand, Russell (2013a) The whole place is a deeply encoded temple of hegemonic power, *Guardian*, 24 May. Available online at http://www.theguardian.com/politics/2013/may/24/russell-brand-parliament-illusion, accessed on 2 February 2015

Brand, Russell (2013b) What I made of *Morning Joe* and *Question Time*, *Guardian*, 28 June. Available online at http://www.theguardian.com/culture/2013/jun/28/russell-brand-morning-joe-question-time, accessed on 2 February 2015

Brand, Russell (2013c) We deserve more from our democratic system, *Guardian*, 5 November 2013. Available online at http://www.theguardian.com/commentisfree/2013/nov/05/russell-brand-democratic-system-newsnight, accessed on 2 February 2015

Brand, Russell (2013d) I always felt sorry for her children, *Guardian*, 9 April. Available online http://www.theguardian.com/politics/2013/apr/09/russell-brand-margaret-thatcher, accessed on 2 February 2015

Brand, Russell (2013e) My life without drugs, *Guardian*, 9 March. Available online at http://www.theguardian.com/culture/2013/mar/09/russell-brand-life-without-drugs, accessed on 2 February 2015

Brand, Russell (2013f) Russell Brand on revolution: We no longer have the luxury of tradition, *New Statesman*, 24 October. Available online at http://www.newstatesman.com/politics/2013/10/russell-brand-on-revolution, accessed on 24 March 2015

Brand, Russell (2014a) *Revolution*, London: Century-Random House

Brand, Russell (2014b) Answer time, 12 December. Available online athttp://www.russellbrand.com/2014/12/answer-time/, accessed on 2 February 2015

Clements, Jo (2009) Shameless Russell Brand laughs of Sachsgate as 'larking around' on money-spinning stand-up tour, *Mail Online*, 20 January. Available online at http://www.dailymail.co.uk/tvshowbiz/article-1122086/Shameless-Russell-Brand-laughs-Sachsgate-larking-money-spinning-stand-tour.html, accessed on 2 February 2015

Davies, Nick (2014) *Hack Attack: How the Truth Caught up with Rupert Murdoch*, London: Chatto & Windus

Klein, Naomi (2014) *This Changes Everything: Capitalism vs. the Climate*, New York: Simon and Schuster

Mindich, David (2005) *Tuned Out: Why Americans under 40 don't Follow the News*, New York: Oxford University Press

Morgan, Piers (2014) The TV tantrum that shows why 'revolutionary' Russell Brand is really just a revolting hypocrite, *Daily Mail*, 3 December. Available online at http://www.dailymail.co.uk/news/article-2859473/PIERS-MORGAN-TV-tantrum-shows-revolutionary-Russell-Brand-really-just-revolting-hypocrite.html, accessed on 2 February 2015

Pew Research Center for the People and the Press (2004) Cable and internet loom large in fragmented political news universe, 11 January. Available online at http://people-press.org/reports/, accessed on 2 February 2015

Pew Research Center for the People and the Press (2012) In changing news landscape, even television is vulnerable, 27 September 2012. Available online at http://www.people-press.org/files/legacy-pdf/2012%20News%20Consumption%20Report.pdf, accessed on 24 March 2015

Press Association (2014) Russell Brand says he is 'volatile person' after dispute with journalist, 2 December. Available online at http://www.theguardian.com/culture/2014/dec/02/russell-brand-volatile-person-rent-journalist-snide, accessed on 2 February 2015

Sawyer, Miranda (2008) Brand on the run, *Observer*, 9 November. Available online at http://www.theguardian.com/media/2008/nov/09/russell-brand-sachsgate, accessed on 2 February 2015

Schudson, Michael (1992) *Watergate in American Memory: How we Remember, Forget and Reconstruct the Past*, New York: Basic Books

Schulman, Michael (2014) Follow the leader, *New Yorker*, 15 December. Available online at http://www.newyorker.com/magazine/2014/12/15/follow-leader, accessed on 2 February 2015

Steel, Mark (2014) If you think Russell Brand's new book *Revolution* is confused, you should read what his critics have to say about it, *Belfast Telegraph*, 1 November. Available online at http://www.belfasttelegraph.co.uk/opinion/columnists/mark-steel/if-you-think-russell-brands-new-book-revolution-is-confused-you-should-read-what-his-critics-have-to-say-about-it-30709726.html, accessed on 2 February 2015

Urquhart, Conal (2012) Johann Hari leaves *Independent* after plagiarism storm, *Guardian*, 20 January. Available online at http://www.theguardian.com/media/2012/jan/20/johann-hari-quits-the-independent, accessed on 10 March 2015

YouTube (2013) Jeremy Paxman vs Russell Brand. Available online at https://www.youtube.com/watch?v=hYM7SzJMKns, accessed on 2 February 2015

YouTube (2014) *The Trews*. Available online https://www.youtube.com/watch?v=-XOVRnr_7zM, accessed on 2 February 2015

Zelizer, Barbie (1992) *Covering the Body: The Kennedy Assassination, the Media and the Shaping of Collective Memory*, Chicago: University of Chicago Press

Zelizer, Barbie (2008) How communication, culture and critique intersect in the study of journalism, *Communication, Culture and Critique*, Vol. 1, No. 1 pp 86-91

Note on the contributor
Sarah Niblock is Professor of Journalism and Head of the Department of Social Sciences, Media and Communications at Brunel University London, UK. She is the author of numerous books and articles on journalism, popular culture, musicology, visual culture and gender, including *Prince: The Making of a Pop Music Phenomenon* (Ashgate 2011, co-authored with Stan Hawkins). She began her career in local journalism in 1987 and continues to write for national and international outlets, as well as giving public talks and appearing on the radio.

Section 2:
The Witty Ways of Literary Journalists

The Savage Wit of Hunter S. Thompson

Garry Whannel

Hunter S. Thompson (1973: 121) believed a sense of humour was the main measure of sanity. American novelist Tom Wolfe called Thompson the greatest comic writer of the 20th century (McKeen 2008: 360). *Rolling Stone* editor Jann Wenner called Thompson's *Fear and Loathing in Las Vegas* (1973) the funniest piece of American prose since William S. Burroughs's *Naked Lunch* (1959) (ibid: 177). Thompson's humour is dark – Thompson himself commented: 'Almost any kind of humor I like always has a touch of melancholy or weirdness in it. I seem to be alone, for instance, in considering Joseph Conrad one of history's great humorists' (Torrey and Simonson 2008: 44). Thompson's style spawned imitators, none of them remotely successful – the only person who can write like Hunter is Hunter.

Thompson's work attracted much favourable comment. Journalist David Halberstam said 'his work is touched by genius and transcends mere journalism' (see Thompson 2000: ix). Critic Richard Ellmann highlighted a 'kind of Rimbaud delirium of spirit' in Thompson's writing, which 'only the rarest of geniuses could achieve' (ibid: xii). Actor Johnny Depp (see Wenner and Seymour 2007) declared that 'Hunter was a genius who revolutionised writing in the same way that Marlon Brando did with acting'. Historian and editor of some of Thompson's collections, Douglas Brinkley (Thompson 2000: xx), recognised the comedy in the writing, commenting: 'Behind the complex personality ... lurks a trenchant humorist with a sharp moral sensibility.' US Democratic Party political campaign director Frank Mankiewicz said the book, *Fear and Loathing on the Campaign Trail '72*, was the most accurate and least factual ever written about American politics.

Although Thompson's work has garnered critical acclaim, his career encompassed just three books widely acknowledged as classics. He never ceased to write short journalistic pieces but never realised his ambitions as a novelist. His public persona (drink and drugs, wild and unpredictable behaviour, and gun ownership and use) began to obscure his writing. According to many biographical accounts, he could be great fun and good company (Carroll 1993; Cowan 2009; Cleverly and Braudis 2008; McKeen 2008; Steadman 2006; Wenner and Seymour 2007). As those same accounts make clear, he could also be petulant and abusive with his various girlfriends and assistants, and viciously rude in print even about his close friends, yet almost every writer also speaks of him possessing the polite manners and courtesy of the southern gentleman.

In this chapter, I draw upon Thompson's work over five decades, and commentaries on his life and work. In examining his humour, I have focused particularly on his most elaborate and successful work of journalism, the day-by-day coverage of the 1972 presidential election campaign, which originally appeared as a series of articles in the music journal *Rolling Stone*, and then subsequently in book form as *Fear and Loathing on the Campaign Trail '72*.

The back story

Thompson showed symptoms of being very bright, and also a handful, from an early age – he was in trouble with the law at age eight, for causing damage (Perry 1992: 7). He was a voracious reader who often sat up reading until the middle of the night (ibid: 9). In 1952, when Thompson was 15, his father died. Subsequently, he was expelled from school after involvement in a robbery. Serving as an air force electrician in 1956, Thompson became sports editor of a military base newspaper. He hastily studied technical terms in journalism textbooks, to appear knowledgeable and experienced (ibid: 25). After leaving the air force in 1958 he worked as a journalist, including a spell reporting from South America. It was only in 1965 that he made a national breakthrough. He was commissioned to write an article about the motorcycle gang the Hell's Angels, for the magazine *The Nation*. Within a week of publication he received seven book offers (McKeen 2008: 101), which led to the highly successful book *Hell's Angels* (1967). This enabled him to move his family to Colorado where he had already rented, and subsequently bought, a house and land in Woody Creek. Owl Farm was to be his main home for the rest of his life.

Between 1967 and 1983 he reached his creative peak and wrote three major works – *Hell's Angels* (1967), *Fear and Loathing in Las Vegas* (1971), *Fear and Loathing on the Campaign Trail '72* (1973). His stylistic breakthrough came in a commission from *Scanlan's Monthly*, who teamed Thompson up with English artist Ralph Steadman, a partnership that lasted for much of Thompson's life. The resultant piece, 'The Kentucky Derby is decadent and depraved' (Thompson 1970a) was dubbed by Thompson's friend, Bill Cardoso, as 'gonzo', a term that became the label for Thompson's style. Although the relationship between Thompson and Steadman could be turbulent, they remained friends, Steadman at one point publishing *Jones of Colorado*, a series of sketches of Thompson's cat (Steadman 1995). Steadman's input was central to the project that became *The Curse of Lono* (Thompson 1983) and Thompson did much of his best work when Steadman was involved (Steadman 2006). Thompson also wrote a series of long features for the music journal *Rolling Stone*, which boosted both the journal and his own reputation (for example, Thompson 1970b, 1971).

For a while Thompson held together a frail synthesis of a journalistic sensibility, an ethnographer's eye and ear, a satirist's wit, a brutal imagination, and a novelist's style. After 1983, these elements never remained in balance long enough for Thompson to write an original book – his post-1983 books were anthologies of short journalistic pieces, letters and other fragments and reprints. He lost the necessary consistency of focus. Increasingly he retreated to his tranquil and remote Woody Creek home, and cranked-up lifestyle in which drink, drugs, cars and guns were significant elements. McKeen recounts that 'he breakfasted on bloody marys and beer, and drank Wild Turkey and Chivas by the tumbler but he was rarely shit-faced' (McKeen 2008:203). Friend Russell Chatham commented: 'Hunter took his work seriously, if not himself, and he was extraordinarily well-read. He was a much deeper, more serious person than the public, I think, even now, suspects' (ibid: 257). The contradictions persisted – Thompson continued to fire guns, verbally abuse friends, and drive *while* drinking, whilst according to close friends Michael Cleverly and Bob Broadis maintaining his polite style (2008: xvi). Alan Rinzler commented:

> Hunter was a nasty, selfish, obsessive drug and alcohol addict who behaved horridly in private and public, but he was also a highly sensitive, acutely intelligent observer and critic of society, government, politics and journalism. Not only that, he could be very charming in a kind and courtly southern way (cited in Bingley 2010: ix).

Eventually, in 2005, with his health deteriorating, and mobility limited, Thompson carried out the act he had been predicting for around thirty years, and committed suicide by shooting himself.

Literary sources

He read voraciously, but the writers most referenced are largely American and almost entirely male. He favoured those who were outsiders or who wrote about outsiders (Nelson Algren, William Burroughs, Scott Fitzgerald); champions of the oppressed (Jack London); social critics and sexual libertines (Henry Miller); those with a macho adventurer element (Ernest Hemingway); and the pugnacious (Jimmy Breslin, Norman Mailer). Jack Kerouac, as an iconoclast, an outsider, a producer of spontaneous prose, a drug user, and long-term alcohol abuser, is clearly a precursor for Thompson's own writing and life. Reportedly, while learning the craft of writing, Thompson spent long hours typing out passages of F. Scott Fitzgerald, author of *The Great Gatsby* (1925) while George Orwell, author of *Animal Farm* (1945) and *Nineteen Eighty-Four* (1949), also influenced his relatively plain prose style. He frequently quoted William Faulkner's comment that the best fiction is 'far more true' than any journalism. He admired the journalism of H. L. Mencken (1880-1956), whose obituary for William Jennings Bryan, the Democratic candidate for the US presidency, in

1896, 1900 and 1908, Thompson said, 'ranked as the most savage and unnatural thing ever said on the death of a famous or any other person' (Torrey and Simonson 2008: 129). This obituary helped inspire Thompson's own obituary of President Nixon, which Brinkley regarded as 'the most devastating critique of a politician since H. L. Mencken's obituary' (see Thompson 2000: xv). Throughout his writing career, Thompson cared about style – considering the weight, rhythm, cadence and mood of every sentence. Typically, visitors to his Owl Farm kitchen would be asked to read his material out loud, and he would correct accordingly, consulting the audience about the impact of specific words. He quoted Mark Twain on the issue: 'The difference between the almost-right word and the right word is … the difference between the lightning bug and the lightning' (Thompson 2003: xv).

The New Journalism, gonzo, and the invention of 'Hunter'

The term 'New Journalism' denotes a set of writing, diverse in topic and approach, with a literary approach to journalism, a break with the dominance of objectivity, a convergence of the techniques of journalism and fiction, and a willingness to experiment and challenge conventions. The form developed during the late 1950s and 1960s and was anthologised and analysed in Tom Wolfe's collection *The New Journalism* (1973) (see also Mosser 2012; Nuttall 2007; Weingarten 2005).

If 'gonzo journalism' is a meaningful term (and it is really a term that applies to only the one writer) then what does it mean? McKeen (2008: 73) comments on Thompson's 'preoccupation with *getting the story*. In fact *getting the story* became the story. His writing could be classified as meta-journalism, journalism about the process of journalism'. Part of the technique grew out of desperate, last-minute deadline pressure. Thompson's style included raw field notes, documents, conversations, editors' notes, and author interviews to augment more honed prose. Gonzo placed the writer at the centre and, according to Nick Nuttall required 'fierce subjectivity' (2007: 136). Tom Wolfe (1973: 195) said of the Kentucky Derby article that Thompson 'usually casts himself as a frantic loser, inept and half-psychotic'. Nuttall suggests (2007: 137) that the writing constructs an 'atmospheric authenticity' built on 'feelings, emotions, sensations'. Steadman emphasises the visual dimension and provocative impact of gonzo, asserting: 'It's got to upset people. It's no good otherwise' (cited in McKeen 2008: 167). Timothy Ferris (in Thompson 2003: xiv) emphasises both humour and anger: 'It is also, like all real humor, essentially serious. At its center resides a howling vortex of outrage and pain.' Brian McNair (2012: 583) sums up Thompson's achievement as 'breaking down the false barrier between truth and fiction, objectivity and subjectivity, journalism and art'.

Thompson's early writing is disciplined and restrained. As gonzo developed the author became a leading character, whether semi-disguised as 'Raoul Duke' or 'Dr Thompson' and assumes a life of its own. Thompson invented the wild drug-gobbling, drink-guzzling, violent and unpredictable persona as a caricature of his own tendencies, but then increasingly felt the need and pressure to live up to it. Thompson kept his own Duke, fed and watered him until he grew into a monster. Unlike the monster constructed by Dr Frankenstein who escapes into the wild, Thompson remained chained to his own creation, who would generally appear after enough drink and chemicals had been consumed. Ironically, while many writers who drank tended to write until the drink took over, Thompson's *modus operandi* involved drinking until the writing took over.

As the Thompson mythology grew, it became the substance – self-mythologising feeding the myth, the constant recycling of second-hand accounts, the inevitable tendency for the sensational stories to be more compelling than footage of a man sitting at a keyboard working, until the writing recedes from full view (see, for example, Carroll 1993; Cowan 2009). Increasingly 'Hunter' gets between us and the story. Alan Rinzler writes that 'the public spectacle of Hunter as the King of Gonzo – a brain-addled, angry, deeply depressed, self-destructive lout – has prevailed in the popular consciousness while the real story of this ground-breaking prose artist and investigative journalist has all but disappeared' (see Bingley 2010: v).

Fear and Loathing on the Campaign Trail '72: Does humour belong in political journalism?

It is in *Fear and Loathing on the Campaign Trail '72* that the balance between the various elements of Thompson's writing – a journalist's sensibility, an ethnographer's eye and ear, a satirist's wit, a brutal imagination, and a novelist's style – are at their most effective both aesthetically and politically. In the remainder of this chapter, I will focus on this book and on the humour within the journalism.

Gonzo cannot exist without humour. This is more than just the voice of the prankster, the parodist, the joke-teller or the caricaturist at work. It has to do with comic vision. Thompson (2000: xxi) wrote: 'Muhammad Ali, one of my very few heroes, once took the time to explain to me that "there are no jokes, the truth is the funniest of all".' Some of Thompson's humour consisted simply of spotting some of the absurdities of campaign life, as when one key aide explained that 'the reason people didn't vote for Ed Muskie [a candidate for the Democratic Party's presidential nomination] here is that they didn't have any reason to' (Thompson 1973: 124), or when a Muskie campaign manager explained that his instructions were 'that the Senator should never again be put in a situation where he has to think quickly' (Thompson 1973: 154).

In *Fear and Loathing on the Campaign Trail '72*, the humour is deployed to underpin the journalism. There are many pen pictures of behind-the-scenes figures of spin-doctors, media managers and campaign directors, yet none are quite as evocative as Thompson's frequently abusive descriptions of McGovern campaign director Frank Mankiewicz. I now have three inter-related lines of inquiry: how are 'politics' and 'journalism' constructed in this account, and in what forms does humour appear?

Politics and humour, Thompson-style

Thompson's politics involve sympathy for the outsiders, oppressed and downtrodden, a regard for maverick individualism, a romantic faith in the democratic vision of Thomas Jefferson, the principal author of the 1776 Declaration of Independence, a melancholic regret for the death of the American Dream, and, perhaps surprisingly, patriotism. He cites the beating of demonstrators by Chicago police during the 1968 Democratic Convention as a formative experience, although he has never felt able to write at length about it: 'For two weeks afterwards, back in Colorado, I couldn't even talk about it without starting to cry – for reasons I think I finally understand now, but I still can't explain' (Thompson 1973: 42).

Thompson believes most politicians should be treated with contempt. Although, according to Thompson (1973: 94), 'The prevailing attitude among journalists with enough status to work Presidential Campaigns is that all politicians are congenital cheats and liars,' he claims the private cynicism of journalistic gossip rarely gets aired in public. Thompson (ibid) identifies this gulf between the public coverage of politics and the private world of political discourse, referring to the '…living rooms around Washington where the candidates, their managers and various ranking journalists are want to gather for the purpose of "talking serious politics" – as opposed to the careful gibberish they distil for the public prints'. The double standards involved are shown as integral to the political process: Thompson (ibid: 199) suggests that Hubert Humphrey, who stood unsuccessfully as the Democratic candidate against Richard Nixon in the 1968 presidential election, 'would go crazy with rage and attempt to strangle his press secretary if he ever saw in print what most reporters say about him during midnight conversations around barroom tables'.

The Thompson style disrupts coziness by writing what he thinks, often in brutal terms. In one of Thompson's most quoted lines, he said: 'Hubert Humphrey is a treacherous gutless old ward-heeler who should be put in a goddamn bottle and sent out with the Japanese Current' (ibid: 129) and declared: 'There is no way to grasp what a shallow, contemptible, and hopelessly dishonest old hack Hubert Humphrey really is until you've followed him around for a while on the campaign trail' (ibid: 199). Of Senator Ed Muskie's campaign, he comments that 'he talked like a farmer with terminal cancer trying to borrow money on next year's crop' (ibid: 138). Thompson's most potent venom is directed at Humphrey and Muskie – seen as pro-war figures who had sabotaged the Gene McCarthy anti-war campaign for the nomination in 1968. The careers of both figures effectively came to an end during the 1972 race for the Democratic presidential nomination. Seldom has the revenge of a writer been as brutal or as final.

Thompson also gains great amusement from spoofing the gullible, such as telling young Nixon supporters that the highly respected NBC anchorman John Chancellor gobbles LSD. Following the success of this last stunt, Thompson says: 'I was tempted to start babbling about Walter Cronkite: that he was heavily into the white slavery trade…' (ibid: 337).

The most striking device Thompson uses is that of imaginative fantasy. For instance, he develops a fantasy about Muskie's use of Ibogaine (a psychedelic substance), after he noticed a supposed similarity between the symptoms of the drug, outlined in a laboratory report, and Muskie's behaviour. He reported a rumour (which he later acknowledged starting) that Muskie's strange behaviour might be as a result of his Ibogaine use, commenting:

> … that he had developed a tendency to roll his eyes wildly during TV interviews, that his thought patterns had become strangely fragmented, and that not even his closest advisors could predict when he might suddenly spiral off into babbling rages, or neo-comatose funks (ibid: 145).

Thompson was amazed when evidence emerged that some people were taking this seriously, and that tales were re-circulated as if true. Although he had frequently embellished description with comic invention, he felt compelled to signal flights of fantasy more clearly by such formulations as 'My God, why do I write these things?' Thompson suggests that a sense of humour is vital to recognise these factual/fictional leaps in his writing. (Torrey and Simonson 2008: 159). This need for a sense of humour provides a significant clue to the issues of factual/fictional, objective/subjective, truth/invention raised in some analyses of Thompson's writing (see Mosser 2012, Winston 2014).

Journalism and humour, Thompson-style

Thompson (ibid: 44) mocks the quest for objectivity: 'Most journalists only *talk* about objectivity, but Dr. Duke grabs it straight by the fucking throat,' and makes it clear that he is nothing other than subjective, declaring: 'With the possible exception of things like box scores, race results and stock market tabulations, there is no such thing as Objective Journalism. The phrase itself is a pompous contradiction in terms.' Thompson and fellow *Rolling Stone* journalist Timothy Crouse, who produced a superb book on the political press, *The Boys on the Bus* (1973), consistently produced good, well-informed reporting. Well in advance of many other journalists, they identified the disciplined and efficient grassroots campaign organisation as a hidden strength of the campaign of George McGovern, the Democratic presidential nominee (Thompson 1973: 62). Later in the year, Thompson (ibid: 220) also discovers what he describes as a 'flat-out byzantine spook story' involving the Humphrey campaign planning to obtain clandestine last-minute funding from shadowy figures based in Las Vegas. The story was subsequently confirmed. The author as loser, struggling with deadlines, also makes frequent appearances:

> Failure comes easy at a time like this. After eight days in this fantastic dungeon of a hotel, the idea of failing totally and miserably in my work seems absolutely logical (ibid: 135).

The resort to gonzo techniques is constructed as growing out of deadline pressures:

> Only a lunatic would do this kind of work: twenty-three primaries in five months; stone drunk from dawn to dusk and huge speed-blisters all over my head. Where is the meaning? The light at the end of the tunnel? (ibid: 177).

One piece is described as ...

> '...one of the most desperate, last-minute hamburger jobs in the history of journalism – including the first known experiments with large-scale Gonzo journalism – which we accomplished, in this case, by tearing my Ohio primary notebook apart and sending about fifty pages of scribbled shorthand notes straight to the typewriter (ibid: 178).

Yet the sequence in this style, derived from Thompson's notebook, between pages 184 and 190, is one of the most effective parts – the balance between gonzo and mainstream journalism is neatly maintained. The devices of brutal humour and self-reflexive revealing of production processes do not divert from the focus on the main narrative of the presidential race. Indeed, the combination of these elements precisely serves to enable a powerful view of the political process from the inside.

As a former sports journalist, Thompson utilises American football as a humorous metaphor for political contestation to good effect: 'There is not much difference in temperament between a good tight end and a successful politician. They will both go down in the pit and do whatever has to be done – then come up smiling and occasionally licking blood off their teeth' (ibid: 79). Boxing, too, constitutes a useful source for bringing out the destructive aspect of politics. Observing Ed Muskie, Thompson (1973: 116) remembered 'the nervous sense of impending doom in the face of Floyd Patterson when he weighed in for his championship re-match with Sonny Liston in Las Vegas'.

Animals and humour: Putting 'nature' back into 'culture'
One of the most striking stylistic mannerisms in Thompson's writing is the frequent use of animal imagery, in which people's behaviour is described with reference to the basic drives and instincts of animals. So Hubert Humphrey is 'a treacherous brain-damaged old vulture' (Thompson 1973: 244) while working for Ed Muskie is like 'being locked in a rolling boxcar with a vicious 200-pound water rat' (Thompson 1973: 243). Even Thompson's own favoured candidate is described as 'that hare-brained bastard McGovern' (Thompson 1973: 244). According to Thompson, 'This world is full of dangerous beasts – but none quite as ugly as a lawyer who has finally flipped off the tracks of Reason' (Thompson 1973: 34). In order to campaign, a politician has to 'run around the nation like a goddamn Methedrine bat' (Thompson 1973: 88).

These humorous animal similes and metaphors are sometimes extended, as when Thompson discusses the need of a jackrabbit for adrenaline as similar to that of the political journalist (Thompson 1973: 13) or when he compares a politician with a rutting elk:

> …a man on the scent of the White House is rarely rational. He is more like a beast in heat: a bull elk in the rut, crashing blindly through the timber in a fever for something to fuck (Thompson 1973: 359).

There follows a detailed description of the condition of the bull elk in these circumstances: '…their eyes glaze over, their ears pack up with hot wax, and their loins get heavy with blood.' And Thompson concludes: 'A career politician finally smelling the White House is not much different from a bull elk in the rut' (ibid).

The animal behaviour referenced is often to do with basic drives – for food, for sex. Thus does Thompson re-insert nature into the culture of politics, utilising humorous animal similes and metaphors to strip away the veneer of civilised and mannered behaviour and reveal the raw emotions below the surface. Thompson consistently used this form of animal imagery throughout his writing career and in his very last piece for *Rolling Stone* (11 November 2004) referred to George Bush Jr as 'talking like a donkey with no brains at all'.

Conclusion: Smashing through the conventions of politeness

Thompson's writing was always situated between fact and fiction, actuality and fantasy, journalism and polemic. In his early writing the caustic wit had yet to find a consistent voice. In the later work, the focus became more diffuse and only on occasion could it hit its targets with forensic accuracy. For a period, at his peak, in the first half of the 1970s, the elements of his writing – journalism, humour, fantasy, and polemic – hit a balance. The resultant alchemical reaction produced by the collision of these elements forged a striking, disturbing and often hilarious lens through which American politics and society could be viewed. He utilised a savage wit to smash through the conventions of politeness and respect that characterised political journalism, reminding his readers of the venal and corrupt motives of the power-seekers.

References

Bingley, Will (2010) *Gonzo: A Graphic Biography of Hunter S. Thompson*, London: SelfMadeHero

Burroughs, William S. (1962) *The Naked Lunch*, New York: Grove Press

Carroll, E. Jean (1993) *Hunter: The Strange and Savage Life of Hunter S. Thompson*, London: Simon & Schuster

Cleverly, Michael; and Braudis, Bob (2008) *The Kitchen Readings: Untold Stories of Hunter S. Thompson*, New York: Harper Perennial

Cowan, Jay (2009) *Hunter S. Thompson: An Insider's view of Deranged, Depraved, Drugged out Brilliance*, New York: Lyons

Crouse, Timothy (1972) *The Boys on the Bus*, New York: Random

Kerouac, Jack (1957) *On the Road*, New York: Viking Press.

McKeen, William (1991) *Hunter S. Thompson*, Boston, Massachusetts: Twayne

McKeen, William (2008) *Outlaw Journalist: The Life and Times of Hunter S. Thompson*, London: Aurum

McNair, Brian (2012) Johnny be Gonzo, *Journalism Practice*, Vol. 6, No. 4 pp 581-583

Mosser, Jason (2012) *The Participatory Journalism of Michael Herr, Norman Mailer, Hunter S. Thompson, and Joan Didion: Creating New Reporting Styles*, Lewiston, New York: Edwin Mellen Press

Nuttall, Nick (2007) Cold-blooded journalism: Truman Capote and the non-fiction novel, Keeble, Richard and Wheeler, Sharon (eds) *The Journalistic Imagination: Literary Journalists from Defoe to Capote and Carter*, London: Routledge pp 130-144

Perry, Paul (1992) *Fear and Loathing: The Strange and Terrible Sage of Hunter S. Thompson*, New York: Thunder's Mouth Press

Steadman, Ralph (1995) *Jones of Colorado*, London: Ebury

Steadman, Ralph (2006) *The Joke's Over: Bruised Memories – Gonzo, Hunter Thompson and Me*, London: Heinemann

Stephenson, William (2012) *Gonzo Republic: Hunter S. Thompson's America*, London: Continuum

Thompson, Hunter S. (1967) *Hell's Angels*, London: Penguin

Thompson, Hunter S. (1970a) The Kentucky Derby is decadent and depraved, *Scanlan's Monthly*, Vol. 1, No. 4 June pp 1-12

Thompson, Hunter S. (1970b) The Battle of Aspen: Freak power in the Rockies, *Rolling Stone*, 1 October pp 30-37

Thompson, Hunter S. (1971) Strange rumblings in Aztlan: The murder of Ruben Salazar, *Rolling Stone*, 29 April pp 30-37

Thompson, Hunter S. (1971) *Fear and Loathing in Las Vegas: A Savage Journey to the Heart of the American Dream*, illustrated by Ralph Steadman, New York: Random House

Thompson, Hunter S. (1973) *Fear and Loathing on the Campaign Trail '72*, San Francisco: Straight Arrow Books

Thompson, Hunter S. (1974) Interviewed by Craig Vetter, *Playboy*, November

Thompson, Hunter S. (1977) Fear and loathing in the graveyard of the weird: The Banshee screams for buffalo meat, *Rolling Stone*, 15 December pp 48-59

Thompson, Hunter S. (1979) The Kentucky Derby is decadent and depraved, *The Great Shark Hunt: Strange Tales from a Strange Time*, New York: Summit Books

Thompson, Hunter S. (1983) *The Curse of Lono*, New York: Bantam

Thompson, Hunter S. (2000) *Fear and Loathing in America: The Brutal Odyssey of An Outlaw Journalist, 1968-1976*, edited by Brinkley, Douglas, London: Bloomsbury

Thompson, Hunter S. (2003) *Kingdom of Fear: Loathsome Secrets of a Star-Crossed Child in the Final Days of the American Century*, London: Allen Lane

Thompson, Hunter S. (2011) *Fear and Loathing at* Rolling Stone*: The Essential Writing of Hunter S. Thompson*, edited by Wenner, Jann S., London: Allen Lane

Torrey, Beef and Simonson, Kevin (eds) (2008) *Conversations with Hunter S. Thompson*, Jackson, Mississippi: University Press of Mississippi

Weingarten, Marc (2005) *The Gang that Wouldn't Write Straight: Thompson, Didion and the New Journalism Revolution*, New York: Crown

Wenner, Jann S. and Seymour, Corey (2007) *Gonzo: The Life of Hunter S. Thompson: An Oral Biography*, London: Sphere

Winston, Matthew (2014) *Gonzo Text: Disentangling Meaning in Hunter S. Thompson's Journalism*, New York: Peter Lang

Wolfe, Tom and Johnson, E. W. (eds) (1973) *The New Journalism*, New York: Harper and Row

Note on the contributor

Garry Whannel is Professor of Media Cultures at the University of Bedfordshire, UK. His most recent publication is *The Trojan Horse: The Growth of Commercial Sponsorship* (with Deborah Philips, 2013). He has written on game shows, celebrity, and the royal family. He developed the concept of vortextuality to analyse major news events – the Beckham wedding, the death of Princess Diana and the Michael Jackson trial. Other books include *Culture, Politics and Sport* (2008), *Media Sport Stars, Masculinities and Moralities* (2001), and *Fields in Vision: Television Sport and Cultural Transformation* (1992). His current research interests include political comedy, and representations of science and scientists.

Sarcasm, Satire, and Irony: The Literary Journalism of Three Spanish Women

Novia Pagone

Humour, generally in the form of satire and irony, has been present in Spanish literary journalism at least since the nineteenth century; Mariano José de Larra (1809-1837) is considered its master practitioner. As the country headed towards its authoritarian mid-20th century, writing about life in Spain became more urgent and decidedly less humorous. As the dictator, Francisco Franco, approached his end and censorship weakened, however, liberal journalism enjoyed new life. It was at this time, in the early 1970s and afterwards, that humorous literary journalism, previously dominated by male writers, emerged again. Female journalists also appeared at this time, mainly writing for mainstream, usually left-leaning, publications. During the period of transition to democracy in Spain (1975-1982), mainstream journalism by women generally ended up in the Sunday supplements or the arts and entertainment pages, rather than in the international politics section. Women, also, did not serve on editorial boards at this time (Fagoaga and Secanella 1987). When their work was included on the opinion page or even the back page, it was most often a piece permeated by sarcasm and satire.

I will argue, then, that humour – and, of course, talent – gave women writers entrance to the mainstream editorial pages, beginning in the mid-1970s. Furthermore, through essays, columns and interviews on topics as diverse as immigrant labour, abuses in prisons, dating services, and elections, humour has contributed to establishing and expanding the presence of female perspectives in the public sphere. Three of the most recognised of these women journalists – Maruja Torres, Rosa Montero, and Empar Moliner – whose work spanned the democratic transition to the contemporary moment, used irony and satire as key ingredients in making their sociocultural and political critiques effective and accessible.

Maruja Torres: The people's journalist

To mark the twentieth anniversary of the death of Franco and the beginning of Spain's transition to democracy, in 1995 the daily newspaper El País printed a series of articles, interviews, and chronicles remembering the years of the transition. Collected in *Memory of the Transition* (Juliá et al 1996), these pieces trace the waning years of the dictatorship, from before the death of its leader up to the entrance of Spain into the European Union in 1986. All the triumphs and defeats of the new democracy were considered, plus there was a brief look at the post-transition. Each of the twenty-six chapters portrays a specific key event of the transition period: including the death of Franco in 1975, the 1976 Atocha murders, the attempted coup on 23 February 1981, and the 1982 election victory of the Spanish Socialist Workers Party. Each chapter includes a six- to sixteen-page chronicle on the chapter focus; an interview, averaging four to six pages; a three- to four-page article of historical or economic or cultural analysis; one or two testimonial accounts, averaging two to three pages; and a two-page satirical column by Maruja Torres.

While various journalists and scholars who experienced the transition, including a few women, write the majority of the contributions[1] the last word of each chapter is always given to Torres's sharp tongue. A preliminary editor's note points out that Torres provides an 'ironic and enjoyable counterpoint' (1996) at the end of each chapter (all translations from the Spanish by the author, unless otherwise noted). Indeed, Torres's focus on trivial news and gossip accentuates the weightiness of the articles that come before it. However, as Jesús Ceberio[2] indicates in his prologue, Torres's essays also explore popular culture's relationship to the political and societal changes that occurred during the transition. She was juxtaposing the progressive currents of society, in Spain and elsewhere, with the often slow-moving realm of the state (Juliá et al 1996: 9-11).

In her columns for this series, Torres covered diverse areas of society as she comments on moments in the life of the culture. For example, in '(Bad) habits and (awful) customs' (1996c), Torres offers a brief criticism of the customs and traditions of Spain under Franco. She juxtaposes the fact that divorce remained illegal in Spain, despite being legalised in other Catholic countries, with the news of certain celebrities who had spoken up in favour of divorce, including Sara Montiel, who had divorced in 1963. While Torres's discussion of celebrity gossip and other topics that are typically considered 'light' could be dismissed as simple entertainment or even fluff, her chronicles serve a serious purpose. They challenge the established order, whether that order is dictatorial or democratic, and satirise the frivolous – in order to draw the reader's attention back to serious matters beyond the façade of popular culture.

Her choice of titles for her articles, in particular, draws on popular culture with references to fairy tales, cultural traditions, and popular pastimes. These sarcastic and familiar beginnings give way to biting criticisms of some aspect of social, cultural or political life related to each chapter's topic. Her essays are part social chronicle, part humoristic note, part opinion column, and part historical recap. Additionally, and most importantly, by participating in a major effort to remember this significant recent history, Torres and her point of view became part of the public discourse on the transition.

From the very first column of the series, 'Sleeping beauty prepares to eat breakfast', we see how Torres's use of humour – and her ability to combine serious and frivolous topics – allows her to discuss serious news without alienating the reader who may be looking for entertainment. The 'sleeping beauty' of the title becomes a personification of Spain in the years just preceding Franco's death, and illustrates 'the agony of Francoism': 'the death of Carrero Blanco ... shook the citizenry with the idea that things could change in this lethargic country. For better or for worse, but change: perhaps the sleeping (and sad) beauty we had become was beginning to agitate in her bed'[3] (1996a: 39).

Torres then moves on to seemingly less political news in this first column, all the while maintaining the background noise of political change. She recalls the premiere of Carlos Saura's film *Cousin Angelica* (1974): 'With a *facing the sun* attitude, Saura put the arm of *Cousin Angelica*'s Falangist in a cast' and notes that 'fascists bombed the cinemas where the film was shown in Spain' (1996a: 40, italics in the original). Torres uses 'facing the sun' with double meaning here. It was the title of the Falangist anthem, something locals would certainly recognise, but it also could carry a meaning similar to 'looking toward the future'. For fascists, this would certainly mean looking toward their future victory over the Republican (leftist) soldiers in the civil war. Torres uses the title of the fascist anthem against them to describe liberal film director Saura's attitude: he disables the Spanish fascist in the film by putting his arm in a cast.

As she observes the slackening of strict no-skin rules in film, including the fact that Ana Belén showed her breasts in *The Love of Captain Brando* (1974), Torres remarks: 'Even the *folclóricas*, these able explorers of political change who always know which side to take when the time comes, ended up conceding interviews in which you couldn't escape knowing their opinion about nudity and, good gracious, the Vietnam war' (1996a: 40). Torres's fake-mocking tone, indicated by her 'good gracious' comment, informs the reader that although the actions of the outspoken *folclóricas* and the breast-baring Ana Belén may seem ordinary to a liberated 1995 audience, in late 1973 both constituted challenges to the ailing dictatorship and indicated a changing society.

These events, together with the assassination of Carrero Blanco, the Prime Minister and long-time confidant of Franco, on 20 December 1973, marked the beginning of the transition out of dictatorship, even if another almost two years would pass before the death of its leader. Torres reconfirms her observation of the changes that had begun at the end of 1973 in several articles. She mentions the elimination of the obligatory No-Do documentaries (1996b: 64), celebrities and others in favour of divorce (1996c: 87), and the death of the 'Great Executioner/Executant', as she refers to Franco (1996d: 117).[4] Of course, Torres assures readers that not all the news was good. For example, she remarks that immediately after Franco's death 'an unidentifiable cloud settled over the country, a bubble of unreality that was, at the same time, genuinely bitter' (1996d: 117). She specifically refers to the censorship experienced by the press at that time, the closing of several magazines, the public reading of a manifesto supporting the Spanish opposition (signed by various intellectuals from outside Spain), the clamour for amnesty, and the 'terrible and hopeful confusion in the air' (1996d: 118). Through this portrait of a country in turmoil, Torres sets the scene for the tumultuous years to follow, but also introduces enough pop culture references and society gossip to put the political situation in a broader and more personal context.

As we arrive in 1978, the year of ratification of the constitution, in the column 'Bingo, love, and soccer' Torres weaves together news of the slow birth of the 'Magna Carta', as she dubs the constitution, with mention of the feminist lawyer Cristina Alberdi's protest over the relegation of a woman to second place in the succession of the crown, and the acceptance of the first woman into the Royal Academy of Spanish Language. The fact that these two items are included indicates that they were newsworthy at the time, suggesting an increased presence of women in the public sphere. However, in the same sentence as the news regarding the Real Academia, Torres remarks that 'a passion burned in the hearts of Spaniards: bingo' (1996e: 341).

The juxtaposition of such a landmark event as admitting the first woman into the venerated male dominion of the Royal Academy with such an insignificant fact as the popularity of bingo is a hallmark of Torres's writing, but it also proves destabilising for the reader. Should we think that her aim is to trivialise everything? Or does she include these trivial details in an effort to represent all aspects of life and society at that time, equally mocking the most unimportant aspects as well as the most important? Or is she simply playing with her audience in the hope of entertaining?

For an answer, it may be instructive to look to another great chronicler of Spanish life, Francisco Umbral (1932-2007). In his study of Francisco Umbral's regular columns, Paul Julian Smith observes that 'Umbral's chronicle acquires its unique status by refusing to discriminate between aesthetic and banal objects, engulfed as they both are in a journalistic *roman fleuve* or (Umbral's term) "novelised memoir" indistinguishable (or so it appears) from life itself' (1998: 327). While Torres's writing style and point of view differ from Umbral's, Smith's analysis of Umbral's work sheds some light on our own examination of Torres's columns for *Memory of the Transition*. She often contrasts a serious news item, such as the creation of the 1978 constitution, with a less serious report on celebrity gossip such as Elizabeth Taylor's diamonds, Jacqueline Onassis's new job in publishing, or the display of politician Felipe González's 'succulent thighs' during a soccer match between members of Congress and journalists. This last bit of admiration of the 'succulent thighs' of the then-leader of the Socialist Party and future Spanish prime minister, in addition to injecting a sassy tone at the end of the article, signals a change in attitude toward the political establishment in the 1990s. It also demonstrates the friendlier relationship between the press and the subjects of their reports, not to mention the lack of censorship.

Torres's columns of 1982, the year that marks the end of the transition to democracy, commemorate the new era by enlightening her readers on the travels and scandals of the royal families of Britain, Holland, Monaco, and Spain, the first visit of a Pope to Spain, the terrible floods, some literary news, the debut of the popular 1980s band Mecano, and sightings of American film and television celebrities. However, in a piece titled 'The Socialist Victory', Torres's column significantly does not cover the victory of the Socialist Party. Torres's description of the Pope's visit does tend toward the political: 'John Paul II condemned abortion and divorce before thousands of faithful followers.' This constitutes her entire portrayal of his visit, wedged between news of floods and the success of Fernando Fernán-Gómez's play *Bicycles are for Summer*. She includes one more bit of political news, buried in the last paragraph: 'Santiago Carrillo[5] left the Spanish Communist Party, but Sean Connery revisited his role as 007 in *Never Say Never Again*, and Carmen Romero[6] returned to her position as professor of literature and language in a secondary school in Madrid' (1996f: 554). This combination of serious information that would merit an entire column on its own – Carrillo's departure from the Communist Party – with obscure or frivolous news highlights Torres's style. She saves her opinion for the final sentence, which further illuminates her methods: 'That is to say, the era of the *technocrat* was beginning, and we didn't even notice' (1996f: 554).

By using the first person plural, a common feature of Torres's writing, she includes herself among her readers, reminding everyone that they were too busy reading about royal shenanigans and the stars of the American television show *Dallas* to take note of the significant political change. Her column is as much a chronicle of the year's events as it is of the public's complacency towards their government. In this way, Torres manages to criticise everyone while leaving the reader entertained and perhaps with a knowing smile at the end of the article. Careful readers will successfully read between the lines, while the less savvy will enjoy what's written on the page. By punctuating the end of each column with this type of statement and a sarcastic tone Torres paints a picture of an apathetic citizenry.

Reflecting on the years after the transition, her article 'The path of wisdom' begins as a nostalgic overview of the transition years but quickly turns into a list of personal 'minor complaints', those things that have become worse over the years:

> Seen from here, traversing in reverse the accumulated images that illustrate how much of the past has led us to this moment – like revisiting a ride through a tunnel that leads to total darkness – you discover the different stages of our growth as a people who recovered their dignity not the day the dictator died – that day what we recovered was hope – but the first time one approached the ballot box. … Our country, the day that it walked

upright to decide its future peacefully, carried inside it an intimidated infancy, a repressed adolescence, a frustrating adulthood, a premature old age. And nevertheless, with all this, it was capable of galloping confidently toward the other side of the tunnel, toward the light, confident that there it would find, together with liberty, a world in accordance with what we all had dreamed (1996g: 705).

I cite this long passage because it captures the weary hope of a nation that had experienced its share of repression and was working towards democracy. Torres leaves aside humour at the beginning of this commentary and trades it in for a bit of proud remembrance, using the first person plural to include herself in that vital moment. As the article continues, Torres offers her readers a personal judgement of the period in question and topics that are important to her. She catalogues her complaints this way:

That the socialist establishment's cult following of the opera and the new gastronomy have obliged us to taste bitterness at the hands of the tenors who have sung [the Spanish standards] *Granada*, *Amapola*, and *Malagueña*⁷ without penalty in massive concerts sponsored by the cultural institutions on duty and to eat salt cod with raspberries. That chastity has become fashionable again. That menopause arrived when I had just purchased a stock of Tampax ... (1996g: 706).

She admits at the end of her long list that even these little deceptions have a good side: 'Those who were proclaiming "long live Spain" have been put in their place and those of the salt cod with raspberries have gotten theirs, too.' Her mention of the proclaimers of 'long live Spain' refers to the old guard who conceived Spain as one and indivisible, rather than a patchwork of autonomous regions, as it was reimagined during the transition. Those who eat 'salt cod with raspberrries' alludes to the new guard, the modern, hedonistic progressives. In the end it appears that Torres chooses neither one side nor the other.

Although she herself is a progressive woman on the left, she expresses in her columns a desire to remain independent and uncategorised through her equal-opportunity critiques. The inclusion here and in other columns of personal and non-personal memories and news items does make for a sort of novelised memoir, in the style of Francisco Umbral, or at least a surreal look back at an intense period of history. More importantly, though, it is representative of Torres's point of view, and for that matter the point of view of the average person who may remember that the day the constitution was signed was also the day when their favourite singer announced big news in his personal life. Torres's unusual combination of pop culture with serious events, and her sharp sarcasm, make her columns appeal to the everyman/woman, as if she is remembering for all the people, not just for the scholars or the politicians or others in power.

Rosa Montero: Defender of the marginalised

While Torres delivers her opinions with a wink and a hearty laugh, mainly on politics and popular culture, Rosa Montero takes a slightly more serious tone, albeit with enough sarcastic wit to bring a smile to readers. She, like Torres, expresses her opinions without reservation, but she does so with a less playful and more righteous tone. Furthermore, Montero's work during the transition period was prolific, appearing almost daily in *El País* and making her one of the more prominent journalists at that time. In addition to her excellent interviews for the newspaper's Sunday magazine, Montero's work included special assignment reports for events such as the Pope's 1982 visit to Spain and a series of columns that occupied the coveted back page of the newspaper during several months in 1979.[8] In that space she offered her opinions to the public on a range of issues. It is these columns that allowed Montero the most flexibility in terms of choosing a topic and developing her writing style.

García Álvarez comments that it is through Montero's columns that she begins to 'penetrate the field of column writing with a profound sense of social responsibility and consciousness of the immense value that this writing has in the press, especially in a newspaper like *El País*. That's why she believes that she should be attentive to the possible injustices that exist and to the downtrodden' (2006: 177). Indeed, Montero uses the prominent back page of *El País* to speak out on behalf of those who do not have a voice, a power that was unavailable to her before the transition to democracy. It is this sense of social responsibility on behalf of the marginalised, often combined with satire and sarcasm to drive home her point, that made Montero one of the more popular and respected journalists in Spain during the transition. She maintains this position today.

For example, in an article titled 'Men and women', Montero defends women and their reproductive rights, a common topic in both her nonfiction and fiction. The subject of the piece is a pill that had recently been developed to ensure the masculinisation of the foetus. Women could take the pill once they were pregnant and guarantee that their child would be male. Montero condemns the very thought of such a pill, calling it 'unbelievable and demented', and she argues that men are at their wits' end in trying to find a solution to women's liberation. She sums up the situation this way: 'Women escape their control, the deceptive male supremacy disappears, half of humanity rebels and enters the competition. And paralysed by the stupor, the only thing that occurs to men is to reduce the number of enemies, contain the feminine assault with the excuse of the birth rate' (1979a). Further on, Montero highlights how the role of women changed during the transition. She observes:

> Women today, we look around, we choose, we change boyfriends, we are effectively independent because we are also economically independent. The wife market has ended and so too have the tears on the pillow of the unmarried woman, those tears of insecurity and desperation, and not of love as they insisted on telling us. We women, in the end, act the way the

men used to, and that scares them and it makes them unstable like birds with buckshot in their wings.

Montero aims her final criticism at those conservative men who invent 'ludicrous pills' as they cling to the macho, Superman stereotype of what it means to be a man. Instead of a strong man who entices women into his protective embrace, she says, 'they have produced a Superman that is hollow and a bit dumb, too muscular for the current taste, and dressing suspiciously in red and blue, the colours of Fuerza Nueva'.[9] She insists that men are determined to 'Superman-ise' themselves because they are terrified of the changes occurring in society and for that reason 'many nights one can hear a "flap-flap-flap" in the air … it's the last supermen of this era, barely blind bats who bang themselves against the wall'.

As one might expect, several letters to the editor appeared in the weeks following the publication of Montero's column, some in favour and some opposed. One man commented on Montero's Superman analogy: 'The Superwoman has been born. Many nights one can hear the "flap-flap-flap" in the air; it's the continual movement of the wings of the Superman and the Superwoman, who flap their wings frenetically to fly higher. Too bad neither of them realises that they are tied to the same chain' (Fonseca 1979). Two women wrote in support of Montero's opinion: 'It's an article that hundreds of thousands of us women would endorse.' These same women took a moment to criticise the male writers of another published letter that simply said: 'What's the problem, girl?' (Javier and Olivares 1979). The women observe: 'Men, when they don't have an argument, they resort to an illogical argument, that is to say, an insult or a stupid remark' (Tablado and Moñino 1979). Likewise, a male reader expresses his solidarity with Montero and women in general: 'I am tired of the constant negative propaganda against women, whether subtle or obvious. … Rosa Montero's article was really entertaining and I think it's fantastic' (García 1979).

I mention these letters because it was significant that a relatively open and public dialogue existed on a topic that, before the transition, would have been censored. The fact that Montero sparked such a discussion also is noteworthy because it shows that she wielded a certain amount of power through her writing, and could influence public discourse on one of the central issues of the cultural transition in Spain.

In a second example, 'Felipe's grey hairs', Montero takes on the leaders and propaganda of each party before the 1 March 1982 general elections, the first since the constitution was launched in 1978. She considers each party in turn before arriving at the subject alluded to in the title – Felipe González and his grey hair. Montero comments that she's tired of the Central Democratic Union leader Adolfo Suárez never being photographed sitting down:

> They plaster our city with photos of a president who is always found by the camera in a full-on hustle and bustle in the middle of parliament, as if the

guy was always talking and doing at every moment and there wasn't any time to rest (1979b).

She tolerates the Democratic Coalition Party's 'pendants coloured the green of hope – insect green-nausea-green that add a majestic note to the urban street lights' and are reminiscent of 'medieval flags' (1979b). All this commentary leads up to the real problem, though: 'It's possible to quietly suffer all this, because what really hurts are Felipe's grey hairs' (1979b). She remarks that just a year-and-a-half before, Felipe González was a different man:

> González was, in the last campaign, a healthy, bare-chested man, with a young air about him, ready to renovate the rancid halls of government, because in that moment it seemed like the entire country wanted to change. ... But I'm telling you that in just a year and a half, oh dear! Felipe has lost his colour and has been made grey. Oh how the man has aged. ... That air of a presidential fifty-year-old and the grey hairs that have taken over his ears. ... he has become a man made ashen by the glow of the presidency (1979b).

She finishes her fake-sad rant about Felipe's grey hairs with one final blow: 'the grey hairs of the socialists are sad because of the interior wrinkles and folds they signify, because they represent that premature old age that is devouring us all' (1979b). In certain quarters during the transition period, it was common to hear this sentiment: that the transition was a little too quick and easy and could lead to deep cynicism in the longer term. Montero's framing of the issue around the metaphorical ageing of the man who would be one of Spain's longest-serving leaders (1982-1996) reveals her own perception and disappointment that the party leader might be compromising his ideals in exchange for power. At the same time she references the widely-used metaphor of Spain as a person passing rapidly through life's major stages, an idea explored in our previous discussion of Torres's work, and one that appeared often in the nonfiction and fiction of writers of the period.

Although both Montero and Torres use humour as a tool in their writing, on topics that are obviously serious in nature, Montero approaches her readers in a straightforward way. She is less playful towards her readers, and assumes a posture that reminds us more of an activist making a point than an irreverent aunt commenting on the news of the day. Although the examples of her work here are from 1979, her style continues in a similar vein in her columns and interviews in *El País* today. That consistency persists in Montero's work, as there exists a certain symbiosis between the topics covered in her journalism and those explored in her many works of fiction, such as *Absent Love: A Chronicle* (1979), *The Delta Function* (1981), and *Beautiful and Dark* (1993).[10]

Empar Moliner: Observer of the everyday [11]

The new millennium brought younger writers into the public sphere, and the focus on remembering the transition period began to fade ever so slightly, even as people continued to remember the civil war (1936-1939) and the dictatorship. Among these writers, Empar Moliner is probably most well-known to a Catalan audience – she writes primarily, although not exclusively, in Catalan, and regularly appears on Catalan radio and television. While her radio and television personality often presents a more radical and irreverent Moliner,[12] her essays and fiction maintain a more measured tone, and humour and serious criticism come together harmoniously. Still, Moliner often approaches her readers with a 'check this out' and 'can you believe this guy' informal attitude. Because of this attitude, and her observance of everyday life, she could be compared to Quim Monzó, one of Catalonia and Spain's more internationally-known satirists. More informal than Monzó, and a bit less philosophical, she nevertheless manages to connect with her public to bring important issues to light.

In her collection of essays *In Search of a Man for Friendship and Possibly More* (2005), Empar Moliner reveals the inner workings of the hiring process for immigrants looking for work as maids, consults a fortune teller on the future of the Catalan language, tests the practicality of the Barcelona municipal government's campaign to get people to walk more, and checks out a dating service, all with the purpose of reporting her findings to the public. She does so with a wry wit and an air of adventure, taking to the streets to find out what's happening. In her essay about the immigrant women looking for work as maids, 'From which country do you want her?', Moliner places herself in the scene as she describes what she observes. Unlike in most of the other essays in the collection, Moliner does not give much explicit commentary about her experience. Instead, she lets her interactions with the women speak for her.

For example, Rosa, a Peruvian woman who volunteers at a convent, explains that many of the women who arrive there have been taught to be submissive and to accept sexism. She recounts the story of one Peruvian woman in particular whose husband brought her and their children to Spain and then left them there, returning to their country for another lover. Rosa explains: 'Many women come here because a placement agency keeps part of their wages, which are already scarce. Another problem is that those who just arrived think that hiding the truth will make it easier for them to get a job. For example, they "kill" their husband and children because they think that it's better to say they are alone' (2005: 9). Rosa also explains that 660 euros per month is about the maximum that women get paid to work as live-in maids.

Through Rosa's eyes, both Moliner and the reader get a glimpse of the reality of trying to find a job as a female, Spanish-speaking immigrant in Barcelona. Immigration and the status of immigrants consistently appear in Spanish newspapers as important political, social, and cultural issues. Moliner's essay provides insight into one aspect of the experience of immigrants and allows readers a peek into a place most will never set foot. Because she tells the story of her experience with a fiction writer's style – but a journalist's eye for factual details – readers relate to the personal stories of the women she encounters, while also being provoked to consider another perspective on a contemporary social topic.

While a number of essays in *In Search of a Man* cover serious news topics, others highlight and make fun of contemporary cultural practices. These include Moliner's experience at a dating agency, recounted in the essay from which the collection takes its title. Moliner describes her experience replying to a series of detailed personal questions using a one-to-five scale to indicate each attribute's importance to her: 'She wants to know if I smoke and if I drink alcohol, if I like animals and the status of my estate. (I don't dislike animals, I own an apartment and a moped. I drink and I don't smoke.)' (2005: 169). After more questions along these lines, Moliner expresses her frustration in an aside: 'There aren't any widowers or separated men that spend the day in the bar, from what I can tell' (2005: 170). Later, when Eva ventures the question: 'How important is sex to you in a stable relationship?' Moliner replies: 'If I say five, will I look bad?' and ends up answering 'four, because I'm feeling romantic this year' (2005: 170). In the end, rather than paying the service for the name of her match, Moliner uses the public forum of the newspaper to send a message to the guy, asking him 'to be unethical' and write to her immediately if he happens to be reading the article.

Her use of humour throughout the piece serves to communicate her opinion that real connections occur through direct contact, rather than through answering some questions in an office or online. Moliner maintains her 'gal on the street' style throughout the collection, revealing a similarly direct and often sarcastic tone with which she informs and entertains her public.

Conclusion

Empar Moliner's style of commentary, both in writing and in broadcasts, demonstrates the success of the path created by female trailblazers such as Maruja Torres – and other journalists of the transition period such as Manuel Vázquez Montalban. It also confirms that the rich tradition that began in the 1970s with humour magazines such as *Hermano Lobo* and *Por favor*, and continued with increasing freedom in mainstream publications, has taken root and will continue to be a valuable source of social and political criticism in the future.

Notes

[1] The journalists and scholars who contributed as writers include Vicente Molina Foix, Victoria Prego, Santos Juliá, Raymond Carr, Rosa Montero, Manuel Vázquez Montalbán, Juan Luis Cebrián, Jorge M. Reverte, Manuel Vicent, Javier Marías, Juan Marsé, Nativel Preciado, Almudena Grandes and Soledad Alameda

[2] Jesús Ceberio was director of *El País* from 1993 to 2006. He authored a preliminary note that appeared in *El País* at the start of the run of these articles in the newspaper. The same note appears at the beginning of the collected volume that was published as *Memory of the Transition* (Juliá et al 1996)

[3] Admiral Luis Carrero Blanco had been named Spain's Prime Minister approximately six months before his assassination by car bomb on 20 December 1973

[4] It's worth mentioning the original Spanish text here because Torres's style is to layer meaning in few words. The original reads 'El Gran Ejecutor'. In Spanish, 'ejecutor' could mean executioner, which would be a fair but dangerous criticism of Franco, at least from this author's point of view, but it can also mean executant or performer, which would also be accurate and less critical

[5] Santiago Carrillo was the long-time, controversial leader of the Spanish Communist Party

[6] Carmen Romero was an active member of the General Workers' Union and eventually became a member of the Spanish parliament. She was also married to the politician Felipe González

[7] Only *Amapola* was written by a Spanish composer. *Granada*, composed by a Mexican songwriter, and *Malagueña*, composed by a Cuban, are works about the Spanish cities Granada and Málaga, respectively

[8] Montero's columns also appeared on the back page of the newspaper more frequently beginning in the 1980s. Those columns are collected in *La vida desnuda* (*The Naked Life*)

[9] Fuerza Nueva was a political party of the extreme right, a relative of the fascist Falangists, that was active from 1976 to 1982

[10] Cristina de la Torre and Diana Glad translated *Absent Love*, Kari Easton and Yolanda Molina Gavilán translated *The Delta Function*, and Adrienne Mitchell is responsible for the translation of *Beautiful and Dark*

[11] Excerpts of this section were originally published by the author in 2012 in *World Literature Today*, Vol. 86, No. 2 pp 56-59

[12] For example, see her recent rant as a regular commentator on the morning show on TV3, the Catalan public television channel: http://www.ccma.cat/tv3/alacarta/programa/A-Soraya-Saenz-de-Santamaria-d/video/5250091/, accessed on 1 February 2015

References

Fagoaga, Concha, and Secanella, Petra María (1987) *Umbral de presencia de las mujeres en la prensa española*, Madrid: Instituto de la Mujer

Fonseca, Carlos (1979) Rosa 'Superwoman', *El País*, 22 March 1979. Available online at http://elpais.com/diario/1979/03/22/opinion/290905207_850215.html, accessed on 1 February 2015

García, José M. (1979) Marxismo y feminism, *El País*, 28 March 1979. Available online at http://www.elpais.com/articulo/opinion/MONTERO/_ROSA/Marxismo/feminismo/elpepiopi/19790328elpepiopi_13/Tes, accessed on 1 February 2015

García Álvarez, María Felicidad (2006) El lector intratextual en las columnas de Rosa Montero, Grohmann, Alexis and Steenmeijer, Maarten (eds) *El columnismo de escritores españoles*, Madrid: Editorial Verbum pp 175-197

Javier, Francisco and Olivares, Miguel (1979) Qué pasa, Rosa? *El País*, 18 March 1979. Available online at http://elpais.com/diario/1979/03/18/opinion/290559606_850215.html, accessed on 1 February 2015

Juliá, Santos, et al (eds) (1996) *Memoria de la transición*, Madrid: Taurus

Moliner, Empar (2005) *Busco senyor per amistat i el que sorgeixi*, Barcelona: Quaderns Crema

Montero, Rosa (1994) *La vida desnuda: una mirada apasionada sobre nuestro mundo*, Madrid: Aguilar

Montero, Rosa (1979a) Hombres y mujeres, *El País*, 14 March 1979. Available online at http://elpais.com/diario/1979/03/14/ultima/290214003_850215.html, accessed on 1 February 2015

Montero, Rosa (1979b) Las canas de Felipe, *El País*, 21 February 1979. Available online at http://elpais.com/diario/1979/02/21/ultima/288399603_850215.html, accessed on 1 February 2015

Smith, Paul Julian (1998) Modern times: Francisco Umbral's chronicle of distinction, *Modern Language Notes*, Vol. 113, No. 2 pp 324-338

Tablado, Pilar and Moñino, Adela (1979) Píldora 'antiniñas', *El País*, 22 March 1979. Available online at http://elpais.com/diario/1979/03/22/opinion/290905208_850215.html, accessed on 1 February 2015

Torres, Maruja (1996a) La bella durmiente se dispone a desayunar, Juliá, Santos et al (eds) *Memoria de la transición*, Madrid: Taurus pp 39-40

Torres, Maruja (1996b) Los cambios y las sombras, Juliá, Santos et al (eds) *Memoria de la transición*, Madrid: Taurus pp 63-64

Torres, Maruja (1996c) Usos (malos) y (pésimas) costumbres, Juliá, Santos et al (eds) *Memoria de la transición*, Madrid: Taurus pp 87-88

Torres, Maruja (1996d) No hay mal que cien años dure, Juliá, Santos et al (eds) *Memoria de la transición*, Madrid: Taurus pp 117-118

Torres, Maruja (1996e) Bingo, amor y fútbol, Juliá, Santos et al (eds) *Memoria de la transición*, Madrid: Taurus pp 341-342

Torres, Maruja (1996f) Empieza la 'política-tecno', Juliá, Santos et al (eds) *Memoria de la transición*, Madrid: Taurus pp 553-554

Torres, Maruja (1996g) El camino de la sabiduría, Juliá, Santos et al (eds) *Memoria de la transición*, Madrid: Taurus pp 705-706

Note on the contributor
Novia Pagone received her doctorate in Hispanic Studies from the University of Chicago. After an enjoyable two-year stint teaching at Knox College in Galesburg, Illinois, she opted for an administrative position at the University of Chicago where she is currently the Associate Dean of Students at the Institute for Molecular Engineering. She continues to pursue her research interests in literary journalism, fiction, and the film of contemporary Spain. Novia would like to thank Dr Cristina Carrasco for her generosity in reviewing the original translations of Empar Moliner's work.

Humour in the Mexican Illicit Drug Trade-Related *Crónicas*: A Way of Pointing the Finger at Injustice

Ave Ungro

Humour has always been based in subjects that are generally considered negative, such as immorality, corruption, and ideological fanaticism. The reasons for this may vary. The Mexican scholar Eduardo Parrilla Sotomayor, who has done extensive work on Mexican satire, parody and irony, explains that humour has historically played not only a corrosive but subversive role. The conflict between false pretensions and crude reality has always been a fertile ground for irony (2009: 13).

Yet it is risky to make public fun of 'serious matters' and sometimes there are unexpected consequences, as we saw so regrettably in France on 7 January 2015 when intolerance for religious irreverence cost some of France's most respected and controversial cartoonists their lives. They were among the twelve people killed during a lunchtime attack on the offices of the Paris-based satirical magazine *Charlie Hebdo*. This tragic attack reminded us of the importance of understanding cultural frictions in communication, and of the power that humour has to explain the world. It also reminds us that humour can cause divisions between people: the creators of humour and their objects of fun; the ones who accept the humour and those who see it as an insult.

This chapter will focus on humour in Mexican literary journalism related to the illicit drug trade. At first glance the illicit drug trade seems an odd subject for humour, as it often involves violence and death. To be more precise, I will analyse the humorous discursive expressions and utterances in the contemporary Mexican *crónicas*,[1] a type of human interest story, defined in more detail later in this chapter. My aim is to examine how humour has helped Mexican *cronistas* – the authors of the *crónicas* – to disentangle the complex patterns of Mexican power structures. Moreover, I aim to examine how the *cronistas* wield the power invested in them by their readers.[2]

In academia humour has been researched from many different angles, including literature (Bakhtin 2009 [1965]), linguistics (Simpson 2003), psychology (Freud 2002 [1905]), and humour as a social phenomenon (Billig 2005). Humour is also present in journalism, a fact that scholars in media and communications studies have too often left unnoticed. This analysis mainly draws upon Andrew Goatly's ideas on meaning and humour (2007 and 2012), Martha Elena Munguia Zatarain's approach on laughter in Mexican literature (2012) and Roger Bartra's philosophy on the Mexican character (2005).

In the first section a definition of the genre '*crónica*' will be given. The second section will concentrate on a discussion of the Mexican character and how it is reflected in Mexican humour, as well as in the *crónicas*. I will also reflect on how, through discursive and societal contradictions, certain humorous aspects of the Mexican illicit drug trade are revealed, such as laughing about death. In the third part I will focus on the humorous tropes in the *crónicas*. In discussing these tropes, metaphors will be touched upon briefly and irony more thoroughly. I will analyse eleven pieces published between 2004 and 2013 by various journalism outlets[3], chosen according to the following criteria:

1. that the articles treat the subject of the illicit drug trade in Mexico;

2. the authors would be included in the list of *cronistas* compiled by the Gabriel García Márquez Foundation for New Ibero-American Journalism;[4]

3. the *crónicas* would not only be published in newspapers or magazines but also included in anthologies of outstanding Latin American literary journalism or awarded an international award for excellence.

What is the *crónica* and can it be humorous?

The definition of the *crónica* has created debates among scholars. In Oxford Bibliographies, Viviane Mathieux describes the *crónica* as 'a somewhat unstructured genre that combines literary aestheticism with the journalistic responsibility to inform'.[5] There have been three momentous periods for the Latin American *crónica*: the *crónicas de las Indias* in the sixteenth and seventeenth centuries; the *crónica modernista* at the end of the nineteenth century, and the contemporary *crónica*.

For the contemporary *cronistas*, the means of expression has mostly been print media (newspapers and magazines), but nowadays the internet and its formats – blogs, lists, web pages and newsletters – have appeared to take it to a whole new level. The length of the *crónicas* varies and is dependent on the criteria set by the media outlet or publishing company, but in my corpus the shortest text has 862 words and the longest 11,558 words. Although some could characterise the *crónicas* as articles of opinion, columns, political commentaries or essays, they possess certain features that make such identifications insufficient. In one of the few critical studies on the contemporary Mexican *crónica*, Ignacio Corona and Beth E. Jörgensen aim to reflect on its liminal character by stating 'the discourse of the chronicle is contiguous to four subgenres, within which clear-cut borders do not exist: in journalism with reportage and human interest pieces; and in literature with the short story and the essay' (2002: 4). Although a hybrid form, the current *crónicas* aim to mirror reality. They are not fictional, nor do they blend reality and fiction.

In Mexico, there has lately been an increase in professional journalists writing literary pieces. A recent journal issue on Mexican communication (*Revista Mexicana de Comunicación,* June 2013) even asked whether there was a *crónica* boom in Latin America. Noted *cronistas* in Mexico such as Carlos Monsiváis, Elena Poniatowska and Juan Villoro write on topics concerning everyday Mexican life. There are also *cronistas* such as Alejandro Almazán, Diego Osorno and Marcela Turati who mainly concentrate on the dark side of Mexican reality: the beneficiaries and victims of the 'war on drugs' policy, organised crime, human trafficking and illegal drug trafficking.

When analysing humour in Mexican illicit drug trade-related *crónicas*, the first problem we encounter is defining precisely what can be counted as humour and what not. There is no definitive typography or definition. Humour is a cognitive experience, dependent on the context, in which laughter, amusement or surprising connections are produced. Goatly says that in order to understand a joke certain knowledge is necessary: 'This might be knowledge of a language code (a matter mostly of semantics) or background knowledge for making the inferences necessary for getting the joke (a matter of pragmatics)' (2012: 1). I have made my selection of humorous samples based both on semantics (for instance, when the author clearly states that humour has been explored in his writing) and a pragmatic basis (for instance, irony as a common practice in Mexican writing).

Of the ten *crónicas* under investigation, seven explored humour as a communicative resource in order to deliver a message or create recognisable discourses. Texts are of different lengths and often divided into sub-chapters. If we use the term microstructures and macrostructures to separate headings from the rest of the text, then notably only 'Un alcalde que no es normal' ('A mayor who is not normal') by Diego Osorno has humour at a macro-structural level. Maybe the lack of humour in the titles and sub-headings refers to an aspect of authorial choices in the *crónicas*. Out of eighty-seven uses of humour in the whole corpus, only thirty-two times was the humour expressed as an original creation of an author. At all other times, humorous stories, jokes, irony, sarcasm or other utterances were expressed by protagonists of the stories. Deciding whether to rely on their own words or the words of protagonists depends on whether the *cronista* has chosen a style that leans more towards an interview as in Parra's 'La voz de la Tribu' ('The tribe's voice') or a column, as in Villoro's 'La alfombra roja del terror narco' ('The red carpet of the *narco* terror'). The importance of choosing who delivers the message cannot be underestimated. There are concrete social and semiotic implications involved in choosing to include a humorous detail, conversation or phrase (O'Grady, Bartlett and Fontaine 2013). For this reason *cronistas* combine the testimonies of the people they interview with their own contemplations, as in Almazán's 'Carta desde La Laguna' ('A letter from La Laguna').[6]

> One of the few businesses to come out ahead in the war of La Laguna is the undertakers. Just this afternoon the skull of a young hit man was 'blown up' – and the employees of about ten undertakers fought over the deceased. 'We are vultures and scrounging is what we do,' said one, who told relatives of the goon that he was the best repairman of heads. Another employee offered the service of express cremation, a good offer at a time when hired gunmen have a bad habit of going to cemeteries to shoot the living during a burial. ... I did not know which part of the story was a joke.[7]

The author is highlighting the absurdity of undertakers profiting from a situation which common sense says should not be profitable. In a humorous way Almazán is criticising the supply-and-demand capitalism that justifies this kind of monetary gain.

Interestingly enough, the *cronistas* sometimes become the figures of fun in their stories. This happens with Guillermo Osorno, who in his *crónica* 'Santa Muerte' ('Saint Death') tells us of people in a crime-ridden neighbourhood of Mexico City who worship a saint that is supposed to incarnate death. After he receives the statue of Santa Muerte as a birthday present, and is warned to be cautious as these things are not a joking matter, he gets scared. Osorno recognises the difficulty of continuing to write the *crónica* about Santa Muerte, and asks a rhetorical question: 'How should one continue writing under so many threats?'

Different theories consider the social or cultural aspect of understanding humour: what seems funny to the members of one social or cultural group might not have the same effect on members of other groups. For example, in most foreign countries the nicknames of the heads of Mexican organised crime, also known in jargon as 'drug lords' or 'drug kingpins', are not translated. But all those names have meaning either in Western popular culture or in the Spanish language. Knowing those meanings makes it funny to read names such as those listed by Almazán's informant in the 'Carta desde la Laguna' ('A letter from La Laguna'): el Chapo (Shorty), el Toro (Bull), el Gitano (Gipsy), el Rambo y el Saico (Psycho). When we start to translate these names, they strike us as hilarious, but the humour becomes darker when we realise that these are serial killers, criminals, and drug traffickers. These nicknames also create a distance between reality and our perception of it. When Mexicans read about people called Rambo or Psycho, it makes them feel as if these villains live in some sort of television show or film that should be taken as a spectacle. I will come back to the danger of this perspective later.

As I have already referred to the importance of the cultural element in the analysis of humour in Mexican literary journalism, let's for a moment concentrate on what is considered specific to Mexican humour and the Mexican way of life in general.

Mexican humorous character

It would be a difficult task to describe what constitutes the Mexican character, what makes the Mexican way of living and experiencing the world unique. First, the concept of nation can be ambiguous and misused in Mexico: it is a country of many languages, religions and world views. Roger Bartra, a noted Mexican sociologist and anthropologist, refers to this multifaceted state when he locates the 'national character' mostly in the dominant groups of the society – since they have the tools and desire to unify people under a dominant discourse (2005: 14). All the same, Bartra says he has never been concerned about a 'typical Mexican' (ibid: 20). Regardless of his reluctance to search for stereotypes, Bartra has worked exhaustively on the diversity of the Mexican character and has often found it rewarding to work with humour (ibid: 25).

Considering the conclusions of researchers who have investigated the Mexican character, it is surprising how often we come face-to-face with Mexican melancholy, as opposed to humour and laughter. Emilio Uranga, a Mexican philosopher, ties melancholy to the Mexican mindset and does not see it as idiosyncratic because melancholy could be considered a typical human condition (2005: 152) Bartra narrows down the area where melancholy spreads its 'tentacles' and sees a melancholic attitude in all Latin American literature (2005: 51). Martha Elena Munguía Zatarain, a Mexican scholar in linguistics and literature studies, reasons that Mexican melancholy has been caused by the inferiority of an unoriginal and violent nation (2012: 26). A chain of notions can be constructed after so many suggestions of melancholy: sad > tragic > tragicomic > comic. The Mexican as a tragicomic character could be analysed in Mexican literature, poetry, journalism and pop culture. Probably the most famous archetype of a Mexican tragicomic figure is the fictional character Cantinflas, a peculiar man from a poor peasant family who in film and on stage offered a critique of Mexican society's injustice (Garizurieta 2005: 124).

But melancholy is only one side of the coin. In contrast Munguía claims the Mexican character is mainly festive and marked by constant laughter (2012: 61). In the *crónicas* the authors refer to the joyful character of the protagonists (most appear to be happy rather than melancholic). The protagonists of the *crónicas* seem to value laughter. For instance, when Emiliano Ruiz Parra chronicles the life of Javier Sicilia, a Mexican poet and peace activist whose son was murdered by drug gang members, the person who unfolds in front of our eyes is described as joyful and full of jokes. Sicilia also portrays a priest friend as someone pleasant because he was always joking a lot (Ruiz Parra 2015).

Sometimes the festive mixes with the sad or tragic in Mexico; this contradiction is decisive in trying to understand Mexican humour. It is illustrated in one of the most celebrated Mexican festivities, Día de los Muertos or the Day of the Dead, a 'time to honour death while mocking it with great abandon' (2003:

198). To a certain extent death is not only seen as normal, but even funny. This festival offers a serious and necessary reminder and consolation to most Mexican people – nobody escapes death, however high their societal position. Neither is there a class-related escape from the *calaveras* (literally: 'skulls'), humorous epitaphs dedicated to the 'memory' of a living person (Brandes 2003). This ambivalent relationship of Mexicans towards death can be contemplated in the *crónica* 'Santa Muerte' ('Saint Death') by Guillermo Osorno, in which he becomes astonished by how much comfort death can give people who see it every day. It does not matter whether there is an elderly granny or a convicted serial killer in front of the statue of Santa Muerte, a 'false saint' not yet approved by the Catholic religion: both show the same kind of devotion. Maybe even someone from a foreign culture would find it funny when Osorno describes the tattoos of a serial killer who is devoted to Santa Muerte: the Virgin of Guadalupe, a Christ, an elf, a witch, the Santa Muerte – and, in the middle of all those mystic characters – the convict himself and his wife, kissing passionately (Osorno 2006: 211).

The serial killer Osorno depicts is an indication of how hard it can be in Mexican society to separate one doctrine or dogma from another, as they are so often blurred together. The barriers that seemingly exist between beliefs and moral conditions also merge. So in the end the author makes the reader ask: is there actually something more important and more valuable than a human life? What are the rules people play by, and what is the name of this game? We might see here a subtle critique of a Mexican character so multifaceted in nature and actions that it is possible to see it as neither victim nor culprit.

Closely connected to this aspect of the Mexican character is the unification of the low with the high, the popular with the exclusive, and the vulgar with the sophisticated – the grotesque. *Cronistas* explore this territory most often by extensive exposition of local jargon, slang, vulgar expressions or double meanings, expressed by people from all economic and educational levels. Drug dealers, accomplices, peasants, people from the higher social stratum – they all share the need to symbolise their complex ideas with the help of charged words. One of these is 'la chingada', a word that is hard to translate, and to which Octavio Paz has dedicated a whole convoluted deliberation in the essay 'Los hijos de la Malinche' (Paz 2005). It is with an emancipated smile that a Mexican reads Diego Osorno's *crónica* 'Un alcalde que no es normal' ('A mayor who is not normal') where the main protagonist, the mayor of the city of San Pedro, Garza Garcia, says: '*Chingado, hombre.*' There might even be a moment of true human equality inscribed in this phrase that to some might seem hilarious, hopeful or just ironic (Osorno 2012).

Humorous tropes in the *crónicas* about the illicit drug trade

Kenneth Burke has popularised a distinction of four types of rhetorical figures or 'four master tropes': metaphor, metonymy, synecdoche and irony (Bateman 2014: 125). The *crónicas* apply tropes often, a circumstance that can be explained by the very nature of the *crónica* as a genre of literary journalism. Figures of speech, allegory, symbols and other tools of literary language also appear in the *crónicas* as tools in delivering humorous messages. I will now concentrate on metaphors and then on irony as the most frequent manifestations of humorous tropes in our corpus.

Metaphors

In the seminal book *Meaning and Humour – Key Topics in Semantics and Pragmatics* (2012), Andrew Goatly categorises seven basic similarities and overlaps between metaphors and humour. More specifically he compares metaphors and irony. It is, therefore, relevant to link any study on humour with a study of metaphors. Goatly has also investigated the relationship between metaphor, culture and ideology to see how metaphors affect our thinking and social behaviour (2007: 3).

In the *crónicas*, the presence of humorous metaphors can be detected in titles such as 'La alfombra roja del terror narco' ('The red carpet of drug terror') and 'El teatro del crimen' ('The theatre of the crime'). However different from their literal meaning in texts, these titles make clear reference to the field of entertainment and seem to indicate the controversial attitude towards Mexican organised crime held by both Mexicans and foreigners. Both *crónicas*, in their titles, ridicule the institutions, government, media corporations and others who have started to relate to organised crime as a form of entertainment discourse. The *cronistas* ask readers: do you really see organised crime as an item from the red carpet or theatre? Is that acceptable to you?

Goatly names several groups of metaphors that carry an ideological cost. Among those groups the most commonly used ones in our corpus are metaphors of emotion, power, and humans as animals. From metaphors related to emotions, for instance, happiness and hope are light and sadness and pessimism are dark. Accordingly, Villoro describes how the Mexican way of governing has produced a 'grammar of shadows' and Mexican authorities govern from the shadows. He does not explain further, but because of the shadow metaphor we easily detect his pessimistic view on the current state of Mexican politics (Villoro 2008). In the *crónica* by Martinez, locals from the borderlands are trying to survive next to big organised crime groups that mostly concentrate on trafficking drugs. The locals see their own niche in selling illegal trips to the United States. They see the illegal immigrants as an easy source of income and are never worried about the transients' fragile security. This is reflected in the metaphor they use as a nickname for illegal immigrants, 'los pollos' or 'chickens', a metaphor that has a negative connotation as someone cowardly or weak. The hard reality of life for people associating with organised crime, a shadowy government and indifferent co-citizens is well presented by metaphors that even at first glance seem humorous (Martinez 2012).

Irony

When the Mexican scholar María Eugenia Flores Treviño interviewed people from the city of Monterrey she concluded that they use humour, laughter, jokes, irony and self-irony because these seem to offer them an opportunity to dissolve social hierarchies and discursive tones. The irony offers them a world of equality, even though ephemeral and ideal. She adds that most people use irony when speaking of the economic situation, religious beliefs, crime, the authorities and consumerism (2009: 98). The same tendencies can be observed in the illicit drug trade-related *crónicas* where the authors and their interviewees use irony as an effective way to fight against established discourses.

One of the most illustrative *crónica*s using irony is 'La alfombra roja del terror narco' ('The red carpet of drug terror') by Juan Villoro. The main target of his black humour is Mexican authorities who have never won a democratic election and who raffle hope for the future as if at some sort of fair. He also scrutinises the citizens of Mexico by claiming that they would rather maintain the idea of drug trafficking as something distant, 'a theme park where they luckily do not have an entrance', rather than look around. Nor does Villoro ignore Mexican media institutions. In his opinion they are not presenting an alternative discourse and, therefore, are full of ignorance. He interprets the media's attention to organised crime, presented as a form of entertainment, as a symptom of a hypocritical and sick society. He paraphrases the famous axiom by Andy Warhol about 'fifteen minutes of fame', saying that in Mexico everyone receives fifteen minutes of impunity. In the beginning of the piece the reader is entertained by his sharp portrayal of the problems related to violence and the ruthless logic of the illegal drug trade. The tone gradually veers into a cry for sanity and for reforming the commonly accepted discourse (Villoro 2008).

Salvadorean *cronista* Oscar Martinez, who has focused many of his *crónicas* on human and drug trafficking in Central America and along the Mexico/US border, critiques dysfunctional countries with the help of the people who live there. In the *crónica* 'Un pueblo en el camino a la frontera' ('A village on the way to the border') he relates anecdotes from simple people forced to accept the cruel reality where they live. One of the men whom he interviews takes him along to buy some cocaine, and during the purchase the drug dealer notes in a sarcastic way that buying cocaine in their village is easier than buying tortilla (Martinez 2012).

This is a type of 'narco-wit' that shows how ordinary citizens forced to engage in organised crime see their activity – a normal process of buying and selling. Although funny, it is an obvious critique of both criminal activity and Mexican consumerism. The hopelessness of this situation – where the lines fade between permitted and prohibited, necessity and greed, good and evil – is described by an inhabitant of the same village in this way:

Remember that if you see someone with a face of a Mafioso, Mafioso they are; if you see a man with a big car and take him for a dealer, dealer he is; and if you see someone who you think is a good person, they are Mafioso.[8]

The *crónica* 'Un alcalde que no es normal' ('A mayor who is not normal') raises the question of what is sane and what could be considered crazy, abnormal. The author discovers through the adjectives 'crazy' and 'normal' a clever pattern to examine the madness or sanity of his protagonist's society. The mayor of a Mexican city claims himself to be definitely 'crazy' or 'not normal', because he tries to do things differently and fights against organised crime with unorthodox methods. He also makes fun of things considered 'normal' in Mexican society, such as how Mexican politicians buy space in the media (Osorno 2012).

Ironically, it is not clear by the end of the article whether the mayor is crazy or if he is acting exactly the way he is expected to. His so-called unorthodox methods, including potential collaboration with organised crime, find support among the citizens of the town he governs. Is this normal or crazy?

Conclusion

The Mexican character, which various scholars have described as melancholic and tragicomic, gives rise to characteristics of humour in Mexican writing. Several qualities of humour that stand out in Mexican literature and creative journalism are noticeable in the *crónica*, a liminal genre that falls between journalism and literature.

In Mexican *crónicas* about the illicit drug trade, *cronistas* employ humour to point at injustice in society. Concrete issues and the conversation around them are being mocked. Often we see a harsh critique of economic gain at the expense of human integrity, and frank judgement of the controversial attitude towards the illicit drug trade as a form of entertainment. *Cronistas* can find or use humour in a variety of topics; there are no thematic boundaries to the expression of humour.

Notes

[1] As the definition of the contemporary *crónica* goes in my opinion beyond the general understanding of the English term 'the chronicle', the original Spanish word is applied throughout the research. However, there are scholars, such as Ignacio Corona and Beth E. Jörgensen, who translate the word into English simply as 'the chronicle' (Corona and Jörgensen 2002).

[2] This chapter will not cover the complex and substantial history of the Mexican illicit drug trade nor will it give a statistical overview of the current *status quo* of the problem because it would be an enterprise beyond its scope. For further reading, see *El siglo de las drogas: el narcotráfico, del Porfiriato al nuevo milenio*, by Luis Astorga (2005) and *Vacíos de poder en México: El camino de México hacia la seguridad humana*, by Edgardo Buscaglia (2013)

[3] The eleven *crónicas* under investigation are 'Carta desde la Laguna' ('A letter from La Laguna') by Alejandro Almazán, 'La caja negra del comandante Minjárez' ('Officer Minjárez's black box') by Sergio González Rodríguez, 'Un pueblo en el camino a la frontera' ('A village on the way to the border') by Óscar Martínez D´Aubuisson, 'El

teatro del crimen' ('The theatre of crime') by Fabricio Mejía Madrid, 'Un alcalde que no es normal' ('A mayor who is not normal') by Diego Enrique Osorno, 'Santa Muerte' ('Saint Death') by Guillermo Osorno, 'Juegan a ser sicarios' ('They are playing being serial killers') by Daniela Rea, 'La voz de la tribu' ('The tribe's voice') by Emiliano Ruiz Parra, 'Los pobres de Estados Unidos' ('The poor of the Unites States') by Wilbert Torre, 'Los "narcos" pobres' ('The poor *narcos*') by Marcela Turati, and 'La alfombra roja del terror narco' ('The red carpet of drug terror') by Juan Villoro

4 The name of the foundation in Spanish is La Fundación Gabriel García Márquez para el Nuevo Periodismo Iberoamericano (FNPI). It is a non-profit institution that aims to improve journalistic standards and reinforce democracy and development in Ibero-American and Caribbean countries. The foundation organises workshops and seminars and gives out annual international awards

5 See http://www.oxfordbibliographies.com/view/document/obo-9780199766581/obo-9780199766581-0092.xml, accessed on 2 February 2015

6 All translations from the Spanish are the sole responsibility of the author

7 Original texts in Spanish: 'Entre los pocos negocios que han salido ganando con la guerra de La Laguna están las funerarias. Apenas esta tarde en que le volaron medio cráneo a un joven sicario, empleados de unas diez funerarias se disputaron al muerto. "Somos buitres y buitrear es lo que hacemos", me dijo uno que presumió a los familiares del matoncillo contar con el mejor reparador de cabezas. Otro trabajador ofreció el servicio de la cremación exprés, una buena oferta hoy en día en que los pistoleros a sueldo han agarrado la mala costumbre de ir al cementerio para dispararles a los vivos en pleno entierro. ... no supe qué parte de la historia era broma'

8 Originally in Spanish: Acuérdese, si usted ve a alguien aquí con cara de Mafioso, es Mafioso; si ve a un señor con su gran carro y cree que es narco, es narco; y se ve a alguien y cree que es buena persona, es Mafioso

References

Almazán, Alejandro (2013) Carta desde la Laguna, *Gatopardo*, March. Available online at http://www.gatopardo.com/ReportajesGP.php?R=185, accessed on 2 February 2015

Astorga, Luis (2005) *El siglo de las drogas: el narcotráfico, del Porfiriato al nuevo milenio*, Mexico City: Plaza y Janés

Bakhtin, Mikhail (2009 [1965]) *Rabelais and His World*, Bloomington: Indiana University Press

Bartra, Roger (2005) *La jaula de la melancolía: Identidad y metamorfosis del mexicano*, Mexico City: Penguin Random House, third edition

Bateman, John A. (2014) *Text and Image: A Critical Introduction to the Visual/Verbal Divide*, Oxon: Routledge

Billig, Michael (2005) *Laughter and Ridicule: Towards a Social Critique of Humour*, London: Sage

Brandes, Stanley (2003) Calaveras: Literary humour in Mexico's Day of the Dead, Narváez, Peter (ed.) *Of Corpse: Death and Humour in Folklore and Popular Culture*, Logan: Utah State University Press pp 221-238

Buscaglia, Edgardo (2013) *Vacíos de poder en México: El camino de México hacia la seguridad humana*, Mexico City: Debate

Corona, Ignacio and Jörgensen, Beth E. (eds) (2002) *The Contemporary Mexican Chronicle: Theoretical Perspectives on the Liminal Genre*, Albany: State University of New York Press

Flores Treviño, María Eugenia (2009) La burla u la risa en la ironía: sus funciones en el habla de Monterrey, Parrilla Sotomayor, Eduardo (ed.) *Ironizar, parodiar, satirizar: Estudios sobre el humor y la risa en la lengua, la literatura y la cultura*, Mexico City: Ediciones Eón pp 87-101

Freud, Sigmund (2002 [1905]) *The Joke and Its Relation to the Unconscious*, New York: Penguin Classics

Garizurieta, César (2005) Catarsis del mexicano, Bartra, Roger (ed.) *Anatomía del mexicano*, Mexico City: Random House Mondadori pp 121-130

Goatly, Andrew (2007) *Washing the Brain: Metaphor and Hidden Ideology*, Amsterdam and Cambridge: Cambridge University Press

Goatly, Andrew (2012) *Meaning and Humour: Key Topics in Semantics and Pragmatics*, Cambridge: Cambridge University Press

González Rodríguez, Sergio (2004) La caja negra del comandante Minjárez, Aponte, David et al *Viento rojo*, Mexico City: Random House Mondadori pp 83-97

Martínez D´Aubuisson, Óscar (2012) Un pueblo en el camino a la frontera, Darío Jaramillo (ed.) *Antología de crónica latinoamericana actual*, Madrid: Alfaguara pp 558-573. Available online at https://cronicasperiodisticas.wordpress.com/2008/11/21/un-pueblo-en-el-camino-a-la-frontera/, accessed on 21 June 2015

Mejía Madrid, Fabrizio (2012) El teatro del crimen, Carrión, Jorge (ed.) *Mejor que ficción. Crónicas ejemplares*, Barcelona: Anagrama pp 265-274

Munguía Zatarain, Martha Elena (2012) *La risa en la literatura Mexicana (apuntes de poética)*, Mexico City: Bonilla Artigas Editores

O'Grady, Gerard, Bartlett, Tom and Fontaine, Lise (eds) (2013) *Choice in Language: Applications in Text Analysis*, Bristol: Equinox Publishing

Osorno, Diego Enrique (2012) Un alcalde que no es normal, Agudelo, Darío Jaramillo (ed.) *Antología de crónica latinoamericana actual*, Madrid: Alfaguara pp 509-529. Available online at http://www.gatopardo.com/ReportajesGP.php?R=72, accessed on 21 June 2015

Osorno, Guillermo (2006) Santa Muerte, Silva, Miguel and Molano, Rafael (eds) *Las mejores crónicas de Gatopardo*, Mexico City: Debate pp 213-215

Parrilla Sotomayor, Eduardo (ed) (2009), *Ironizar, parodiar, satirizar: Estudios sobre el humor y la risa en la lengua, la literatura y la cultura*, Mexico City: Ediciones Eón

Paz, Octavio (2005), Los hijos de la Malinche, Bartra, Roger (ed.) *Anatomía del mexicano*, Mexico City: Random House Mondadori pp 159-178

Rea, Daniela (2014) Juegan a ser sicarios, Taibo II, Paco Ignacio et al (eds) *El cáncer del crimen organizado*, Mexico City: Albatros pp 121-124

Ruiz Parra, Emiliano (2011) La voz de la tribu, *Gatopardo*, June. Available online at: http://www.gatopardo.com/ReportajesGP.php?R=90, accessed on 2 February 2015

Simpson, Paul (2003), *On the Discourse of Satire: Towards a Stylistic Model of Satirical Humour*, Amsterdam: John Benjamins

Torre, Wilbert (2012) Los pobres de Estados Unidos, Bosch, Lolita (ed.) *Nuestra aparente rendición*, Mexico City: Random House Mondadori pp 133-135

Turati, Marcela (2012) Los 'narcos' pobres, Bosch, Lolita (ed.) *Nuestra aparente rendición*, Mexico City: Random House Mondadori pp 251-257

Uranga, Emilio (2005). Ontología del mexicano, Bartra, Roger (ed.) *Anatomía del mexicano*, Mexico City: Random House Mondadori, pp 145-158

Villoro, Juan (2008) La alfombra roja del terror narco, *Clarín*, 29 November. Available online at http://edant.revistaenie.clarin.com/notas/2008/11/29/_-01811480.htm, accessed on 2 February 2015

Note on the contributor

Ave Ungro is a doctoral student at the University of Helsinki, Finland. She gained a Master's degree in Spanish Philology after graduating from the University of Tartu (Estonia). Her work on the Mexican illicit drug trade-related *crónicas periodísticas* aims at revealing how literary journalism can mirror important societal changes, the illicit drug trade being currently one of the most controversial, important, social and political issues in Mexico. Her main research areas are Critical Discourse Studies (CDS), Media and Communication Studies and Cultural Studies.

Section 3:
The Politics of Being Funny

A Mirror and a Pen: Millôr Fernandes's Legacy and the Role of Humour in Brazilian Journalism

Nicolás Llano Linares

One of the most prolific humorists in Brazil, Millôr Fernandes (1923-2012) was a journalist, cartoonist, dramatist, translator and visual artist whose influence extended throughout the country's cultural scene. Known for his sceptical view of the world, Millôr – as he was commonly known – has become a major reference point in the study of the intersecting threads between political commentary, independent media outlets and humour in Brazilian media discourse. This chapter focuses on two phases of Millôr's journalistic work during the military dictatorship (1964-1985): *Pif-Paf* magazine, an unconventional independent journalistic enterprise that used humour as its main resource to critically dissect the defining traits of the Brazilian political system; and the seminal O *Pasquim* (1969-1991), an alternative weekly magazine that has been acknowledged as the main vehicle for independent, countercultural and alternative voices, at a time when censorship and political persecution were common.

Will the real Millôr Fernandes please stand up?
Considered by many the essential cultural commentator on Brazilian culture in the twentieth century, Millôr Fernandes wrote – and illustrated – an unconventional and utterly hilarious comprehensive picture of Brazilian social, political and cultural life. Born on 16 August in 1923, in the suburban neighbourhood of Méier in Rio de Janeiro as Milton Viola Fernandes, his story began with a calligraphic mistake made by the notary who registered his name. The functionary miswrote the upper horizontal stroke of the letter *t*, placing it over the *o*. He also left the final trace of the letter *n* undone, thus transforming the name into Millôr, a name Fernandes would embrace from 1938. His mother's death when she was just 36 – his father had passed away at the same age – was an episode he would often describe as a breaking point in his life. It was the moment he stopped believing in God and adopted scepticism as his

guiding principle. Fernandes felt he had 'come into the world to distrust the established things even though they had been accepted since always' (Fernandes 2013: 89).

His life in the news media started early. When he was nine his uncle sold his first drawing to a newspaper in Rio (*O Jornal*). In 1938, he started working for *O Cruzeiro* magazine, the biggest and most important weekly publication of the first half of the century, doing a variety of jobs. Before turning 18 he was already a popular writer for *A cigarra* magazine, under the pseudonym Emmanuel Vão Gogo. He also wrote a column under the same name for the *Diario da Noite*, and worked as director (writing, editing and illustrating) of two literary and cartoon publications (*O Guri* and *Detetive*). He returned to *O Cruzeiro* in 1943, along with a new wave of collaborators, giving a massive boost in popularity to the already important magazine. The figures were telling: from 11,000 copies sold per week, circulation surged to more than 750,000 after they joined (Moreira Salles 2003).

Millôr's defining features started to surface early: addressing a broad range of themes, the use of a variety of genres and techniques and, above all, his profound knowledge of the Portuguese language, articulated as a grammatical and syntactic disobedience that eventually would become the cardinal element of his discursive style (Fernandes 1975). 1945 saw the launch of the '*Pif-Paf*' section in *O Cruzeiro*, written until 1963 as Vão Gogo. During the first ten years of its publication it was illustrated by Péricles Maranhão. This would be a milestone in the life of Fernandes; from then on he would be the most popular and idiosyncratic journalist in the country.

There are a variety of *Millôrs* to analyse: the celebrated and self-taught translator, the inventive playwright, the magnificent illustrator and cartoonist. Also worth discussing is his impact on popular culture. One of his most popular legacies is his supposed invention of the beach sport *Frescobol*.[1] We could focus on the multiple dimensions of Millôr's work and probably never manage totally to grasp his influence and contribution to the cultural life of the country. His work navigated from politics, culture, and literature to science and religion. No topic seemed out of his domain. He had so many facets, all in which he excelled, that to call him versatile would be an understatement.

Millôr in context: Humour in Brazilian journalism

Millôr Fernandes was a rare case in Brazilian journalism. He worked for the biggest and most powerful media outlets, and participated in some of the most alternative and independent journalistic projects of the second half of the twentieth century. To all he brought the same originality and creative approach to text and images. As the writer and journalist Zuenir Ventura commented: 'I don't know if in Brazilian culture there exists another phenomenon like Millôr – someone who, whilst working, writing and drawing, daily or weekly on the printed press, was producing an *oeuvre* with such diversity, extension and quality like the one he produced and still does …' (Ventura 2003: 25). Fernandes defined himself – and his work – 'as a writer without style'. But he certainly left a mark in every genre he tried: illustrations, cartoons, journalism, translations, playwriting, aphorisms, haikus and fables. For all the many masks and social identities he could assume and project, he preferred to be acknowledged and characterised as a humorist and a journalist, for this simple reason: 'Essentially to take out the pretension' (2003: 32).

For Millôr, humour was the critical resource that allowed him to expose and dissect the most ludicrous and senseless aspects of society, and the commonly dishonourable practices of politicians; he considered humour the 'essential constituent of seriousness' (ibid: 278). He knew that humour was just as powerful as the independence, courage, professionalism and integrity in his work. The fact that Fernandes was also a prominent translator, playwright and visual artist helped upset the belief that humour was not equal to cultural and artistic products of the highest aesthetic order.

Written humour has been a part of the Brazilian press since the 1830s. Cartoons were the main type of humour published until the 1930s; magazines such as *Picante* (1834), *Lanterna Mágica* (1844) and *O Diabo Coxo* (1864) were the first weekly and monthly magazines to incorporate different types of graphic and textual humour. The beginning of the twentieth century brought a semi-professionalisation of satirical writers and cartoonists. Magazines were the first printed medium to establish specific spaces for humour (*Rio Branco; Alvorada*). *Folha da Noite* (now *Folha de São Paulo*) was one the first newspapers to have popular cartoonists among its collaborators in the 1930s (Belmonte and his *Juca Pato* character). Although Brazil's journalistic humour was always extremely political, it was not until the 1930s that humorous journalism would be regarded as a powerful tool to uncover the social reality of the country. *Careta* was one of the first publications to acquire notable popularity for publishing humorous texts and images. Many of these critiqued Getúlio Vargas's *Estado Novo* politics (Pimentel 2004).

With the appearance of the journalist Aparício Torelly, known as the *Barão de Itararé* (The Baron of Itararé), Brazilian printed humour strengthened its political stance.[2] Directing and writing the entirety of the *A Manha* newspaper, Torelly's work institutionalised humoristic texts as a tool for political opposition. Even though he did not like the work of the *Barão de Itararé* – Fernandes thought Torelly's fame was more a product of a good marketing campaign from his native state (Rio Grande do Sul) than for actual humorous material – Torelly's work may have paved the way for Millôr Fernandes to become the most important cultural commentator in the country.

According to Elias Thomé Saliba, humorous language in Brazil is bookended by the publication of the *Encyclopedia do riso e da galhofa* (written by the editor Eduardo Laemmert under the pseudonym Pafuncio Semicupio Pechincha) in 1863 and Millôr Fernandes's personal anthology of aphorisms and personal definitions *A bíblia do caos* (*The Bible of Chaos*, 1994). Millôrs's humour takes cues from a wide range of artists, writers and disciplines. However, from a linguistic perspective, Millôr shared a particular sensibility with the work of *Juó Banere* (real name Alexandre Ribeiro Marcondes Machado).

Before the 1950s Brazilian humorists occupied a place somewhere between advertising, press clippings and light theatre – a space filled with the quotidian, the trivial (Saliba 2003), a place without the social and cultural value given to literature and the arts. Humorists fought a long battle against a society that considered their talent and social purpose to be vulgar, never took them seriously and continuously censored them.

Since the beginning of his career as a journalist, Fernandes was famous for his original use of the Portuguese language. His texts are filled with clever inventions, reconfigurations and inversions of logical-semantic units, word uses and semantic structures. According to Zuenir Ventura: 'Few writers in the Portuguese language have explored the syntactic and semantic potential of words – the puns, the game, the polysemy, the vocabulary playfulness – placing those resources in the service of a type of humour that makes [you] laugh and think at the same time' (Zuenir Ventura 2003: 25).

Millôr's knowledge and irreverence towards the established grammatical and syntactic rules of the Portuguese language could be compared to the 1958 version of Pelé, the king of Brazilian football. Pelé, too, was precise, playful and fearless. Branca Granatic (1987) analysed the grammatical and logical-semantic resources in Millôr Fernandes's humour published in *Veja* magazine. According to Granatic, the most common linguistic elements used by Fernandes were: invention and overlapping of words, word fragmentation, repetition, inflection of invariable terms, using adverbs as nouns, appropriation of words and expressions from other languages, coordination of cognate adverbs, nominal syntagmatic shifts, proverbs and the reconfiguration of biblical passages. His most common logical-semantic resources were: *double entendre*, comparison and metaphors, hyperbole, irony, euphemism, antitheses and paradox.

Pif-Paf and the birth of the alternative press

After spending more than 18 years acquiring a devoted audience for his *Pif-Paf* section, the relationship between Fernandes and *O Cruzeiro* came to an abrupt and controversial end. In October 1963, yielding to pressure from the Catholic Church and conservative groups, the magazine printed an editorial accusing Fernandes of having abused its trust and good faith by publishing a 12-page piece called 'Esta é a verdadeira história do Paraíso' ('This is the True Story of Paradise'). The story was Fernandes's version of Adam and Eve. In the editorial, the magazine asked for God's and the Church's forgiveness, promised Fernandes's dismissal and exempted itself from any responsibility, comparing the publication of the piece with an act of sabotage. For Fernandes, the editorial and sudden dismissal came as a surprise. He heard the news from a friend while attending a party for the Countess of Paris in Lisbon.

When Fernandes returned to the country, Brazil was in profound turmoil. Political polarisation had deepened, inflation was hitting record numbers and a number of political and economic reforms proposed by President João Goulart – including legalisation of the Communist Party, the right of the illiterate to vote and agrarian reform – were received by conservative and right-wing sectors as defining steps towards a Communist regime. By February, the country's political commentators were already discussing the imminence of a military coup. On 13 March, the president and some of his ministers publicly presented their proposed reforms during a rally in Cristiano Ottoni Square, in Rio de Janeiro. The main points were:

a) a series of decrees that allowed the government to expropriate farms with more than 500 hectares within 10 kilometres of dams, railroads and highways;

b) the announcement of the control of rental prices;

c) the beginning of a popular movement to reform the foundations of the nation using plebiscites and institutional amendments (Bahiana 2014).

On 31 March, chaos and confusion exploded after several military units rebelled, starting 21 years of military dictatorship. According to Bernardo Kucinski: 'It was the beginning of an ambiguous regime, still undefined between a conservative liberal-civil movement and another military-authoritarian. There was "democratic" speech and a repressive practice. With the powerful weapon of irony, the humorists penetrated the contradiction between word and deed emphasising the grotesque situation' (Kucinski 2003: 26).

Motivated by his sudden dismissal and friendly pressure from some of the most celebrated and original journalists, cartoonists and writers of the time – Claudius, Fortuna, Ziraldo and Jaguar – Fernandes decided to start *Pif-Paf* as a quarterly magazine (Fernandes 2005: 11). He took a loan and began production in his own studio; it was a one-man operation. Fernandes's incorruptible beliefs about freedom of speech and civil liberties, his sceptical attitude towards life in general and his distinctive humoristic style were felt in all eight editions published (Kucinski 2003). Although the magazine was one of the seeds of the alternative press that assumed the role of public opposition during the military dictatorship, it was not exclusively a liberal, humorous and left-wing publication. The range of subjects asserted the universality of his intellectual interests: love and language, biblical themes, philosophical digressions about daily life.

'*Pif-Paf*, a *carioca*[3] point of view, is a quarterly magazine ... of irreverence and critique. We are not in favour or against, we don't have sacred or profane' (*Pif-Paf* 2005d: 1). From the first issue the editorial stance was unmistakably Millôr's, the director solely 'responsible for all the views expressed in the magazine, no matter how crazy, paradoxical, conflictive or stupid they are' (Fernandes 2005: 3). Launched the third week of May 1964, the first issue sold almost 40,000 copies. It had a substantial – and somewhat unexpected – impact on students, journalists, politicians and cultural agents. As the political scientist and journalist Bernardo Kucinski commented: 'Despite focusing on the criticism of societal customs and having been prepared before the coup, *Pif-Paf* was received as a response to the military coup. It quickly became a political magazine, since that was the use its readers and the circumstances made out of its existence' (2001: 28).

During the 1950s the *carioca* press went through a transformation. The increasing capital invested in the sector brought an adaptation of the North American model of labour division inside newsrooms (Sodré 1999) and a transition from a 'political journalism to an informative journalism' (Rocha 2011: 16). Introduced by the *Diário Carioca*, new standards of printed journalism started to be adopted by the majority of newsrooms: the use of images as lead components of graphic designs; defined sections and opinion columns; the division of content based on thematic classifications; and, in news coverage, standardised language based on objectivity and neutrality as fundamental components of the professionalisation of journalism (Rocha 2011). Along with other independent and alternative journalistic outlets of the time *Pif-Paf* navigated against this trend. Millôr's production was too loose to be fixed in restricted discursive spaces, and his style was too idiosyncratic to be considered textbook objective journalism. His beliefs (or lack of them) were always present. His was an editorial-based type of journalism that never intended to disguise the basis of his discourse and social identity, a hybrid between 'factual objectivity and aesthetic subjectivity' (ibid: 95). He was one of the few relevant practitioners to experience the modernisation of journalism in Brazil without having to adapt or change his style, or compromise with the commercial or political interests of the news media conglomerates.

The 1950s was also a transformative decade for Brazilian society. The industrial development promoted by Juscelino Kubitschek's government established the basis for new business and cultural enterprises. The *carioca* point of view was also a social ethos imbued in the magazine's opinions. Even though the capital of the country had moved to the recently-inaugurated Brasília, Rio de Janeiro was still the social, cultural and, to a certain degree, political centre of the country. The imperial past had left its lasting marks, especially in the construction of a cosmopolitan and modern middle class. Brazil's iconic cultural lifestyle, and its media image, was built around a bohemian segment living in Rio's Copacabana and Ipanema neighbourhoods. The lively social relations and close collaboration between artists, writers, intellectuals, journalists and musicians were the main components of a particular universe that was usually apparent in *Pif-Paf*'s pages (Fernandes 2003).

Despite its intricate and ever-changing graphic design, much of the content of the magazine revolved around regular sections: '*Pif-Paf*'s letters' (readers' letters and the magazine's responses); 'In conclusion' (the editorial column written by Millôr, in which he commented on the national and international political situation, mixed with fresh doses of his own daily life in Rio de Janeiro); '*Pif-Paf* analyses a joke' (an always surprising textual deconstruction of a cartoon that shattered assumptions about humour, cultural critique and social conventions);

Pif-Paf (Millôr's classic miscellaneous section 'Now directly from the producer to the consumer'); and 'Dog's world' (a global news overview composed of real and fictitious press clippings served with cold doses of irony and satire). Even though it only lasted eight editions, *Pif-Paf* is remembered for its acute satirical depiction of the politics of the country.

Several *Pif-Paf* features (articles, pieces, cartoons) gained cult status during the dictatorship. One was 'But, at the end, what is freedom?' (Issues 2-3), a critical and satirical commentary about the costs of freedom. It used the Statue of Liberty as a reference: 'But, Freedom exists! Not only does it exist, it is made out of concrete and steel, and is 100 meters high. It was donated by the French to the American [people] in 1886, because at the time the French had many liberties and the American [people] none' (Fernandes 2005: 8). Another was the testimony of Claudius, a *Pif-Paf* cartoonist, about his detention for several days: 'Well, it looks like up until now our pretentious class [journalists] did not have its martyr ... Thank to DOPS[4], for finally remembering us' (*Pif-Paf* 2005: 2).

The magazine came to an end for a number of reasons. Censors reacted to the constant critique of the regime, and what they considered to be a dissemination of extremely liberal moral views. In addition, several published photomontages of ministers and the president were considered offensive by the military regime. The lack of a functional and organised structure, the scarce advertising revenue and the fact that Fernandes, the body and soul of the publication, was 'exhausted in every sense' (2005: 12) were also instrumental in the closing of Millôr's enterprise. The magazine ended in style. In its last edition (27 August 1964), text printed on the back cover – a provocation, some might say – asserted the magazine's approach to the political situation of the country:

> If the government continues to allow certain journalists to speak about elections; if the government continues to allow certain newspapers to criticise its [the government's] financial policies; if the government continues to let some politicians persist in keeping their candidacies; if the government continues to let some people think on their own; and, above all, if the government continues to let this magazine circulate, with all its irreverence and criticism, we will soon be falling into a democracy (Fernandes 1964: 24).

The chief of police of the state of Rio de Janeiro ordered the seizure and closing of the magazine. The ending of the short-lived but highly influential *Pif-Paf* gave way to one of Fernandes's happiest and proudest collaborations. He received a letter asking him to become a regular collaborator for the Portuguese newspaper *Diário Popular* (Fernandes 2004). 'That was how, because of the Brazilian repression, for 10 years I would transform into a Portuguese journalist. They even had a nightclub with my name – *Vão Gogo* – in Lisboa' (Fernandes 2005: 12). *Pif-Paf*, both the column and the magazine, had a strange kind of historical destiny. The magazine was launched a couple of months after the beginning of the Brazilian military dictatorship. Ten years later, his final contribution to the *Pif-Paf* column in the Portuguese newspaper was published on 24 April 1974, the day before the overthrow of António de Oliveira Salazar's regime in Portugal.

When disobedience is done right and succeeds: *O Pasquim*

If *Pif-Paf* was the birth of the alternative press, the weekly magazine *O Pasquim* cemented the ascension of the alternative press during the military dictatorship. Introduced to the public on 26 June 1969, the magazine was a mixture of *Mad*, the *New Yorker* and *Village Voice*. It was created by several of Millôr's previous collaborators and some of the most popular *carioca*[5] writers, journalists and cartoonists of the time: Tarso de Castro, Jaguar, Claudius, Sergio Cabral and Carlos Próseri. In Millôr's words, *O Pasquim* was 'presumptuous, iconoclastic, outspoken, gentle and rude, sensual, incapable, agnostic, restricted and comprehensive, written in an extremely popular language' (Fernandes 2006: 92). The magazine represented the voice of a specific segment of the *carioca* middle class – firmly settled in elite southern neighbourhoods, especially Ipanema – the intellectuals, artists and bohemians who would comprise the core of *O Pasquim*'s collaborators. Their work methods, such as doing interviews in their favourite bars, and their proclivity to turn social and public spaces like the beach, the bar and *carnaval* into loci of creativity and social productivity, left indelible marks on the rise of Ipanema as a cultural instigator, on Rio de Janeiro being recognised as the cultural capital of the country and on the ethos of the magazine.

There were two major factors behind the conception of *O Pasquim* (Fernandes 1977). First, there was Millor's *Pif-Paf*. Its financial independence from major news media companies and economic groups, the use of humour for critical political commentary, the lack of labour divisions and hierarchies inside the newsroom, the articulation of a modern design and the extensive range of subjects were defining elements that impacted not only *O Pasquim*, but several other alternative press enterprises. Secondly, Sérgio Porto – also known as Stanislaw Ponte Preta – the director of the weekly humoristic magazine *Carapuça*, died. *Carapuça*'s distribution company considered continuing to publish under a new set of collaborators, including Jaguar and Sérgio Cabral. Those two knew that Sérgio Porto's style was extremely difficult to emulate and suggested the creation of a new magazine, thus becoming founding members of *O Pasquim*.

The very name *O Pasquim*[6] – meaning a satirical and critical text against the government and also a defamatory and vulgar type of publication – indicated how politicised the public discourse had become at the time. After many names were discarded, Jaguar came up with the idea of naming the magazine after the type of response the right-wing and the military government would have to the editorial content of the magazine: 'They are going to call us a lampoon (defamatory newspaper, injurious pamphlet), thus they will have to invent other names to insult us' (Jaguar and Augusto 2006: 7).

Between the closing of *Pif-Paf* and the beginning of *O Pasquim*, the military dictatorship had become more severe and brutal. Institutional Act No. 5 (AI-5), issued on 13 December 1969 by President Artur da Costa e Silva, and written by the Minister of Justice, Luís Antônio Gama e Silva – one of seventeen such decrees during the regime – amounted to a brutal attack against freedom of speech and the civil liberties of social and student movements. The decree granted exceptional constitutional powers to the president, closed the National Congress and suspended civil liberties, freedom of speech and social organisation rights. It allowed the arrest of any citizen for sixty days – ten in complete isolation – without evidence. It even suspended *habeas corpus*. AI-5 created an open platform for the violation of basic rights; kidnappings, torture, murder and political persecution were recurrent practices used by the Costa e Silva government. 1968 represented the institutionalisation of the military regime assuming its dictatorial nature (Gaspari 2002).

O Pasquim was a success right from the start. The fist issue sold more than 30,000 copies, and five months later they were celebrating selling 100,000 copies per edition. Before the end of its first year, the magazine was selling an average of 200,000 copies per week. For a small independent and countercultural magazine that started with the ambition of becoming a neighbourhood publication – without any financial support from advertisers and the main media conglomerates which backed the other two defining magazines of Brazilian journalism, *O Cruzeiro* (Diários Associados, the media baron Assis Chateubriand's company) and *Veja* (the Brazilian version of *Time* magazine, published by the powerful *Editora Abril*) – its popular impact and longevity was a most impressive achievement. It lasted 22 years – 1,072 issues – and boasted an impressive list of collaborators: Vinícius de Moraes, Ferreira Gullar, Rubem Fonseca, Ivan Lessa, Paulo Francis, Antônio Callado, Rubem Braga, Tom Jobim, Heitor Cony, Oscar Neimeyer, Jô Soares, Caetano Veloso, Luis Fernando Verissimo, Fausto Wolf and Glauber Rocha, among many other national and international artists, writers and cultural figures.

As expected, the dictatorship was not fond of the magazine; for them *O Pasquim* 'was a Communist den filled with drunks, perverts and drug addicts, hell-bent on promoting exotic and subversive ideologies, misguiding the youth and destroying the Brazilian family' (Augusto 2006: 11). Censorship of the magazine became common. It was not unusual for the editors to put together material for two editions at once knowing the number of edits and cuts the censors often applied to its content. Sometimes all the issues on newsstands were confiscated. Several members and collaborators of the magazine were arrested, and others had to leave the country because of political persecution and death threats. It was not easy being on the opposition side of a humourless regime.

Madam Marina was the assigned censor for the magazine. She had the final decision on what could and could not be published. However, because she worked inside the newsroom – a common tactic at the time – the members of *O Pasquim* struck up rather 'friendly' relations with her and between drinks she would approve content that was not 'favourable' to the *status quo* (Augusto and

Jaguar 2006). Eventually she was fired and General Juares Paes Pinto took her place; he was also discharged after having 'missed' an interview with Angela Gillian, an American anthropology professor who stated that racism was still alive in the country. From then on editorial inspection moved to the Army's Centre of Information in Brasília until 1975, the year when censorship supposedly ended.

Millôr's involvement with *O Pasquim* had two distinct phases. Although credited as a founding member due to his involvement from the first issue, the influence of his work and some of the founding members' experience working at *Pif-Paf*, Millôr was only a close collaborator from 1969 to 1972. In the first issue he wrote a text on the difficulty of building a truly independent publication: 'I am not trying to discourage you, but one thing I would tell you: If the magazine is, indeed, independent it's not going to last three months. If it lasts three months it is not really independent' (Augusto and Jaguar 2006: 8). The message was clear: Millôr knew that an alternative and independent voice would not go unnoticed by the censorship apparatus. The article ('Independence, right? You guys are killing me') was a chronological record of his independent journalistic undertakings, his many encounters with censorship and advice from his experience on the complexities the new venture would have to face:

> A) The general establishment that has never been sympathetic to our activities, and definitely doesn't find anything funny about it. B) The advertising agencies that love humour, naturally, only if it's from abroad, from far away, done by *Mad*, published in *Playboy* and filmed by Jacques Tati ... C) The Church ... D) The Family, the Social Classes, The Important People, The Squares ... The Avant-Borings that dress as Avant-Garde, etcetera' (Fernandes 2006: 17).

From the beginning Millôr was involved in the production of the celebrated collaborative interviews that constituted the central section of every issue. He also wrote numerous texts that defied classification, like the majority of his journalistic production. In the 40th issue, he listed all the magazine's slogans and used them to introduce a text that can be described as a mixture of a declaration of principles, a critique of the restrictions of freedom of speech, a characterisation of the irreverent nature of their editorial guidelines and a homage to the fact that the magazine was still alive. In 1972, after several changes in the editorial board, Millôr became the 'president' of the magazine: 'I don't pretend to change anything but to go deeper and make Brazil the funniest country in the world' (Veja 1972: 48). His promotion was highly publicised; even *Veja*, the country's biggest mainstream magazine, gave it a full-page spread.[7] During his run as president (1972-1975), Millôr continued to comment on a variety of themes: '... revising the West's culture and history; deconstructing jokes; parodying [Bernardo Bertolucci's 1972 movie] *Last Tango in Paris* (at the time forbidden in Brazil, like other films such as Woody Allen's *Bananas*); reinventing the vacuum cleaner, eyeglasses and a telephone without the number

9; revising the clichés of the news media; and ... philosophising about the things that could not be philosophised' (Augusto 2007: 8). From a managerial point of view, Millôr's presidency was characterised by the delicate financial situation of the magazine and the increasing censorship and political persecution that affected the functioning of the magazine.[8]

Millôr collaborated with the magazine until 1975. Although it had a distinct non-hierarchical editorial organisation, frictions and conflicts arose between the publication's principal figures. The censorship the magazine had been subjected to since November 1970 came to an end in March 1975. In the celebratory 300th issue, Millôr wrote an editorial ('Without censorship') commenting on the responsibilities journalists had – with or without censorship (Kushnir 2004). The issue was confiscated after it hit the newsstands on the orders of the Minister of Justice, Armando Falcão. After the episode, Millôr proposed to make Falcão the theme of the following issue, but Jaguar and other members of the editorial team disagreed with him, leading to the end of his work with *O Pasquim*.

Beyond all its virtues, *O Pasquim*, and to a certain degree *Pif-Paf*, were also victims of their own humoristic resources. Several analyses of the magazine and Millôr's weekly column for *Veja* magazine (Crescêncio 2012) have shown that in some cases the same tools used to critically reflect on the repression, the growing radicalisation of the dictatorship and the dogmatic tendencies of the left were also used to perpetuate stereotypes of feminist and homosexual movements. These stereotypes were rooted in the nature of Brazil's patriarchal society. Several pieces published in the magazine had a distinct bias. Women were often commoditised and valued simply for their looks, and although the magazine published feminist voices, the final word, a satiric and ironic one, was always the editors' (Soihet 2005).

A 'successful outsider': Closing remarks

In many ways, Millôr Fernandes was one of the last figures to embody the print culture. His practical wisdom in both business and trade, his work ethic and endless energy for more than 80 years helped create the Millôr myth within the country. Without following rules, formats and patterns, he aspired to – and inspired – a model of thought based on freedom and creativity without restraints of any type.

It seems useless to try to classify Millôr's work. Was he a writer, artist or journalist? At his core, he was a humorist – a gifted one. His diversity enabled him to move not only through genres, styles and discourses, but also between social and political classes: exhibiting his opinions and digressing about the common, the holy and the ordinary without any type of compromise. Several factors allowed Millôr Fernandes to keep his journalist enterprises independent: his massive popularity; his unbreakable integrity that led to conflicts with mainstream media outlets and increased his aura as the ultimate iconoclastic commentator; and the fact that neither *Pif-Paf* nor *O Pasquim* had any commitments to a particular political or economic group, thus having complete freedom from any economic or political interests.

For him, being a humorist was based on the idea of confronting static ideas. He was always confronting popular and established beliefs, ideologies and trends. He would engage with the present and past with a sceptical attitude as a way to distance himself from any set political or cultural perspective. He used humour as a linguistic space for complete freedom of thought: 'Humourism is a panoramic vision of the world, it can be practised with everything, at any time, in all forms, in politics, in religion and even in crime' (Fernandes 2002: 571). His dislike for praise was balanced with a long-lasting dedication to parodying himself. Millôr was inclined to understate his influence on generations of journalists, cartoonists and artists. In a well-known aphorism he examined the importance of legacy: 'The only one that has an *oeuvre* is the construction worker.'[9] Although Millôr's work constitutes an authentic 'synthesis of almost all of the modalities of Brazilian humour' (Saliba 2003: 95), he was never comfortable with the categorisation of his work as part of any cultural or artistic canon. Nor did he want to be remembered as a 'thinker, or worse, an erudite' (Fernandes 2013: 198).

Millôr Fernandes's massive body of work can be considered as an alternative history of the last 80 years of Brazilian life. Examined today, his texts still hold the same degree of perspicacity and audacity. Even some of the most dated pieces can be read as illuminating and revealing sociological digressions. He was interested in capturing contradictions, in deconstructing old ideas, in revealing the conflicts and frictions between the moral system and the reality of the country, and in putting a serious veil of critical perspective on the banal and quotidian: 'When you do a type of humour that is close to the philosophical, it is timeless' (Fernandes 2003: 45). With Fernandes, no absolute truth, no self-announced saviour got away. Reading his work today is an educational experience; it teaches you to see not only between the lines, but to doubt why the lines are there in the first place.

For Millôr, assuming and maintaining a humorous attitude – in complete synergy with his sceptical philosophy – allowed him to cultivate a critical, nonconformist and rebellious attitude no matter what the situation in the country. According to Ventura: 'The substratum of all he does is humour, without resentment and bitterness. With that, he transforms himself into a model that helps Brazil be its best (the best thing it has), which is the vocation to laugh – against seriousness, narrow-mindedness, the powerful and ourselves' (2003: 25). Although some of his work was strictly focused on the country's changing political context, the array of themes and genres he explored made him a truly universal writer. He saw humour not as a genre, but as a tool, a resource, an apolitical approach to life in general. In the end, Millôr Fernandes was not the best humorist in the country, but only 'the funniest person of the funniest family of the funniest city of the most mishandled country in the world' (Fernandes 2013: 279).

Notes

[1] A popular type of paddleball Millôr Fernandes claimed to have invented in the 1960s. The game does not have a winner, rules or points. He was an avid player and supporter of the sport

[2] A name he created based on the battle 'that never happened' between the São Paulo Public Forces (the army of the government) and the revolting army led by Getúlio Vargas in the 1930 military coup

[3] Native or inhabitant of Rio de Janeiro

[4] DOPS: Department of Social and Political Order. Acronym based on Portuguese language

[5] Some of the defining collaborators of the history of *O Pasquim* were not born in Rio de Janeiro (Ziraldo, Henfil, Luis Carlos Maciel) but were so adapted to the middle class bohemian-intellectual *carioca* lifestyle that they were considered *carioca* by essence and not by origin

[6] From the Italian term '*pasquino*' which signifies a satirical, critical text, or injurious pamphlet

[7] He wrote for *Veja* magazine between 1968 and 1984 and later from 2004 to 2009

[8] In the final weeks of 1970, several staff members of the magazine were detained for two months. During that period – known as '*O Pasquim's flu*' – Fernandes worked as ghost writer, writing as his incarcerated colleagues

[9] The phrase is a play on the use of the word *obra* (*oeuvre*) in Portuguese. It can signify both an intellectual product and a construction project

References

Branca, Granatic (1987) *Os recursos humorísticos na obra de Millôr Fernandes*. Master's Thesis presented at São Paulo's University, Faculty of Philosophy, Letters and Human Sciences, São Paulo, Brazil

Crescêncio, Cintia Lima (2012) Movimentos de quadris e movimentos feministas: Millôr e feminismo, *História: Debates e Tendências*, Vol. 12, No. 2 pp 238-259

Fernandes, Millôr (1975) *Trinta anos de mim mesmo*, São Paulo: Círculo do Livro S.A., third edition

Fernandes, Millôr (1977) *Millôr, o inventor da liberdade de Imprensa no Pasquim*, São Paulo: Círculo do Livro SA

Fernandes, Millôr (2002) *Millôr Definitivo. A Bíblia do Caos*, Porto Alegre: L&PM Editores

Fernandes, Millôr (2003) *Cadernos de Literatura Brasileira: Millôr Fernandes*, Rio de Janeiro: Instituto Moreira Salles

Fernandes, Millôr (2004) *Pif-Paf*, Coutinho, João Pereira (ed.) Lisboa: O independente

Fernandes, Millôr (2005) *PIF-PAF Quarenta anos depois. Coleção fac-simil das 8 edições da revista Pif Paf de Millôr Fernandes*, Rio de Janeiro: Editora Argumento, second edition

Fernandes, Millôr (2006) Independência, é? Vocês me matam de rir, Jaguar and Augusto, Sérgio (eds) *O Pasquim. Antologia Volume I 1969-1971*, Rio de Janeiro: Editora Desiderata p. 17

Fernandes, Millôr (2013) *Millôr Definitivo. A Bíblia do Caos*, Porto Alegre: L&PM Editores, pocket edition

Gaspari, Elio (2002) *A Ditadura Envergonhada*, São Paulo: Companhia das Letras

Jaguar and Augusto, Sérgio (eds) (2006) *O Pasquim. Antologia Volume I 1969-1971*, Rio de Janeiro: Editora Desiderata

Jaguar and Augusto, Sérgio (eds) (2007) *O Pasquim. Antologia Volume II 1972-1973*, Rio de Janeiro: Editora Desiderata

Kucinski, Bernardo (2001) *Jornalistas e Revolucionários*, São Paulo: Edusp, second edition

Kushnir, Beatriz (2004) *Cães de alugel*, São Paulo: Boitempo Editorial

Pimentel, Luís (2004) *Entre Sem Bater! O humor na imprensa: do Barão de Itararé ao Pasquim21*, Rio de Janeiro: Ediouro Publicações S. A.

Revista Veja (1972) Emfim, um escritor sem estilo, São Paulo: Editora Abril, 20 December, No. 224

Rocha, Silva Lygia Maria (2011) *PIF-PAF: O JORNALISMO QUE RI. Uma análise do campo jornalístico a partir da imprensa alternativa brasileira*. Master's thesis presented at Santa Catarina's Federal University Journalism Department, Santa Catarina, Brazil

Saliba, Elias Thomé (2003) Patrimônio humorístico, Fernandes, Millôr *Cadernos de Literatura Brasileira: Millôr Fernandes*, Rio de Janeiro: Instituto Moreira Salles pp 94-101

Sodré, Nelson Werneck (1999) *História da Imprensa no Brasil*, Rio de Janeiro: MAUAD Editora, fourth edition

Soihet, Rachel (2005) Zombaria como arma antifeminista: instrumento conservador entre libertários, *Estudos Feministas*, Vol. 13, No. 3 pp 591-611

Ventura, Zuenir (2003) Confluências, Fernandes, Millôr, *Cadernos de Literatura Brasileira: Millôr Fernandes*, Rio de Janeiro: Instituto Moreira Salles pp 24-25

Note on the contributor

Nicolás Llano Linares is a PhD candidate in Comunication Sciences at Sao Paulo University. His research interests include food and material culture, media and journalistic discourses and critical explorations of visual culture. He is one of the editors of *Antropologia & Comunicação* (2014), a collection of papers presented at the IX International Seminar of Image Culture – Cultural Images. He is an active member of the research group GESC3: Semiotic Studies in Communication, Culture and Consumption. His latest publications have been focusing on the symbolic links between Colombian culture and violence. He is also a regular collaborator to *Letras Libres* (Mexico) and *Revista Matera* (Colombia) and works as a translator of Latin American and Portuguese literature and essays.

Humour and Identity in Catalonia: The Role of the Satirical Press

Rhiannon McGlade

Catalonia lays claim to a rich, and yet relatively unknown, tradition for satirical publication and cartooning that was deeply imbricated in the twentieth-century social and political evolution of the region. These publications played a significant role in using humour to manipulate existing stereotypes and perceptions to construct and reinforce in-group solidarity. Before the outbreak of the civil war in 1936, the backlash against the humour press typically included censorship, fines and closures. Added to these, incidents of army-led assaults on offices, the declaration of a national state of emergency, and an assassination all suggest that this was a humour being taken very seriously. However, with the installation of Francisco Franco's dictatorship, following the Nationalist victory in the civil war in 1939, all Catalan satire was driven underground or into exile. While the Spanish civil war has received significant academic treatment, one area requiring further examination is the role played by humour during the conflict.

Since jokes rely on shared attitudes in order to communicate their intended messages, we can use humour from a given period to identify existing beliefs within social groups during that particular moment in history. This chapter will introduce readers to the satirical press in Catalonia, charting its rise to prominence from the nineteenth century until the end of the Spanish civil war. It will go on to discuss the cultural work performed by the Catalan tradition and its part in group identity construction and consolidation during the conflict, using indicative examples taken from the two key remaining satirical publications of the time: *L'Esquella de la Torratxa* (*The Cowbell of the Turret*) (1872-1939) and *Papitu* (named after the music critic Josep Maria Pascual) (1908-1937).

The origins of the Catalan satirical press
The arrival of *Un Tros de Paper* (*A Scrap of Paper*) in 1865 – the first humorous weekly published exclusively in the Catalan language – marks the beginning of the Catalan satirical tradition. Lasting for sixty-nine numbers, its publication was

in keeping with a growing sense of cultural and linguistic identity in Catalonia that had taken root by the mid-nineteenth century as part of the revivalist movement known as the *Renaixença*. Despite a short print life in modern-day terms, the magazine's popularity was undisputed, and the various imitations it spawned demonstrated the Catalan public's readiness to read publications in its own language. Spurred on by the success of *Un Tros de Paper*, the publication's editor, Innocenci López, went on to create Catalonia's most iconic satirical periodicals: *La Campana de Gràcia (The Gracia Bell)* (1870-1934) and *L'Esquella de la Torratxa* (1872-1939).

La Campana was first published on 8 May 1870 and promoted the use of vernacular Catalan as opposed to more arcane academic forms. This use of contemporary language, as well as a growing prominence given to caricature, was combined with notably Republican and federalist sympathies that gained the publication a popular following from the outset. However, *La Campana*'s outspoken style and refusal to compromise in its satirical derision of the establishment left it prone to governmental backlash, resulting in countless fines and suspensions during its long history.

It was during one such interruption that López decided to create a stand-in publication to satisfy *La Campana*'s avid readership, and on 5 May 1872 *L'Esquella de la Torratxa* went to print. Following two initial short-lived print runs, *L'Esquella* eventually carved out its own place in the Catalan market and became a full-time publication in its own right. While *La Campana* tended to concentrate on national and international politics, *L'Esquella* concerned itself with ridiculing Barcelona's main political figures. Both retained an anticlerical and republican stance. *L'Esquella* shared *La Campana*'s tumultuous history, but went on to outlive its sister publication by five years. It was forced to close with the arrival of Francisco Franco's dictatorship in 1939.

By the early twentieth century, *La Campana* and *L'Esquella*'s dominance of Catalan satirical publishing had taken root and each boasted healthy circulation figures and contributions from Catalonia's most acclaimed writers and cartoonists.[1] Although many tried, few publications were able to emulate or challenge López's monopoly in the field. There were, however, three notable exceptions, namely *Cu-Cut!* (after the sound of tapping on a table) (1902-1912), *Papitu* (1908-1937) and *El Be Negre (The Black Sheep)* (1931-1936).

Rather than following the ideological position held by the established satirical stalwarts, *Cu-Cut!* combined conservative Catalanism and centralism and was directly at odds with *La Campana* and *L'Esquella*'s republicanism. Following its first number on 2 January 1902, *Cu-Cut!* quickly made a name for itself with the hostile tone of its humour. It seemed no one was safe from the publication's acerbic satire, including the competition. During its lifetime *Cu-Cut!* was an enthusiastic participant in the strident exchanges between Catalonia's principal satirical publications. Nevertheless, despite its distinct ideological stance and brand of humour, *Cu-Cut!* shared many of the experiences of *La Campana* and *L'Esquella*: it enjoyed healthy circulation figures, while also being subjected to numerous fines on account of its uncompromising and confrontational approach.² Undeterred by these financial penalties, the publication continued to push the boundaries.

The magazine's provocative style led to a violent assault on its premises in what became known as the *fets de Cu-Cut!* (*Cu-Cut!* events). A drawing produced in 1905 by one of the publication's staff cartoonists, Joan Junceda, which ridiculed the Spanish army – a common theme in the Catalan satirical press following Spain's humiliating defeat in the Spanish-American War of 1898 – and celebrated a Catalan political victory, was seen as one insult too many. Although the cartoon was retracted before going to print, the damage had been done. On 25 November 1905, three hundred soldiers from Barcelona's garrison, incensed by Junceda's cartoon, attacked the *Cu-Cut!* offices, beating employees and torching typewriters in the street while shouting 'Long live Spain!' and 'Death to the Catalanists!'. The government's subsequent decision to protect the army rebels and suspend constitutional guarantees was met with outrage. In Madrid, the events sparked a ministerial crisis and the proclamation of a law which gave the military power to try by court-martial anyone it deemed offensive. In a modern context, this key – and yet relatively unknown – case study is highly pertinent to current debates concerning the power of humour to shape and/or reflect the socio-political *status quo*.

The strong public reaction to the *Cu-Cut!* events underlined the need for a united front to protect the common Catalan cause. This spurred the political mobilisation of an electoral coalition – *Solidaritat Catalana* (Catalan Solidarity) – that enjoyed the support of Catalanists from across the political spectrum, achieving resounding victories in the local and general elections of 1907. Many of the satirical magazines at the time, attracted to the ideals of *Solidaritat Catalana*, dedicated substantial print space to supporting the group and satirising its opponents. However, despite this influential backing and the fact that *Solidaritat Catalana* was instrumental in consolidating a nationalist movement, a long succession of internal disputes over the issues of regionalism and republicanism meant that politically the group achieved very little (Balcells 1996: 60).

Coinciding with the third anniversary of the *Cu-Cut!* events, *Papitu* (1908-1937) was first published on 25 November 1908. With many of the same staff as *Cu-Cut!*, *Papitu*'s initial stages were marked by the same adversarial style of humour. Following a series of early run-ins with the authorities, the publication's editor Feliu Elias – real name of the well-known cartoonist 'Apa' – was forced into exile in Paris.

A significant part of *Papitu*'s history overlapped with a period of military dictatorship. Following a military coup on 13 September 1923, Miguel Primo de Rivera's rule (1923-1930) was initially portrayed as a transition period to restore social and political order to Spain. Within a few days, however, it became clear that this period was to be far from temporary and would have particularly negative effects on Catalonia, considered by Primo to be a separatist danger. During this time, therefore, Catalonia experienced extensive repression, with the dissolution of all Catalan institutions and the public use of the language and celebrations of Catalan culture banned.[3]

As for the press, Primo installed a system of strict control, with all material requiring approval before being permitted to go to print. In addition, the dictatorship controlled the press by proscribing material for publication as well as disseminating messages through its own newspaper, *La Nación*. As a result, *Papitu* opted to forsake its initial biting political satire in favour of a humour that was predominantly picaresque and scatological. In its final years the magazine was taken over by a syndicate and resumed a political outlook with a markedly propagandist type of humour, which will be discussed below. While *Papitu* did not create the same political controversies as *Cu-Cut!*, and could not boast the longevity of *L'Esquella* or *La Campana*, it was still one of the foremost satirical publications of its time.

Unlike *Papitu*, during Primo's dictatorship *L'Esquella* and *La Campana* continued to create political satire, an approach that led to yet more fines and suspensions. The subsequent financial strain caused by these repeated penalties and periods of blocked income during closures was a harsh reality for López, who was living in a state of near bankruptcy at the time of his death in 1931 (Lletget 2007: 64). Ironically, the arrival of the Second Spanish Republic, so vehemently demanded by *La Campana* and *L'Esquella*, was a significant factor in their decline as both publications suffered from identity crises and a lack of direction. While *L'Esquella* was able to survive and eventually recapture its former popularity, *La Campana* fell victim to the tumultuous political situation that erupted during the 'October events' of 1934. Madrid's repeal of an agrarian reform law ratified by the Catalan government – which had been reinstated under the Republic after more than 200 years – sparked renewed conflict between the two legislative institutions. When the Catalan President, Lluís Companys, rebelled, declaring a separate Catalan state within the Spanish Federal Republic, he was swiftly arrested along with all members of the Catalan government. As a result of subsequent outbreaks of violence between the Catalan police force and the Spanish army, Catalan autonomy was suspended, the Catalan press and language were controlled and martial law was imposed until the following May.

Many of *La Campana* and *L'Esquella*'s contributors were implicated in the October clashes. This, coupled with the aforementioned decline in popularity and financial difficulties, brought about the closure of *La Campana* in 1934. Nevertheless, two years earlier, a new publication, *El Be Negre* (1932-1936), had established itself in the satirical market. The editorial team was made up of the director Josep M. Planes, the editor Màrius Gifreda, and artistic director Valentí Castanys. Among the principal contributors were Catalonia's new generation of celebrated cartoonists including Tísner, Fontanals (Soka) and Castanys himself. Since all articles were published anonymously there was still a great deal of unattributed material. The magazine's format and content were inspired by the French satirical publication *Le Canard Enchaîné* (1915-) and, like *Cu-Cut!* before it,

El Be Negre feared no one and attacked everyone. Despite only being in print for four years, the magazine attained iconic status in Catalan twentieth-century satire due to its political outspokenness and staunch anticlericalism.

With its unceasing raillery of the emerging Republic, the magazine contributed to the destabilisation of the fragile political climate in 1930s Catalonia, and it did so at an increasing cost to both itself and the Catalan movement. According to Carles Fontserè, '*El Be Negre* ... was the right-wing Republican organisation that most contributed to the discrediting of the autonomous institutions led by Francesc Macià and Lluís Companys' (2006: 203). As Solà observes, '[the magazine] mocked everyone and everything, and its steely, shameless and ruthless criticism wreaked havoc amongst the public figures of the time', creating discord at a moment when solidarity was critical (1973: 333).

Whatever its actual role in the shaping of the political climate, *El Be Negre* was made to pay a heavy price for its confrontational style. When Planes published an outspoken anti-terrorism campaign in both *El Be Negre* and the newspaper *La Publicitat*, he was threatened in an open letter in the anarchist labour publication *Solidaridad Obrera*. He was later assassinated by members of the Iberian Anarchist Federation (FAI), on 24 August 1936. Although *El Be Negre*'s success sparked many imitations, these were inferior in quality and largely ephemeral. Indeed, following the magazine's closure, the onset of war and subsequent 36 years of dictatorship spelled the end for the Golden Age of the Catalan satirical press.

Catalan satire and the Spanish civil war

The political polarisation of Spain during the civil war led to significant changes in Catalan satire. Catalonia's decision to form pacts with extremists had damaged its prestige, particularly in the eyes of many of its sympathisers – such as the writer George Orwell – and the divisions and in-fighting that these coalitions created were to help bring about the eventual defeat of the Republicans on 1 April 1939 (Heywood, 1989: 22-23).[4] The war itself, as well as legislative measures, such as the promulgation of the 1938 Spanish Press Law, spelled an untimely end for many satirical magazines.[5] Those publications that did survive were taken over by politically-driven organisations and converted into tools of propaganda for the left, which maintained a stronghold in and around Barcelona. The most influential of these groups was the *Sindicat de Dibuixants Professionals* (Professional Drawing Syndicate [SDP]). Its control over the final years of *Papitu* and *L'Esquella*, as well as a membership which included a large majority of Catalan satirical cartoonists and writers at the time, make it an important factor for an examination of the production of Catalan satirical publications during the civil war.

The SDP was formed in April 1936 when a group of fifty artists came together aiming to 'prevent directors of commercial enterprises and any intermediaries from taking advantage of the professional [artists] they employ' (Fontseré 1978: 354). Although one of many artistic syndicates, the SDP was by far the best represented, with a membership of around 1,800 within its first week (Madrigal Pascual 2002: 281). With the outbreak of the civil war, the SDP began intensive production of anarchist and republican posters and was soon at the forefront of political activity. The syndicate's popularity was, of course, not universal. It was rejected by many of *El Be Negre*'s former contributors who were, for the most part, anti-anarchist and anti-syndicalist (Cañameras 1990: 49).

After electing the *Union General de Trabajadores* (General Workers' Union [UGT]) as its affiliate party, the SDP was put in charge of the party's satirical acquisitions – including *L'Esquella* and *Papitu* – with the intention of transforming each into a political mouthpiece. The change in direction imposed upon these two publications had contrasting effects. Since *Papitu* relied upon a readership that had become accustomed to its particular style and tone, the political alterations imposed by the SDP caused the magazine to lose its audience. *L'Esquella*, on the other hand, underwent a period of relative rejuvenation. In theory, production was now split into two parts, with the SDP taking charge of the graphical content while the *Agrupació d'Escriptors Catalans* (Catalan Writers' Group) – another UGT syndicate – was asked to oversee the text. This new system, however, was not as segregated as it may at first seem, since many cartoonists also contributed to the text, and so for the purposes of these satirical magazines the two syndicates often merged.

As the war took its toll, the SDP suffered from competing internal factions, reflecting a general plight of the left during the conflict. Indeed, the 1937 *fets de maig* (May Days) in Barcelona – during which rising tensions on the left erupted into street battles lasting five days and resulting in some 500 deaths and 1,000 wounded – put an unbearable strain on relations in the syndicate, resulting in disputes that led many communist contributors to be expelled from the SDP.[6] Afraid of being out of work, these cartoonists formed a splinter group known as the *Cèl·lula de Dibuixants del PSUC* (Artist Division of the Unified Catalan Socialist Party).

The dispute reached a climax when, in July 1937, the *Cèl·lula* seized control of *L'Esquella* and – to the dismay of the SDP – all the equipment associated with its publication. After the split from the SDP, the *Cèl·lula* contributed very little to the production of propaganda posters, prioritising its satirical publications. The primary concern became *L'Esquella*, which throughout the rest of the war focused its attention on ridiculing and discrediting members of the Marxist and anarchist movements. Indeed, in line with the accusations levied at *El Be Negre* – linking it to the problems of unity faced by the Second Republic – under the PSUC *L'Esquella*'s humour was even more caustic and divisive, and was seen by some as a Stalinist propaganda machine damaging the unity of the Catalan government (Fontserè 1978: 372; 2006: 331-332).

However, there are those, such as the author and Catalan nationalist Rafael Tasis, who played down the communist influence on *L'Esquella*'s content and, instead, highlighted its political involvement as one of welcome financial support (Tasis 1990: 15-16). In fact, the associated financial help from PSUC allowed for the upkeep of *L'Esquella* until just before the fall of Barcelona, while *Papitu*, which had been kept by the remaining sectors of the SDP, had to be closed due to insurmountable debts. When the Spanish civil war broke out, only *L'Esquella* and *Papitu* were able to sustain some form of reliable readership. By the war's end, neither remained.

'Catalonia is not Spain'

The left-leaning stances of *L'Esquella* and *Papitu* led each publication to voice its own brand of criticism at the traditionally conservative army and Catholic Church. This satirical critique took on increasingly caustic and aggressive tones following the outbreak of the civil war, owing to the popular perception that the Church was supporting the military on the Nationalist side. The Church and the army were subsequently mocked as enemies of the Republic, and by extension Catalonia, in its strategic position as a republican stronghold. Satirising these groups became part of a wider narrative of 'us' and 'them' that was being constructed in the context of war. This differentiation between Catalonia and the rest of Spain (which gained international coverage during the 1992 Barcelona Olympics with the omnipresent graffito 'Catalonia is not Spain') was by no means new. Following almost three centuries of influence as part of a union with the kingdom of Aragon, between the fifteenth and eighteenth centuries, Catalonia underwent an era of cultural and political decline. This culminated in the abolition of Catalan rights and privileges previously enjoyed by the kingdom, as well as the first of many attempts to eradicate the language through legislation, the Nova Planta Decree (1714). By the eighteenth century industrialisation had taken hold in Catalonia, and the resulting economic development distinguished it from the rest of Spain. This gave the Catalans both a sense of superiority and a confidence to begin to rebel against the Castilian dominance in Spain, which fuelled the fire of mutual suspicion between the two (Balcells 1996: 21).

While historians differ in their assessment of the origins of the animosity, there is reasonable agreement that it can be traced back to the early eighteenth century. However, there are those such as Pabón (1999) and Rovira Virgili (1930) who claim that since Catalanism was not strictly established until the *Renaixença*, 'anti-Catalanism' cannot have preceded it and must, therefore, be considered a nineteenth-century phenomenon. We can see these differing viewpoints as the product of taxonomical disagreements; while a sense of collective identity and solidarity among Catalans certainly predates the nineteenth century, it was not until the early twentieth century that these manifestations were supported by the organised political counterpart of 'Catalanism'.

Humour and identity

The expression of identity is often, and effectively, achieved through humour. Holmes argues that 'one of the most basic social functions of humour [is] that it serves to create and maintain solidarity, a sense of belonging to a group' (2000: 159). Moreover, according to Holmes and Marra, 'humour can contribute to the on-going construction and reinforcement of inter-group boundaries by providing an acceptable means of objectifying or distancing the "other" group' (2002: 393). In national identity construction, Knight observes, 'simple nationalistic satire stresses the distinction of one's own country from others by exaggerating their negative qualities' (2004: 59).

The relationship between humour and identity has at its root the superiority theory of humour – often described as the dominant philosophical tradition in the field of Humour Studies.[7] Drawing on classical methods, in *Leviathan* Thomas Hobbes explains laughter as the expression of 'a sudden glory arising from some conception of some eminency in ourselves, by comparison with the infirmity of others' (1968 [1651]: 5). This view of humour as a form of social corrective was the product of personal and specific social conditioning: a life in which 'the predominant form of humor was raillery within a small group of acquaintances' (Davies 2009: 51).[8] Nevertheless, the key ideas of the superiority approach remain relevant to this chapter's focus on political satire, a humour typified by antagonism and where superiority is a common component.

Several reworkings of the general approach to a humour based on superiority include observations about the effects of humour on group solidarity and the study of the laughter of inclusion and exclusion.[9] We can understand humour's relationship to the framing of identity through Hobbes's theory of superiority, since humour occurs when we perceive ourselves as superior to 'the other' in a given contrast (see Raskin 1985: 36-8; Attardo 1994: 49-50). In their study of superior versus subordinate relationships, Dolf Zillmann and Joanne Cantor (1972) correctly predicted that the subordinate group would appreciate humour involving the temporary domination of their superiors. Holmes and Marra add to the debate by noting that 'making fun of other groups, or rendering aspects of their behaviour in a comical way, effectively drives a wedge between the speaker's group and the butt of the humour' (2002: 392).

Indeed, superiority humour based on the role reversal described by Zillmann and Cantor is often achieved by highlighting the inferiority of those in power, thus implying by contrast the superiority of the (typically) subordinate in-group (McGlade 2013). As a branch of humour concerned with elevation and/or reduction of one individual, group or ideal over another, Hobbes's general concepts of derisive laughter and superiority can be used to support claims for the important role humour played (and perhaps plays) in reinforcing Catalan in-group identity construction. The remainder of this chapter, then, will explore and discuss the implications for identity construction and some of the forms these attitudes took, in the two major Catalan satirical publications of the Spanish civil war: *L'Esquella de la Torratxa* and *Papitu* during the period 1936-1939.

Satirising 'otherness'
The propagandist humour that typified *L'Esquella* and *Papitu* during the civil war saw both the army and the Catholic Church cast in the role of the out-group, or 'other'. Although 'other' is typically used to refer to members of a dominated

out-group, according to Jean-François Staszak (2009), 'otherness is due less to the [actual] difference of the Other than to the point of view and the discourse of the person who perceives the other as such'. In the case of Catalan satire, identity humour that uses, and re-enforces, distinctions between the 'underdog' and the dominant group is built on the idea of a Catalan, Republican in-group that considers its members and values to be superior to those of the Nationalists, and by extension, the army and the Catholic Church. Therefore, the Catalan satirical press can be seen to have consistently 'othered' Madrid as symbolic of Spain and the army and the Church as representatives of the Nationalist 'enemy'. This portrayal was both implicitly and explicitly juxtaposed with the promotion of an in-group comprising a working-class, republican, Catalan populace.

The most common satirical positions taken by both publications towards the army consisted of accusations of drunkenness and a general lack of scruples, particularly among the higher ranks, as well as criticisms of the foreignness of the so-called 'Nationalist' troops. A particularly popular target was Gonzalo Queipo de Llano. Initially a supporter of the left-wing political coalition, the Popular Front, he switched sides and was subsequently a key player in the Nationalist coup, becoming one of Franco's main rivals for power after the uprising. This change of allegiance was seen as the ultimate hypocrisy and, as a result, Queipo was extensively ridiculed in the press. He was typically caricatured with a ridiculously long moustache and a pot-belly that prevented him from fitting into his uniform. In particular, satirists made references to his famous radio broadcasts in Seville 'which were often delivered under the influence of alcohol and were sprinkled with profanity and remarks about his troops' sexual prowess' (Nelson and Hendricks 1993: 304). This behaviour, coupled with Queipo's high rank in the Nationalist army, made him a prime target for humour.

Exaggerated descriptions of his drunkenness and proclivity for prostitutes were juxtaposed with his position of power and pompous nature to create superiority humour based on role reversals, or more specifically the 'inferiorisation' of a superior. References to Queipo were almost always accompanied by some comment related to alcohol. For example, *L'Esquella*'s number published on 10 October 1936, presented a fictitious speech given by Queipo for Radio Sevilla, using a playful pun on the word 'vino' which means both 'came' and 'wine':

> The rebellion *came* along because of the victory of the left. And the victory of the left *came* along because of Gil Robles. And Gil Robles *came* along ... Goodness! In twenty-five words I have used the word *came* [wine] five times. That's strange isn't it? (italics in the original)[10]

The use of italics is employed in the final 'vino' to emphasise the pun and the irony of Queipo's suggestion that his discussion of wine should be strange. These kinds of puns were equally common in *Papitu*, which also milked the theme of Queipo the alcoholic. For example, in one of its descriptions of Radio Sevilla, the magazine produced a humorous pun on the figurative and literal meaning of the word 'font' as a source for information and as a spring or well respectively. In a clear reference to Queipo's drunken and often incomprehensible broadcasts it claims that 'Radio Sevilla cannot be a source for information, because it is a wine cellar'.[11] The same number of *Papitu*, which appeared on 1 October 1936, includes a joke about Queipo trying to ban the Catalan dish of *estofat*. The text, written in the style of a newspaper report, explains that he will not even eat it if it is washed down with sherry, going on to add, 'and that is saying something!'.[12] In both publications any jokes involving Queipo speaking would always appear in Castilian, to highlight his membership of the out-group by virtue of his non-Catalan otherness. Indeed, language was frequently used in this way to reinforce in-group identification due to the well-publicised anti-Catalan attitude of the Nationalists, which sought to eradicate 'separatist' elements in the pursuit of 'absolute national unity, with a single Castilian language, and a single Spanish personality'.[13]

A large amount of the humour directed at the army focused on the nationality of its troops. In many instances, this referred to the forces from North Africa that Franco had used as part of the initial uprising. The reputation of these legionnaires as barbaric savages was due, in part, to the way in which they carried out 'brutal clean-up operations during the occupation of [Republican] towns and cities' (Basilio 2013: 26). This led many satirical publications not only to allude to the unscrupulous behaviour, but also to the underhandedness of the generals who employed these mercenaries. Indeed, *Papitu* dedicated a whole number to the subject in its 'Oriental Special', published on 26 November 1936. Many of the jokes, therefore, had a dual effect, ridiculing the authority figures and belittling those who had trusted in them.

Another aspect of this humour included the intervention, albeit unofficial, from Mussolini and Hitler in support of the Fascist forces. Naturally, the irony of a self-declared 'Nationalist' side that comprised troops from North Africa, Italy and Germany did not go unnoticed by the satirists, and the so-called 'italo-german-luso-moroccan invasion' formed the basis of countless satirical cartoons and written pieces from the time. One of the most common features of comment on the topic was the word 'national' which, when referring to Francoist troops, would typically appear in inverted commas to introduce an ironic tone. It seemed that what made the Republicans' welcoming of international support from the Soviet Union acceptable was this avoidance of fraudulent nomenclature.

The use of identity was key to the construction of humour related to this topic, particularly in the juxtaposition of the 'in' and 'out' groups. Here again it was commonly the emphasis and portrayal of inferiority that was used to attack the Nationalist out-group. An example of this can be seen in the 'Oriental Special' in a text that depicts 'Franco's harem', complete with a German eunuch and an Italian biplane pilot, described as having 'the face of a cherub's bottom that could break your heart'.[14] The idea that the Nationalist troops depended on external players undermined their claims to a strong sense of collectivity. By ridiculing this aspect of the army, *Papitu* and *L'Esquella*'s satirists were not only reinforcing the polarity between the 'in' and the 'out' groups – thus strengthening the collective identity of their 'in-group' readership – but were also highlighting the disjointed make-up of the opposition. The dual 'immasculinisation', through the use of the eunuch and the beautiful pilot, is used to undermine the effect of the international support for the Francoist side, while at the same time adding an acerbic comment on the failure of the Non-Intervention Agreement signed in August 1936 by, among others, Germany, Italy and the Soviet Union.

The anti-clerical leanings of both *Papitu* and *L'Esquella* meant that the Catholic Church, already a long-standing target for much of the Catalan satirical press, continued to be a prime subject of derision with the outbreak of the civil war. Typically, the humour would be directed at the unscrupulousness and hypocrisy of the Church, which whether directly or indirectly was believed to be bolstering the Nationalist cause. This derision often took the form of caricatures of fat, greedy clergymen feeding on the spoils of war. Directly connected to this, another common outlet for the satirical treatment of religion and religious figures was through humour targeting the 'Requetés'. These were the highly religious Carlist militia, predominantly from the region of Navarre, who fought alongside the Nationalists in defence of monarchical and religious tradition. Indeed, religious humour often functioned via a sense of perceived solidarity between the two groups. Since they were identified as a combined enemy, the satirised hypocrisy of the Church was commonly used to imply the moral inferiority and 'otherness' of both.

An example of the nature of this humour can be found in *Papitu*'s section which offered a humorous account of the outbreak of the civil war from the perspective of a fictional Requeté. In the section that appeared in *Papitu*'s 1 October 1936 edition, of note is the entry for 21 July 1936 (in the days during the military uprising that eventually led to the outbreak of civil war), which read: 'Those damn Catalans! Fancy burning churches because inside our brave priests were shooting at the mobs. What barbarism!'.[15] The reference to the burning of churches in Catalonia is a direct allusion to the events during the first days of the July uprising, which saw the torching of religious buildings and the slaughter of members of the clergy following an outbreak of anti-clerical violence in Barcelona. The root of the humour is in the incongruity of labelling the indiscriminate shooting into crowds as 'brave' while being unable to identify the 'barbarism' of the priests' actions. The result is one of ridicule based on the hypocrisy and self-righteousness of the Church's attitude to the conflict. Moreover, in the Requeté's stipulation that it was 'those damn Catalans!' who had burned down the churches, the text contains an example of the use of humour to further polarise group identity, in this case between the Catalan 'in-group' and the Requeté/religious institutional 'out-group'.

The humour draws from a staple image of civil war propaganda that reflects a popular assessment of the Church's direct involvement in the conflict.[16]

Although this involvement was, in reality, principally restricted to rhetoric (Matthews 2012: 86), according to Mary Vincent it is based on a myth engineered by the Republican government to justify often out-of-control anticlerical violence, particularly in July and August 1936 (2009: 68-70). Nevertheless, Vincent does claim that by July 1937 'there was no doubt that the Church would line up with the Rebels against the Republic' (1996: 248). It was, therefore, common to see humorous texts referring to armed clergymen, with descriptions such as 'tonsured priests with Star guns' (*Papitu*, 15 October 1936).[17] In this particular example, where Star refers to Star Bonifacio Echeverria, a common brand of weapons manufacturer, the allusion to the religious hair shearing often associated with medieval Catholic practice is used to heighten the juxtaposition of traditional values with the arguably un-Christian use of weaponry, in an attempt to underline the hypocrisy of the Church's involvement in the war. *Papitu*'s text, then, is acting as both a comic and cathartic reflection on the fighting and as propagandist material in its emphasis and consolidation of commonly held beliefs.

Following the SDP takeover of *Papitu* and *L'Esquella*, print space was increasingly given to overtly propagandist material representing a superior in-group, with the effect of overtly reinforcing in-group solidarity on the Republican side and implying the inferiority of the 'other', Nationalist contingent. This is hardly surprising, since many SDP members working for these publications had also been engaged in the production of propagandist posters during the early stages of the war. Indeed, the centrefold of *L'Esquella* at this time typically depicted a strong working class fighting a brave and just fight against the greedy, drunken and immoral enemy – usually comprising clergymen, soldiers and monarchist supporters. The humour contained within these pieces was still concentrated on an exaggerated negative depiction of the enemy versus a positive, exaggerated, and wholesome depiction of the in-group. As was the case with the humour of the publications on the whole, the intent was to bolster the perceived strength of the in-group while ridiculing the fallibility of the out-group, using exaggeration to further highlight the contrast between the groups.

Although much of the group identity humour that appeared in *L'Esquella* and *Papitu* during the civil war fell under the Republican umbrella of the Popular Front, which led it to attack the national institutions of the army and the Church, these were often delivered as expressions of Catalan identity, which remained a prominent feature in the humour content during the 1936-1939 period. Both publications were able to draw on a history of accusations of anti-Catalan sentiment directed at each institution, which had won them popular approval in Catalonia. Their continued derision of the army and the Church, while maintaining healthy circulation figures, point to a shared existing social attitude towards these institutions in the region.

Humour related to the solidarity between the two identified 'out-groups' of the Church and the army was used to further the construction or reinforcement of the Catalan Republican in-group identification. Through the established 'othering' of both groups individually, another satirical approach was to underline the relationship between the two, with the effect of emphasising the inferiority of both in their association with one another. An example of this can be found in the 'Carnet d'un requetè', where the journal describes the 'campaign against the infidels'. This phrase is used in connection to the belief on many fronts that the Nationalist fight was a crusade to restore the sense of moral decline that had been brought about by the progressive and liberal reforms of the Second Spanish Republic. In this entry, the Requeté waxes lyrical about the days of the Grand Inquisitor, Tomás de Torquemada (1420-1498), a clear allusion to the years of the Spanish Inquisition. This serves to highlight both his traditional attitudes and to connect him with the negative reputation for violence and suffering associated with the Inquisition. The piece is heavily laden with ironic tones when again, unable to recognise the cruelty of his own organisation's behaviour, he instead laments the unexpectedly high number of 'infidels', asking: 'How many women and children have we had to shoot because they were not following the word of God?'[18] Continuing to describe the so-called 'crusade' he rejoices, announcing:

> Everything will be fine. We Christian forces have received reinforcements. Moors and the legions have joined together to help us in our crusade for the purity of the Catholic faith and for the reign of the Pope. Everything will be for the greater good of the Holy Roman and Apostolic Catholic Church ... and the sons of Allah will help us to fight the Spanish non-believers.[19]

The incongruity of 'the sons of Allah' joining in the fight for a Christian crusade ridicules the Carlists. The reference to the North African troops has similar effects to those outlined above in relation to the army. Indeed, the mention of these military reinforcements as part of a religious crusade highlights the collaboration between Church and army against Spanish republican supporters. By ridiculing the combined efforts of the 'out-groups', the humour also serves to reinforce a sense of solidarity among members of the identified 'in-group' by highlighting the moral inferiority of the 'other'.

Conclusion

The Nationalist victory in the civil war in 1939 marked the end of a significant chapter in the rich history of the Catalan satirical tradition. Although it would continue under various guises during the Franco regime and beyond (McGlade 2016 forthcoming), it would never enjoy the same monopoly and influence of the Golden Age that spanned the first third of the twentieth century.

As we have seen, the satire directed at the institutions most associated with the right – the Church and the Nationalist army – was based on underlining the Church's lack of ethics and the incompetence of the Rebels, as opposed to the Republican side who were typically depicted as strong, righteous defenders of liberty. These themes remained fairly constant in the satirical press throughout the war, and demonstrate how humour can be used to highlight the unsatisfactory behaviour of the out-group in order to amplify the superiority of the in-group. In this way, several aspects of Catalonia's satirical tradition raised here chime with current debates about the power and influence of humour.

Moreover, since humour relies on shared or recognisable perceptions and messages in order to be decoded or understood, it serves as an innovative historical source in gauging extant social perceptions during any given period. Thus, the depictions of the Church and the army during the Spanish civil war introduced here provide innovative access to areas of public opinion within identified sectors of society from the time. Indeed, although humour continues to be undervalued as a media form worthy of academic attention, the fact that it typically comprises an overall message built on multi-layered encoded meaning, often requiring several unpacking phases, is evidence that it is, in fact, a complex form of communication that benefits from careful consideration.

Notes

[1] During the first years, *La Campana* and *L'Esquella* would sell between 8,000 and 10,000 copies in Barcelona in the first four hours, while the remaining stock was transported to the rest of the region (Lletget 2007: 16). Within the space of a decade the overall figure had grown to approximately 22,000 and in its final stages *L'Esquella*'s circulation reached 68,000 (Foguet 2005: 147)

[2] *Cu-Cut!* sold around 20,000 copies of its first number, with some later reaching 60,000, although its average circulation was between 30,000 and 40,000 (Torrent and Tasis 1966: 350)

[3] It became illegal to hang a Catalan flag and dance the Catalan *sardanes*, and the regime ordered the closure of Barcelona Football Club and the choral society, Orfeó Català (Solà 2005: 95)

[4] When Orwell fought on the Republican side during the civil war, he became 'an intense critic of all political orthodoxies' as a result of the numerous power struggles between the various factions of the left (Black, Conolly and Flint 2008: 533)

[5] Restricted to areas under Nationalist control, the 1938 Press Law did not come in to full effect until the Nationalist victory in 1939, after which it remained the guiding document for censorial practice until 1966 when it was eventually replaced with the so called 'Fraga' Law named after its principal architect, Manuel Fraga Iribarne (1922-2012)

[6] For Francesc Ferrer (2000: 54) so called 'Catalanofòbia' can be found at the time of the Count-Duke of Olivares (1587-1645). However, earlier testimonies exist such as the example of Estefania de Requesenes who, in 1534, writes of her son Luïset 'who wants to be Catalan ... and defends Catalonia's reputation whenever it is maligned' (Guisado 1988: 49). According to Pasamar (2010: 253) some historians trace an 'imagined anti-Catalan policy' back to the fourteenth century

[7] In humour research, superiority theory has also been referred to as 'aggression', 'disparagement' and 'degradation' theory (Banas et al. 2011: 328)

[8] This view was also adopted by the French philosopher Henri Bergson (1859-1941). See his *Laughter: An Essay on the Meaning of the Comic* (1900)

[9] These include an initial study by Dupréel (1928), which was developed and expanded by Wolff, et al. (1934), Middleton (1959), Priest (1966), Zillmann and Cantor (1972; 2007) and La Fave, et al. (2007)

[10] 'Vino la rebellion porque vino la Victoria de las izquierdas. Y vino la victoria de las izquierdas porque vino Gil Robles. Y vino Gil Robles...Carai! En veinte y cinco palabras he empleado *vino* cinco veces. Curioso, ¿verdad?'

[11] 'La Ràdio Sevilla no és una font, perque és un celler'

[12] 'No li passa ni barrejant-lo amb el xereç, que ja és dir'

[13] 'La unidad nacional la queremos absoluta, con una sola lengua, el castellano y una sola personalidad, la española'; Carol Klee and Luis Ramos García, *Sociolinguistics of the Spanish–Speaking World, Iberia, Latin America*, United States: Bilingüe, 1991 p. 15

[14] 'Careta de cul d'àngel que trenca el cor'

[15] '21 de juliol. Aquests maleïts catalans! ... Mireu que cremar esglésies perquè des de dintre els nostres valents capellans tiraven contra la xusma! Quina barbàrie'

[16] An example of this widely accepted view of clerical involvement in the conflict can be found in Ken Loach's film *Land and Freedom* (1995), which depicts priests firing from the bell-towers

[17] 'Capellans amb tonsura i pistola marca Star'

[18] 'Quantes dones i criatures hem afusellat perquè no feien cas de la paraula divina'?

[19] 'Ara tot anirà bé. Les forces cristianes hem rebut reforços. Moros i tercio se'ns han ajuntat per ajudar-nos en la nostra creuada per la puresa de la fe católica i pel regne del Papat. Tot sia per al major bé de la Santa Església Catòlica, Apostòlica i Romana... Que els fills d'Alà ens ajudin a combatre els espanyols increints...'

References

Attardo, Salvatore (1994) *Linguistic Theories of Humor*, New York: Mouton de Gruyter

Balcells, Albert (1996) *Catalan Nationalism: Past and Present*, London: Macmillan

Banas, John A., Dunbar, Norah, Rodriguez, Dariela and Liu, Shr-Jie (2011) A review of humor in educational settings: Four decades of research, *Communication Education*, Vol. 60, No.1 pp 115-144

Basilio, Miriam (2013) *Visual Propaganda, Exhibitions, and the Spanish Civil War*, Farnham: Ashgate

Bergson, Henri (1900) *Laughter: An Essay on the Meaning of the Comic.* Available online at https://archive.org/details/laughteranessay00berggoog, accessed on 17 March 2015

Black, Joseph, Conolly, Leonard and Flint, Kate (eds) (2008) *The Broadview Anthology of English Literature: The Twentieth Century and Beyond: From 1900 to World War Two*, 7 Vols, VIa, Toronto: Broadview Press

Cañameras, Jaume (1990) *Conversa amb Bartolí*, Barcelona: Abadia de Montserrat

Davies, Christie (2009) Humor theory and the fear of being laughed at, *Humor*, Vol. 22, No. 1 pp 49-62

Dupréel, E. (1928) Le problème sociologique du rire, *Revue Philosophique*, Vol. 106 pp 213-60

Ferrer, Francesc (2000) *Catalanofòbia. El pensament anticatalà a través de la història*, Barcelona: Edicions 62

Foguet Boreu, Francesc (2005) Una història de la revolució i la contrarrevolució (1936-1939). Tria de textos publicats a /Esquella de la Torratxa, *Llengua i Literatura*, No.16 pp 89-154

Fontserè, Carles (1978) El sindicato de dibujantes profesionales, Miravitlles, Jaume (ed.) *Carteles de la República y de la Guerra Civil*, Barcelona: La Gaya Ciencia pp 353-377

Fontserè, Carles (2006) *Memòries d'un cartellista del 36 (1931-1939)*, Barcelona: Proa

Guisado, Maite (ed.) (1988) *Cartes íntimes d'una dama catalana del segle XVI. Epistolari a la seva mare la comtessa de Palamós*, Barcelona: La Sal

Heywood, Paul (1989) Why the Republic lost, *History Today*, Vol. 39, No. 3 pp 20-27

Hobbes, Thomas (1968 [1651]) *Leviathan*, Harmondsworth: Penguin

Holmes, Janet (2000) Politeness, power and provocation: How humour functions in the workplace, *Discourse Studies*, Vol. 2, No. 2 pp 55-82

Holmes, Janet and Marra, Meredith (2002) Humour as a discursive boundary marker in social interaction, Duszak, Anna (ed.) *Us and Others: Social Identities Across Languages, Discourses and Cultures*, Philadelphia: Jon Benjamins pp 377-400

Klee, Carol and Ramos García, Luis (1991) *Sociolinguistics of the Spanish-Speaking World, Iberia, Latin America*, United States: Bilingüe

Knight, Charles (2004) *The Literature of Satire*, Cambridge: Cambridge University Press

La Fave, Lawrence, Haddad, Jay and Maesen, William A. (2007) Superiority, enhanced self-esteem, and perceived incongruity humour theory, Chapman, Anthony and Foot, Hugh (eds) *Humour and Laughter: Theory, Research and Applications*, New Brunswick: Transaction pp 63-92

Lletget, Isabel (2007) Memòries de la família Lletget López (1872-1942), *Revista bibliográfica de geografía y ciencias sociales*, Vol. 718, No. 12 pp 1-160

McGlade, Rhiannon (2013) *Seriously Funny: Towards an Interpretative Framework for an Analysis of Catalan Satirical Cartoons in the Twentieth Century*. Unpublished doctoral thesis, University of Sheffield

McGlade, Rhiannon (2016, forthcoming) *Catalan Cartoons: A Cultural and Political History*, Cardiff: University of Wales Press

Madrigal Pascual, and Ángel, Arturo (2002) *Arte y compromiso: España 1917-1936*, Madrid: Fundación de Estudios Libertarios Anselmo Lorenzo

Matthews, James (2012) *Reluctant Warriors: Republican Popular Army and Nationalist Army Conscripts in the Spanish Civil War, 1936-1939*, Oxford: Oxford University Press

Middleton, R. (1959) Negro and white reactions to racial humor, *Sociometry*, Vol. 22, pp 175-183

Nelson, Cary and Hendricks, Jefferson (eds) (1993) *Edwin Rolfe: Collected Poems*, Illinois: University of Illinois Press

Pabón, Jesús (1999) *Cambó: 1876-1947*, Barcelona: Alpha

Pasamar, Gonzalo (2010) *Apologia and Criticism: Historians and History of Spain, 1500-2000*, Bern: Peter Lang

Priest, R. F. (1966) Election jokes: The effects of reference group membership, *Psychological Reports*, Vol. 18 pp 600-602

Raskin, Victor (1985) *Semantic Mechanisms of Humor*, Dordrecht: D. Reidel

Rovira Virgili, Antoni (1930) *El nacionalismo catalán*, Barcelona: Minerva

Solà, Lluís (1973) *Un segle d'humor català*, Barcelona: Bruguera

Staszak, Jean-François (2009) Other/otherness, Kitchin, R. and Thrift, N. (eds) *The International Encyclopedia of Human Geography*, Amsterdam: Elsevier pp 43-47

Tasis, Rafael (1990) *Les presons dels altres: Records d'un escarceller d'ocasió*, Barcelona: Pòrtic

Torrent, Joan and Tasis, Rafael (1966) *Història de la premsa catalana*, Barcelona: Bruguera

Vincent, Mary (2009) 'The keys of the kingdom': Religious violence in the Spanish civil war, July-August 1936, Ealham, Chris and Richards, Michael (eds) *The Splintering of Spain: Cultural History and the Spanish Civil War, 1936-1939*, Cambridge: Cambridge University Press pp 68-89

Vincent, Mary (1996) *Catholicism in the Second Spanish Republic*, Oxford: Clarendon Press

Wolff, H. A., Smith, C. E. and Murray, H. A. (1934) The psychology of humor: A study of the responses to race disparagement jokes, *Journal of Abnormal and Social Psychology*, Vol. 28 pp 341-345

Zillmann, Dolf and Cantor, Joanne R. (1972) Directionality of transitory dominance as a communication variable affecting humor appreciation, *Journal of Personality and Social Psychology*, Vol. 24 pp 191-198

Zillmann, Dolf and Cantor, Joanne R. (2007) A disposition theory of humour and mirth, Chapman, Anthony and Foot, Hugh (eds) *Humour and Laughter: Theory, Research and Applications*, New Brunswick: Transaction pp 93-116

Note on the contributor

Rhiannon McGlade is Lecturer in Catalan Studies and Director of the Centre for Catalan Studies at Queen Mary, University of London. Her book, *Catalan Cartoons: A Cultural and Political History*, is due for publication with the University Wales Press. She completed a BA at Sheffield University in 2007 in Hispanic Studies with Catalan Philology. She then completed a Master's at the University of Birmingham in International Studies (Diplomacy) before returning to Sheffield to study for her PhD (completed in 2013). Her research focuses on the role of political cartoons in cultural studies, with a particular interest in the Catalan tradition.

Monarchy, Army and Catholic Church in the Spanish Satirical Press: From Franco's Death to the Socialist Government (1975-1982)[1]

Josep Lluís Gómez-Mompart, Dolors Palau-Sampio,
José Luis Valhondo-Crego and María Iranzo-Cabrera

Satirical press during the Spanish transition to democracy

The two periods of splendour of twentieth-century Spanish satirical journalism – which began in and developed throughout the nineteenth century – were, first, during the Second Republic until the onset of the Spanish civil war (1931-1936) and, second, from the waning years of the Franco dictatorship (from 1972 to Franco's death on 20 November 1975) through the early years of the transition to democracy until October 1982 and the first PSOE (Spanish Socialist Workers' Party) government of which Felipe González was Prime Minister. The former period is deemed to be the golden age of contemporary satirical press while the latter is often referred to as the silver age, not because its publications (which were not so prolific) were less important than the earlier ones, or because their socio-cultural impact was smaller, but because the political circumstances were not remotely comparable (Bordería et al 2010). The latter period was marked by the death rattles of the dictatorship, the early years of the reign of King Juan Carlos I – imposed by the Franco regime's pseudo-parliament, the *Cortes Españolas*, two days after Franco's death – and the beginnings of the complicated and violent[2] installation of a democratic regime in Spain.[3]

Article 2 of the Press and Print Law of 1966, principally authored by Franco's Minister of Information and Tourism, Manuel Fraga Iribarne, and vaguely stipulating 'respect for persons and institutions' – and accordingly open to rather arbitrary interpretation by government institutions – remained in force until 1 April 1977. The regulations deriving from the law clamped down on freedom of expression, imposing administrative penalties and sanctions ranging from hefty fines through to impounding of issues, closing down the publication in question and, in some cases, imprisonment.[4] This repression explains in large part why the satirical press was less critical than it would have liked to have been of the three most representative institutions of power in traditional Spain: the monarchy, the army and the Catholic Church. In the republican years of the 1930s, Spanish satirical journalism was merciless in its pillorying of the monarchy and the Church, and somewhat less so in the case of the military. In the period that concerns us here, the crackdowns on anyone who questioned or mocked the crown or the army instilled fear and self-censorship among journalists (Bordería et al 2015).

Nevertheless, four weeklies stood out in the 1970s. They presented current affairs in the form of ironical or satirical texts and cartoons, thus making a decisive contribution not only to the good mood of readers but also through their influence in the nascent political culture of the day, introducing colloquial vocabulary and parodic language into the public discourse of democracy. The best cartoonists and the most caustic wits among the journalists and writers worked for these publications, namely the progressive liberal *Hermano Lobo* (1972-1976), the anarchist-popular *El Papus* (1973-1987), the communist libertarian *Por Favor* (1974-1978), and the moderate left *El Jueves* (since 1977). Apart from the Madrid-based *Hermano Lobo*, the other three were published in Barcelona. Journalism in this city was more progressive, with younger journalists who admired and closely followed the European press. Also Catalan society was – in geographical and structural terms – further away from the old regime's most antiquated and rancid powers and the powerful bureaucratic-administrative apparatus of the capital of Spain.

The howls of *Hermano Lobo*

Hermano Lobo (*Brother Wolf*) made its appearance on 13 May 1972,[5] with a large staff of young people on the payroll, some of whom had entered the fray working for *La Codorniz* (*The Quail*), a Franco-era publication founded by Miguel Mihura in 1941. They were led by the cartoonist Chumy Chúmez but the idea for the new magazine's name came from another great humorist, Manolo Summers. Chúmez had wanted to call it *El huevo duro* (*The hard-boiled egg*) but, for some incomprehensible reason, it did not get past the censors. Nevertheless, Chúmez had no editorial responsibility because he did not possess a press card issued by the regime, which was essential if he were to occupy the editor's chair, so the job went to the journalist Ángel García Pintado. He was appointed by José Ángel Ezcurra, who was also editor of the leftish weekly news publication *Triunfo*. Unlike Chúmez, García Pintado wanted something more than just a humorous magazine: the humour had to be critical too. Apart from Chúmez and Summers, other outstanding cartoonists were Gila, Ops (Andrés Rábago), Forges and (El) Perich. They were backed up by two well-known journalists, Manuel Vicent – who subsequently defined the magazine as 'critical, acid and sarcastic' (Mora 2000) – and Cándido (Carlos Luis Álvarez), as well as the writer Francisco Umbral. It was an immediate success: the 100,000 copies of the first print run fell short of demand. Only a few weeks later circulation rose to 150,000 (Fontes y Menéndez 2004: 527).

However, six months after it first appeared – by which time Bernardo de Arrizabalaga Amoroto had become the new editor and Chumy Chúmez had been relieved of his job as content manager – the magazine began to languish. By 1974 it was graphically impoverished but bolstered in literary terms by the contributions of some of the best journalists from *Triunfo* including Eduardo Haro Tecglen, Manuel Vázquez Montalbán, Luis Carandell, Diego Galán, Rosa Montero and the philosopher Fernando Savater. The formula only worked for two years, and 6 June 1976 saw the wolf's demise. Although *Hermano Lobo*'s bites did little damage to the dictatorship in its final years, its howls sometimes bothered the regime. It responded by filing several complaints, issuing warnings, imposing two fines and seizing two editions.

The swipes of *El Papus*

The first number of the satirical magazine *El Papus*[6] appeared in the week of 20 September 1973. It was published by Elf Editores and printed by TISA, which produced the conservative Catholic daily *La Vanguardia*, property of the Count of Godó, who also owned TISA. The editor of another humorous publication, *Barrabás*, Xavier de Echarri, and the delegate from TISA-*La Vanguardia*, Carlos Navarro, held a meeting with the underground cartoonists Ivà (Ramon Tosas Fuentes), Òscar (Nebreda) and the illustrator Gin (Jordi Ginés), asking them to design a trial issue. The future owners were pleased with almost everything that resulted, although they did veto the well-known left-wing journalist Manuel Vázquez Montalbán.

Most of the *El Papus* (*The Bogeyman*) staff were outstanding cartoonists: JA (Jordi Amorós), Oli (Enrique Oliván), Marcel Bergés, Miguel Esparbé, Vallés, Snif (Joan Barjau), the duo (Enrique) Ventura and (Miguel Ángel) Nieto, Carlos Giménez, Tha (Josep August Tharrats), (Carlos) Killian, (Miquel) Ferreres, Kalondi, Luis Rey, Manel, Llobet, L'Avi (Lluís Recasens), Ramón, Ludovico (Arnaldo Ballester), Adolfo Usero, Sappo (Manuel Vázquez), Curcó (Víctor Luna) and the Onomatopeya collective, which specialised in photomontage. Cartoons by South American artists including (Guillermo) Mordillo, Tabaré (Gómez), Pierino (Ricardo Galluci) and Roberto Fontanarrosa were also acquired through agencies. Working with them were the journalists Antonio Franco, Maruja Torres, Albert Turró, Enric Bañeres, Cristina Dachs, Francesc Arroyo, Enric Sopena, the writer Joan de Segarra and the rock star Ramoncín.

In its almost fourteen years of publication, the magazine sold 584 numbers. It began with a print run of 150,000 copies and reached a peak of 400,000 in February 1976. The wit and talent of its graphic and textual content won it the 1976 Yellow Kid Award, presented in Lucca, Italy, for the world's best comic magazine. However, its mordant criticism of the powers-that-be and the most fanatical remnants of the Franco regime, couched in caustic, imaginative colloquial language, drew continuous threats from the ultra-right as well as a terrorist attack by the Triple A (Anticommunist Apostolic Alliance) group, which sent a letter bomb to the office on 20 September 1977 that killed the concierge, Joan Peñalver, who was hand-delivering it to the editor. It was the only magazine to suffer a terrorist attack during the transition.

The overriding reason for its success was its provocative content or, in other words, the easy, idiomatic sarcasm with which it reflected on facts already known to its readers through other branches of the media. A survey carried out with one hundred *El Papus* readers – as recounted in Maria Iranzo's PhD thesis (2014) – shows that six out of ten people read it because of the 'spleen it vented on the system' and, more specifically, against the apparatus of government. While half the readers said that the publication did not influence their way of thinking, the other half said *El Papus* helped to give shape to their ideology, either reaffirming it (32 per cent) or modifying it (12 per cent). This would suggest that – in the case of some people at least – satirical language contributed towards a change in political culture, with the shaping and diffusion of a certain kind of political idiom.

The satirical swipes of *El Papus* – seeking, within its restricted freedoms, to emulate the French magazines *Hara-Kiri* and *Charlie Hebdo* – resulted almost every week in administrative inquiries and criminal charges being laid, as well as the impounding of some fifty issues. The government decreed two temporary suspensions of the publication at times coinciding with its biggest circulation: from July to October 1975 and March to June 1976. It was also hauled before two military tribunals after publishing two covers poking fun at the armed forces.

The malice of *Por Favor*

The first number of *Por Favor* (*Please*) went on sale at a very delicate political moment in the final years of the Franco regime, namely on 4 March 1974, two days after the execution by garrotte of the young Catalan anarchist Salvador Puig Antich, following a summary military trial full of irregularities. Only two months earlier, Carlos Arias Navarro had been sworn in as Prime Minister, replacing Admiral Luis Carrero Blanco who had been assassinated in a spectacular attack by ETA on 20 December 1973. 'The magazine's political and moral humour was cutting edge, lampooning all the falsehoods of the regime in every dimension: individual, collective, public and private' (Vázquez Montalbán 2000: 14).

Although the journalist Eduardo Arce figured as nominal managing director, in practice the boat was captained by a communist (PSUC) militant, Manuel Vázquez Montalbán, and the cartoonist El Perich, a 'fellow traveller', as non-card-holding party sympathisers were called at the time, together with the libertarian writer Juan Marsé, who was editor-in-chief. Other well-known professionals also contributed, among them the journalists Antonio Álvarez Solís, José Martí Gómez, Maruja Torres, Rafael Wirth, Soledad Balaguer, Ángel García Pintado and Luis Vigil; the intellectuals Joan Fuster, Fernando Savater,

Joan de Sagarra, Josep Ramoneda, Domènec Font and Amando de Miguel; and numerous excellent cartoonists, including Forges, Cesc, Martínmorales, El Cubri, Guillén, Máximo, Núria Pompeia, Romeu, Vallés, Vives, Tom, Outumuro, Cebrián, Bolinaga, Bach, Kim and Ludovico. Moreover, famous graphic humorists abroad – for example, the Argentine artists Joaquín Salvador Lavado (Quino) and Roberto Fontanarrosa, and the French humorist Jean-Marc Reiser – also offered their work.

Although the humorous discourse of *Por Favor* was the most stylised and refined of the day, and featured several feminists (Maruja Torres, Núria Pompeia, and Soledad Balaguer), it was guilty, like other publications at the time, of machismo in its contents. It may not have been quite as male chauvinist as the rest but – as Jessica Lluch (2014) has shown – the female body was used on some of its covers as sexual bait for political matters. It had four different publishers, Punch Ediciones, Garbo Editorial, Cumbre and Planeta who produced 219 weekly issues, the last seven without some of its star contributors, including El Perich, Vázquez Montalbán, Forges and others who had left the magazine because of its parlous economic situation and certain disagreements with the management.

Por Favor's explicit vitriol led to weekly battles with the Ministry of Information and Tourism, which was outraged by its audacious and politically radical pillorying. It was impounded on several occasions and, on others, pages were censored. Several heavy fines were imposed and it was closed down on two occasions, all of which ate away at its finances to such an extent that it was eventually put up for sale (Vázquez Montalbán 2000: 14). The first suspension of *Por Favor*, only three months after it appeared, lasted four months, from 24 June to 25 October 1974, and the editor was fined 250,000 pesetas (Fontes and Menéndez 2004: 550). The pretext was a cartoon by Vives, showing a waiter handing Jesus Christ the bill at the end of the Last Supper.[7]

The jibes of *El Jueves*

The humorous weekly *El Jueves* (*Thursday*), which first appeared in May 1977, just a month before the first elections of the transition – in which all the parties had been legalised except the Catalan nationalist party Esquerra Republicana de Catalunya (Republican Left of Catalonia) – has endured to the present day. The first 26 numbers were published by Formentera, an initiative of the entrepreneur José Ilario, who also launched *Barrabás* (1972) and *Por Favor* (1974). The publishing house Grupo Zeta bought *El Jueves* in October 1977 and retained it until 1982 when its outstanding cartoonists, José Luis Martín, Òscar Nebreda and Jordi Ginés (Gin), acquired it and called their publishing operation Ediciones El Jueves.

In December 2006, the publisher RBA acquired 60 per cent control of the magazine. On 4 June 2014, some of its best known cartoonists – Albert Monteys, Manel Fontdevila, Bernardo Vergara, Paco Alcázar and Isaac Rosa – decided to leave in protest when the company vetoed and changed a cover already approved by the editorial board. It showed King Juan Carlos placing a crown full of excreta on the head of his son and heir. These artists, and another eighteen who also left, went on to publish the monthly online satirical magazine *Orgullo y Satisfacción* (*Pride and Satisfaction*).

A good number of the *El Jueves* cartoonists had previously worked for *El Papus* and/or *Por Favor*, including Òscar, Ivà, Gin, El Perich, Forges, El Roto (formerly Ops), Romeu, Ventura and Nieto, Ja, Oli, Martínmorales, Vives, Kim and Tom. During its long, four-decade span many other humorists have contributed, including José Luis Martín, Dino, Trallero d'A, Raf, Bosch, Nitka, Mariel, Toni Batllori, Maitena, Marika, Malagón, Julio Rey, Juan Álvarez, Carlos Azagra, Manel Barceló, Fer, Rubén Fernández, José María Gallego, Guille and Guillermo.

The circulation of *El Jueves* grew from the initial 50,000 copies to more than 200,000 with No. 785 in 1992, after which the number dropped to 90,000 in 2002 and, twelve years later, about 40,000 (Barrero 2014). Less elitist than *Por Favor* and less populist than *El Papus*, the magazine has a progressive, anti-clerical, moderate-left editorial line, and a basically cynical attitude to political parties in general. It observes a hands-off policy *vis-à-vis* the crown and the army, for which it shows some deference.

The facetious jibes of the magazine, less aggressive and sarcastic than those of its peers, in part because it has always existed in a democratic system, have caused fewer problems with the authorities. Nonetheless, its covers have been seized by court order on three occasions, including two of the early numbers in June and July 1977, because they ridiculed democracy and showed the Pope fighting with Bishop Lefebvre, respectively. In 2007 (No. 1,573) another was seized, for showing the then-Prince of Asturias (currently King Felipe VI) fornicating doggy style with his wife Doña Letizia, while gleefully speculating on their chances of getting a 'baby cheque' of €2,500 from the socialist government of José Luis Rodríguez Zapatero.

Institutions in the mirror of the satirical press

The monarchy, army and Church were all present but unequally treated in the pages of Spain's leading satirical magazines between 1975 and 1982. For all the different nuances in their ideological orientation, *Hermano Lobo, El Papus, Por Favor* and *El Jueves* largely coincided when it came to the targets of their more intense satire. With a fledgling monarchy and an army protected by the threat of government reprisals and suspensions, the Church was the main butt of their scathing humour. This was particularly true before the day that became known as 23-F, that of the attempted *coup d'état* led by Lieutenant Colonel (Guardia Civil) Antonio Tejero on 23 February 1981.

This lenience towards the monarchy and the army also contrasts with the jibes aimed at the political and entrepreneurial classes and the starchier, more reactionary strata. Self-censorship and self-control overshadowed these publications, as recognised in a cartoon published by *El Jueves* in 1982. It showed a man proclaiming: 'In Spain there is freedom of expression and you can say anything,' giving as an example the possibility of mocking anything outside the country without mentioning domestic issues, and added: 'You don't like the British monarchy, the Chilean army is horrible and the Polish Church is right-wing.' But speaking about matters close to home was forbidden. It is not difficult to see signs of circumspection in humorists' approaches to sensitive subjects that may have incurred anything from fines to government-decreed suspension, as some cartoonists admitted (Tubau 1977). One also notes a search for alternative ways of presenting controversial issues, counting on the complicity of readers who could divine the crux of the matter in abstract or obscure references (Peñamarín 2002).

The monarchy: Consensus over the figure of the King

Of the three institutions under discussion, the monarchy not only has the smallest presence in the pages of the satirical press but is also treated with most forbearance. During the transition, the political and economic elites agreed to construct and feed to Spanish public opinion a positive image of consensus concerning the figure of King Juan Carlos I. Self-censorship won the day even in the satirical magazines. In *El Jueves*, which was subsequently known for its merciless parodies, the prevailing humour took the form of innocuous, naïve witticisms, inspired by the king's diplomatic activity and his 'nice guy' attributes.

Perhaps the clearest proof of this kid-glove treatment of the monarchy was the absence of graphic caricatures in *Hermano Lobo* and the delay of their appearance until 1977 in *Por Favor* (even then, the only two cartoons it published offered a palatable image) and until 1984 in *El Papus*. For all the typical digs at the lifestyle and privileges of the European monarchies (especially Caroline of Monaco and, in England, Prince Charles's marriage to Lady Diana), the only explicit criticism of the indolence and high living of the Spanish royal family appeared at the end of 1982, taking advantage, as its author (JA) said, of the vacuum of 'power' after the recent Socialist Party (PSOE) victory. The date is no trivial matter, as the magazine waited for the election of the first left-wing government to attack the monarchy, as well as PSOE hypocrisy, from the standpoint of basically republican principles.

In *Hermano Lobo*, mention of the recently-crowned monarch was confined to neutral terms and subjects such as the royal agenda (in *Las coplillas de Don Luis* [Carandell] – *The Little Ditties of Don Luis*) or, indirectly, through general references to the institution but steering clear of the incumbent or, in the case of Manuel Vicent and Francisco Umbral, allusions to a hypothetical Third Republic, of which Umbral ironically wrote early in 1976: 'Who told you another republic is coming now, you drunken sod, you union-loving, bloody anarchist, liberal, heathen fool?' (No. 203, March 1976). One exception was Ramón, who decried the entrenchment of old ways and institutions when he referred to the 'programme of the first government of the monarchy and Franco's twenty-somethingth' (No. 196, February 1976). Another was Lord, who criticised the role of the press for its part in imposing a 'monarchic and aristocratic image that isn't good for the country, that the country doesn't want and that the monarchy probably doesn't want either because it knows this could work against it' (No. 185, November 1975).

With five exceptions, the pages of *Por Favor* were almost devoid of references to the crown before the first democratic elections of June 1977. A notable exception is a cartoon by Máximo (No. 110, August 1976) showing the three powers on a winner's podium. The top position is occupied by the Church, represented by a cardinal sitting on his throne, complete with pastoral staff. Kneeling before him and praying with bowed head is a king while, in third place, behind the cardinal, is a general in full dress uniform including a Kaiser's helmet. The triad of powers is resignedly contemplated by a father and his small son. In those years *Por Favor*'s oblique references to the monarchy, with very restrained humour, is understandable if one bears in mind that the first time the magazine published anything related to the crown it alluded to statements made by the king's father, Don Juan de Borbón, in the newspaper *ABC*. As a result, it was seized for the first time (No. 35, March 1975).

The coup attempt of 23 February 1981 had its effects on the two satirical magazines remaining in the market. *El Jueves* bent over backwards in praising King Juan Carlos with an appreciative assessment of his television appearance. It then presented the crown as the only institution capable of safeguarding democracy, and the king as the only Spaniard able to deal with the putschists. The fear of Spanish citizens during the attempt was mercilessly ridiculed by the magazine, which was yet another way of lauding the king's role. A notable example is a cartoon by Tom in which a citizen, still lying in bed and clinging to his transistor radio after the coup scare, heaves a sigh of relief and declares that he is a monarchist ('23F. We went to bed republicans and woke up monarchists'). The editorial team of *El Papus* also recognised the king's good work in facing down the military, although the magazine subsequently found fault with his submission to the Establishment, which it expressed by presenting him as something of a loser. Ivà was the least restrained of the cartoonists in his criticisms of the Head of State but, even so, he resorted to indirect rhetorical and graphic strategies. He was followed in his daring by L'Avi and JA.

The Army: Indirect references and attempted coup

The army, one of the mainstays of the Franco regime, was a recurrent motif throughout the period that concerns us. Nevertheless, as with the monarchy, far from any direct criticism or fine-honed satirising of the power and performance of Spain's military hierarchy and its visible heads, the focus was international, a resort to foreign affairs as an indirect strategy and a wink at readers, in order to escape the heavy hand of the Press Law. In this regard, *El Papus* and *Hermano Lobo* tended to refer to military leaders and dictators such as Jorge Videla, in Argentina, or Augusto Pinochet, in Chile.

In the absence of more explicit invective against the Spanish military, *Hermano Lobo* opted for a general anti-militarist line, questioning through apparently innocuous jokes the presence of United States bases in Spain and the Vietnam War. It also alluded – this time with a considerable load of mordancy and black humour through the cartoons of Gila, Summers and El Roto – to much thornier issues, for example firing-squad executions, which were not abolished in Spain until the end of the dictatorship. Neither did *Por Favor* ignore this issue. It tackled the execution of an ETA militant by means of a cartoon by El Perich, showing a statue of Justice with long bloodied fangs, announcing: 'Two death sentences have been decreed in Barcelona' (No. 55, July 1975).

Por Favor covered initiatives such as the founding of the Unión Militar Democrática (Military Democratic Union), a clandestine organisation of military officers trying to democratise the armed forces, but did so without comment and not a trace of jest or irony. The army (especially) and for good measure the Guardia Civil and the police were simply out of bounds.

Between 1975 and 1977, the army, which vehemently opposed the legislative changes being introduced, took centre stage in the pages of *El Papus*. Then, after a break of three years, it was in the limelight once again when the magazine's interest in coup rumours peaked in the early 1980s. A closer look shows that the main attributes depicted in its coverage of the army were abuse of power and its malevolent nature, followed by its subjugation of civil society.

Before the attempted coup, *El Jueves* gave most of its attention to the Amnesty Law and Operation Galaxy (an aborted military coup attempt in 1978). The opinion columns inveighed against the amnesty for denying justice to the victims of the Franco regime, although the figure of Franco was treated with condescension and, at most, a few touches of irony. In the case of Operation Galaxy, *El Jueves* scoffed at the spinelessness shown by the government and the legal system in the light sentences meted out to the would-be putschists, one of whom, Tejero, went on to try again with 23F. The magazine expressed no direct criticism of the army as an institution, either in its comic strips or in the editorial texts, while the convicted perpetrators were disparaged, but indulgently. It was not until the 1990s that any direct reference to the army appeared again, this time in Ivà's comic strip series 'Historias de la puta mili' (Bloody Conscription Stories).

The Church: A broadside against hypocrisy and sexual moralising

The Church is by far and away the institution with the greatest presence in the texts and cartoons in the magazines discussed here. It is also that which received the widest variety of nuance in its treatment, depending on the particular period. In 1975 and 1976, *Hermano Lobo* revealed the strictures of balancing acts when seeking to cover, in an anticlerical, progressive publication, the conflicts between traditionalists and the so-called post-conciliatory sectors, or the battle between Church and state arising from fines imposed on priests as a result of their sermons. Irony, with dashes of sarcasm, became the best way of dealing with the two countervailing powers, as shown in the following fragments mocking the reactionary outcry against more progressive positions like that held by the then-President of the Spanish Episcopal Conference, Monsignor Tarancón: 'Tarancón, the firing squad anon,' in response to his liberalising stance; 'Tarancón, you're modern and red and you'll land in hell when you're dead ... Save your soul and keep those little commie priests at bay ... I don't know how long it is since you killed a republican, excommunicated an egghead or burned one of those hussy witches' (No. 152, April 1975).

In another article, Francisco Umbral turns to the parable of the camel and the needle's eye in defence of the social doctrine of the Second Vatican Council, represented by Tarancón, against the ultra-conservatives whom Manuel Vicent depicts as upholding the values of the Christian Reconquest (No. 189, December 1975). Apart from these questions, Vicent steers clear of matters of sexual morality and misses no chance to draw attention to the 'fine discernment' of the Catholic Church 'many of whose men are in the more advanced political and social movements' although 'the sex department or the Dicastery of the Lower Belly is behind the times' (No. 195, January 1976).

Most of the digs at the Church during the transition period refer to its resistance to giving up its privileges as the bulwark of moral prescription in matters pertaining to divorce, abortion, sexual education and conduct, gender equality, contraception, Church funding and Church-state relations. In the case of *El Papus*, the Church was a focus from the beginning, especially in the debate about decriminalising adultery in 1976, and in 1978 and 1979 when the Divorce Law was being drafted. This period featured one of its most successful sections, a weekly comic strip starring the nun Sister Angustias de la Cruz.

The issue of adultery was also taken up in *El Jueves*, which pilloried the conservative, traditionalist position of the Church, sometimes bitterly and on other occasions with some indulgence, while always giving priority to reflecting public opinion. The greater part of Spanish society was fed up with the Church's heavy-handed 'monopoly of conscience' intrusion in so many matters, as a Don Cirilo cartoon shows (No. 3, June 1977). The character is an archetypical old-fashioned village priest, used to wielding power from the pulpit to the confessional, an embodiment of the moral hypocrisy forged in Spain by the National-Catholicism of Francisco Franco's dictatorial regime.

The Church is portrayed in *El Jueves* in the guise of village priests but also as bishops, nuns and personalities from the clerical hierarchy. Noteworthy here are the series '*La historia sagrada contada para los niños*' (Bible Stories for Children) by Ivà and José Luis Martín's 'Dios' (God) which 'unmasked' the Church's moral hypocrisy. The main humorous devices employed by the magazine were parody and irony, and these were more concerned with seeking complicity with the reader than with demolishing the object being sent up. This helped create a united front against the power of the Church.

Por Favor differed from the other publications under discussion, and the traditional anti-clericalism of the left-wing satirical press in Spain (Capdevila

2010). Its texts and cartoons were in tune with the mood of citizens, in that it censured the Catholic Church for its contradictions and double standards much less than for its ideological and political support for the Franco dictatorship. Testifying to this is a two-page spread of Forges' cartoons titled '*Los Eclesiásticos*' (*The Ecclesiastics*) featuring different types of monks and nuns and captioned 'totally bent' (No. 125, November 1976). The fine irony of the superb artist barely touches any of the usual anti-clerical stereotypes. None of the eight frames refers to sexual moralising, and only one of them links a priest with money, showing him behind a cashier's window with a sign saying 'Spiritual director getting down to it.'

In both *El Jueves* and *El Papus*, attacks on the Church gathered momentum after 1977 with the debate concerning the constitution and the funding and privileges it conceded. In this period, too, the Church's alliance between the then-existing ultra-conservative political party Alianza Popular (People's Alliance), many of whose leaders were from the Franco establishment, or the Christian Democrats of Unión de Centro Democrático (Union of the Democratic Centre) became evident. In *Por Favor*, referring to the draft constitution, Martínmorales presented two priests discussing the matter. One of them angrily pronounces: 'Those politicians who drew up that draft constitution have definitely committed a mortal sin' (No. 182, December 1977).

As head of the Catholic hierarchy, Pope John Paul II was a prime target for *El Papus*. It is no accident that the majority of items referring to the Pontiff are clustered in 1982, the year in which he visited Spain. He was one of the magazine's most pilloried characters and featured on nine covers. In the first of these (No. 412, April 1982) Pope John Paul II is shown in a bathing costume under the caption: 'Easter holidays start today.' The Public Prosecutor filed a complaint against the artist Luis Rey and the Art Director, Ramón Tosas (Ivà) while the ultra-Catholic group Warriors of Christ the King issued threats against the magazine's staff.

El Papus depicted the Pope as a freeloading money-grubber and, accordingly, with predominantly unfavourable connotations which highlighted the hypocrisy, the puritanical moralising, and the general iniquity associated with the Church. The diatribe against Pope John Paul II culminated in a call for nothing less than the eradication of the papacy (No. 332, December 1980): '*El Papus* warns you! We got Franco, Girón, Arias and Abril Martorell and now we're going for Suárez!! Then it's your turn, Pope Wojtyla.' The text is also an example of the evolution of *El Papus*'s language from a relatively refined register – also characteristic of *Hermano Lobo* – to a highly colloquial tone with the progressive appearance of expletives and doggerel. Earlier the magazine resorted to highbrow language and slang as euphemisms, and used a considerable array of non-colloquial idioms. What did not diminish was the use of adages and figures of speech, which were scattered throughout the magazine, revealing a rebellious spirit and dissent from the decisions of the respective governments and powers-that-be. This versatility in combining registers testifies to the authors' wide-ranging knowledge of the Spanish language.

Conclusions: Self-policed humour

In the transition years, irony and inoffensive humour won the day over sharp satire in the ways in which the three institutions, monarchy, army and Church, were treated. This style differed considerably from the corrosive lampoonery with which these magazines treated politicians and well-known business figures. Criticism of the crown and the army were all but absent in the main satirical publications, in an exercise more of self-control than self-censorship. The journalists and cartoonists were well aware of the dangers of direct repression after almost four decades of dictatorship. This reality was underlined by the fact that the Head of State was not only the monarch but also Commander-in-Chief of the armed forces.

Unlike the army and the monarchy, the Catholic Church was the main target of sarcastic scoffing. While sympathy was expressed for its liberalising elements, its more fanatical sectors were denounced, as was the Church's unwillingness to loosen the iron grip of its privileged position in the crucial debates defining the state and individual freedoms during the transition.

To sum up, *Hermano Lobo, Por Favor, El Papus* and *El Jueves* were more concerned with civic than clichéd institutional criticism, focusing an ironical and satirical spotlight on the political and economic power-holders and managers rather than the politics of the state apparatus. To avoid fines, impounding, and suspensions, threats which remained enshrined in the Franco regime's Press Law until 1977, and also as a result of certain routines acquired by journalists who feared reprisals from the Head of State and the army, the self-controlled, trade-off style of humour was aimed at a public that knew how to read between the lines.

Notes

[1] This chapter is part of the R&D&I project of the Spanish Ministry for Science and Innovation (CSO2011-27678, 2011-2014) which is titled, El humor frente al poder: la Monarquía, el Ejército y la Iglesia a través de la comunicación satírica en la España contemporánea: 1930-1936 y 1975-1982 (Humour in the Face of Power: Monarchy, Army and Church in the Satirical Journalism of Contemporary Spain: 1930-1936 and 1975-1982)

[2] Between 20 November 1975 and 31 December 1983, the transition's toll was more than 2,663 victims of political violence, 591 of whom were killed, while the rest were hospitalised as a result of their wounds (Sánchez Soler 2010)

[3] The first half of the 1970s coincided with the last years of the dictatorship or late Franco period, while the latter half began with the restoration of Juan Carlos I imposed by the *Cortes Españolas* (1975), followed by parliamentary elections (1977), the constitutional referendum (1978), municipal elections (1979) and the first elections in the Autonomous Regions of the Basque Country and Catalonia (1980)

[4] In 1975, the journalist Josep María Huertas Clavería was condemned to two years in prison for slandering the army in the evening television programme *Tele/eXprés*, with an episode titled 'Vida erótica subterránea' (Underground Erotic Life), in which he reported that many brothels were run by widows of military men. Moreover, the actor and director Albert Boadella, director of the play *La Torna*, which was performed by the group of mime artists Els Joglars, was also sentenced to two years in prison by a military court two months after the premiere of the work which mocked the Guardia Civil

[5] The first number, of sixteen pages, went on sale for fifteen pesetas. By 1974 it had twenty-four pages and cost twenty pesetas, which rose to thirty-five pesetas in the last period of its existence

[6] The name *El Papus* refers to the *papu*, a kind of ogre, bogeyman or, in the Catalan oral tradition, the *home del sac* (man with the sack), a figure cited by adults to frighten children

[7] 'In the first period of suspension decreed by the ministry, the company contributed towards the appearance of another humorous magazine, *Muchas Gracias* (*Thank you very much*), headed by the future film-maker [Francesc] Bellmunt, [the cartoonist] Vallés and [the writer] Joan de Sagarra. This was also in the line of critical political humour but tending more to existential and historical absurdity' (Vázquez Montalbán 2000: 15)

References

Barrero, Manuel (2014) *El Jueves: Revista de la Transición, Revista en Transición*, Sevilla: Tebeosfera

Bordería Ortiz, Enrique; Martínez Gallego, Francesc Andreu; Gómez Mompart, Josep Lluís (eds) (2010) *La risa periodística: Teoría, metodología e investigación en comunicación satírica*, Valencia: Tirant Lo Blanch

Bordería Ortiz, Enrique; Martínez Gallego, Francesc Andreu; Gómez Mompart, Josep Lluís (eds) (2015) *El humor frente al poder. Prensa humorística, cultura política y poderes fácticos en España (1927-1987)*, Madrid: Biblioteca Nueva

Capdevila, Jaume (2010) *Si los curas y frailes supieran. Antología de la caricatura anticlerical*, Barcelona: Ediciones la Tempestad

Fontes de Garnica, Ignacio and Menéndez Gijón, Manuel Ángel (2004) *El Parlamento de papel. Las revistas españolas en la transición democrática*, Madrid: Asociación de la Prensa de Madrid

Iranzo, María (2014) La revista satírica *El Papus* (1973-1987) Contrapoder comunicativo en la Transición política española. El tratamiento informativo crítico y popular de la Transición española, PhD thesis, University of Valencia. Available online at http://roderic.uv.es/handle/10550/39651, accessed on 26 November 2014

Lluch Giménez, Jessica (2014) La representación de la mujer en la prensa satírica: *Por Favor* (1974-1978), *Revista Internacional de Historia de la Comunicación*, Vol. 1, No. 3 pp 71-94. Available online at http://revistainternacionaldehistoriadelacomunicacion.org/, accessed on 4 January 2015

Mora, Miguel (2000) El humor de los tiempos de la penuria triunfa otra vez, *El País*, 9 January

Peñamarín, Cristina (2002) El humor gráfico del franquismo y la formación de un territorio translocal de identidad democrática, *CIC: Cuadernos de información y comunicación*, No. 7 pp 351-380

Sánchez Soler, Mariano (2010) *Una transición sangrienta: Una historia violenta del proceso democrático en España (1975-1983)*, Barcelona: Península

Tubau, Iván (1987) *El humor gráfico en la prensa del franquismo*, Barcelona: Mitre

Vázquez Montalbán, Manuel (2000) Prologue, Claret, Jaume (ed.) *Por Favor. Una historia de la transición*, Barcelona: Crítica pp 9-19

Note on the contributors

Josep Lluís Gómez-Mompart is Professor of Journalism and Communication at the University of Valencia and director of a research team on satirical communication. He is author of Semiotics and the History of Social Communication (1990), Guerra televisada y televisión bélica: Vietnam, El Golfo, Kosovo y Afganistán (2003), Diversidad latina y comunicación panhispana en la prensa en español en Nueva York al inicio del siglo XXI (2008), From Quality Journalism to Speculative Journalism (2009) and, with other authors, *Historia del periodismo universal* (1999), *La risa periodística* (2010), The Changing Identity of British Broadsheets (2013), *La calidad periodística* (2013) and *El humor frente al poder* (2015).

Dolors Palau-Sampio has a PhD in Journalism from the University of Valencia (UV) and is a tenured lecturer and member of the satirical communication research team at the UV. She is author of *Els estils periodístics: Maneres de veure i construir la realitat* (2005), Estilo y autoría en la información, Una aparente ausencia de identidad (2009) and Periodismo ciudadano en las ediciones digitales, una apuesta limitada (2012) and, with other authors, *La calidad periodística* (2013), *Shaping the News Online* (2014), *Appraising Digital Storytelling across Educational Contexts* (2014) and *El humor frente al poder* (2015).

José-Luis Valhondo-Crego is a substitute lecturer in the Faculty of Documentation and Communication at the University of Extremadura and a member of the satirical communication research team at the University of Valencia. In 2011, he published *Sátira televisiva y democracia en España*. He has also published Monarcas, bufones, políticos y audiencias: Comparación de la sátira televisiva en Reino Unido y España (2011) in the *Revista Latina de Comunicación Social* and, with other authors, L'infosatira televisiva e i suoi effeti (2012) in the review *Comunicazione Politica*.

María Iranzo-Cabrera has a PhD in Journalism from the University of Valencia (UV) and is a member of the satirical communication research team at the UV. She is author of *El Papus*: Una revolución satírica que copó la crítica humorística española de julio de 1975 a marzo de 1976 (2014), *El Papus*: Memoria de la mala baba (2013) and Un golpe de risa, la gracia de un golpe: Análisis del golpe de Estado del 23 de febrero de 1981 por la revista *El Papus* (2010) and, with other authors, Humor y periodismo valenciano tras la dictadura franquista: identificación y periodización de las publicaciones (2013).

Once Upon a Time in Manila: Managing Marcos and Martial Rule through Humour

Amy Forbes

> In the beginning there was only a word which stood all alone in the great abyss of darkness. And the word wandered within the sphere of darkness and ignited another word and together they gave birth to more words which created a balance against the darkness. Soon men began to rely on the words to shine upon them, to feed them, and the words failed them not.
>
> Ninez Cacho-Oliveres
> 'The gospel according to journalists'
> 24 February 1982, *Bulletin Today*

Introduction
To a nation of people mired in poverty and misery, fairytales and fables wield a special power that can capture the heart and the imagination. Is it not through these stories that heroes and heroines are transported from despair to redemption? From helplessness to hope? From poverty to riches? The recent political history of the Philippines reads like a fairytale, albeit dark, with all the key components: victims and villains, kings and peasants, conflicts and triumphs, and pure fantasy in spades. There is the ex-president, the once powerful king who is now dead, his corpse encased in wax in a futile quest to preserve his rotting flesh. There is the former first lady, a real-life Cinderella who grew up penniless in a small town, but whose beauty attracted the nation's most eligible bachelor, and who was destined to live in a real palace, to wine and dine with kings and queens of faraway places. And then there are the scribes who chronicle all these events, sharp pens and even sharper wits at the ready.

That the power of a good story is not lost on Ferdinand Marcos is evident in his choice of Imelda as his partner. Years before, as a young congressman from the north, Marcos had cast his eye on the beautiful but poor relation of a fellow politician from the south. Imelda Romualdez was born in Manila to near-penniless parents. The family had had to live in a garage described as a carport;

the flooring was barely a foot from the ground. Her father was an underachieving lawyer who had become a widower with five children, before remarrying and having six more. His second wife, Trinidad, Imelda's mother, would die from pneumonia a few months after giving birth to her sixth child. Stories abound of how the young Imelda grew up in the southern province of Leyte, where she became known as 'the Rose of Tacloban'. Marcos knew that marrying a woman from the south would serve not only to expand his political reach, but that the press would adore beauty.

Marcos had tried for years to woo the press to his side. After winning his first term of office as president in 1965, he is said to have poured millions of dollars into public relations and media for his re-election. This was the first time a Filipino politician acknowledged the key role favourable media coverage could bring to an election campaign.

The Philippine media had always operated as extensions of business empires and were used to defending big business (Rosenberg 1979: 154). Historically, the media experienced uneven periods, of almost total freedom and almost total repression. If the climate was free and prosperous, it flourished. When governments put on restraints, it responded with meek compliance.

Ninez Cacho-Olivares: Confronting pro-government compliance with wit

It was this obsequious compliance that television and print journalist Ninez Cacho-Olivares rebelled against. Born in Zamboanga in the south, Olivares had originally wanted to be a doctor. Her father's work took them to Cebu, where she began a pre-medicine degree at the University of San Carlos. However, she could not stand the smell of formaldehyde and the thought of cutting up dead animals. She said: 'I figured it was so boring to come around and cut up cats and dogs. What I said was I'd rather cut up people and politicians. So that was what happened' (personal communication, 19 August 2014).

Olivares had been a radio personality in Cebu before she moved to Manila to pursue a degree in journalism at the University of Santo Tomas. Before she could graduate, she found work as a disc jockey at Manila Times Radio, a subsidiary of the *Manila Times*, one of Manila's largest and oldest newspaper publishers. From radio it was an easy leap into writing feature stories for the *Daily Mirror* and *The Sunday Times* magazine. Later, she forayed into television as a newsreader for Channel 9. By 1975, martial law was in full swing and no one dared show dissent. Censorship was widely practised and erring journalists were either invited in for questioning, or fired from their positions. Olivares became a household name, and viewers knew her as a fearless broadcaster. Reading outright lies masquerading as glowing reports of Marcos's New Society, she would roll her eyes on screen and smirk. Marcos was an avid viewer of the news and pressured Channel 9 owner Roberto Benedicto to have Olivares moved from the primetime news programme to the late evening news. She said:

> Everybody knew that I was fearless because that was the time of martial rule. I had this habit of while reading propaganda for the Marcos

government. ... I always rolled my eyes, so everybody knew I was against Marcos. That was my way of maintaining my reputation as an independent journalist even under such adverse conditions. Marcos, who kept on watching me even during the late night, and the continued eye roll, had me fired, *tout suite* (ibid).

How Marcos clamped down on the media

When martial law was declared in 1972, Marcos clamped down on all media outlets, arresting and detaining newspaper publishers, editors and journalists. By his own recollection, 52 of the targeted 200 people had been rounded up by the second day of martial law (ABS-CBN News 2012). These included Senators Benigno Aquino Jr, Jose Diokno, and Ramon Mitra, Constitutional Convention delegates from the Liberal opposition party, a governor who interestingly was labelled the country's number one smuggler, a congressman, and various labour leaders. None of those detained were known communists who 'threatened the Republic', the rationale Marcos had used in legitimising his decision to proclaim martial law.

In the last three months of 1972, 8,281 people were 'apprehended and detained': 2,410 allegedly belonged to subversive groups, 2,219 were wanted criminals, and 3,652 belonged to the 'others' category (IRAIA 2012). The senators and 22 Manila-based journalists fell under this 'others' category. Among the media, publishers and journalists arrested were Eugenio Lopez, Jr., Amando Doronila, Chino Roces, Teodoro Locsin, Soc Rodrigo, Luis Mauricio, Napoleon Rama, Rosalinda Galang, Roger Arrienda, Jose Mari Velez, and Max Soliven (Gleeck, Jr. 1987: 116). Some would languish in military camps for years, or be released only upon surrender of their assets to Marcos.

Marcos effectively dismantled the media monopolies, only to turn them over to relatives and cronies, including Imelda's younger brother Benjamin 'Kokoy' Romualdez, who headed the *Times Journal*. The newspaper with the largest circulation at the beginning of martial rule was the *Philippine Daily Express*. This was financed by Marcos fraternity brother and classmate Roberto S. Benedicto, who was also awarded control of the sugar industry and appointed ambassador to Japan by Marcos (Celoza 1997: 97). The *Manila Daily Bulletin*, later renamed *Bulletin Today*, was owned and operated by former Marcos senior military adviser General Hans Menzi. It had been shut down briefly, along with all other newspapers, magazines, radio and television stations when martial law was declared. The story goes that Marcos summoned Menzi to the official presidential residence, Malacañang Palace, and ordered him to reopen the paper but with a new name. Menzi complied, returning with two studies – one for the *Philippine Daily Bulletin*, and the other, *Bulletin Today*. Marcos signed the latter to which he also scribbled 'ok' (Mariano 1995:13). Ninez Cacho-Olivares would write for the *Bulletin Today*. It is here that she used the power of fables, fairytales, religion, popular culture and humour to discuss topics otherwise taboo under the dictatorship.

Martial law was lifted on 17 January 1981, after almost ten years. No one had expected it to last as long as it did. Some commentators speculated that Marcos lifted martial law because he was pressured by the US government (Celoza 1997: 73). His human rights record had been severely criticised as politicians and journalists continued to be detained, with no charges other than that they were 'communist sympathisers'. At the same time his long-time friend Ronald Reagan was about to be inaugurated as the 40th President of the United States, and it would not look good for his new presidency if he could not convince his friend Marcos to restore democracy to the Philippines. And Pope John Paul II was scheduled to visit the country in February to beatify several martyrs, including two who would later be sainted, St. Lorenzo Ruiz and Magdalene of Nagasaki (Sin 1981). Human rights violations and talk of martyrs under martial law certainly gave fodder to the press, something Marcos was all too eager to avoid.

Olivares and *Bulletin Today*: The beginnings

And so it was in late 1981 that Ninez Cacho-Olivares offered her services as a columnist to *Bulletin Today* publisher Hans Menzi. She had bumped into him at a restaurant and said she could do a better job at writing a column than his regulars. He was sceptical:

> 'I know you can do newscasting but I don't know if you can write.' I said: 'Okay. But I bet I can.' I mean I'm always like that, and he said: 'Okay. Send me two articles and I'll let you know' (personal communication, 29 August 2014).

Menzi already had young journalist Arlene Babst writing for him, and she had been trying to convince him to hire more women writers (de Jesus 2012). Babst's writing was beginning to be noticed for its audacity against the regime, and circulation was growing. Menzi was intent on regaining the number one spot from the *Philippines Daily Express*, and having Olivares and other women writers might just be the ticket. Besides, any appearance to suggest that the *Bulletin Today* was not subject to the usual censorship was also good for the government and his friend, the president. Olivares said:

> It was a political column even if it was so humorous, because I just come around and say: 'Once upon a time, there was an evil king who had an avaricious wife…' and everybody knew whom I was talking about. So the column became the talk of the town, and Hans Menzi liked the idea of having me there as a columnist writing humour because it leant credibility to the newspaper (ibid).

Thus began the fairytales and fables and humour, each a not-so-subtle attempt to out-step government censors. Each was written with Olivares's trademark wit and with tongue firmly pressed against a cheek. In 'The wicked witch' (Olivares 1982a: 6), the references to the First Lady are as transparent as

Cinderella's glass slippers. Cinderella complains that the Wicked Witch is spreading false fairy tales about her:

> 'You silly old fool. How dare you give out parchments that say I'm such an extravagant girl? What kind of false fairy tales are you spreading all over town? I do as I'm asked and it's only in my desire to please them that I can be called extravagant.'
>
> 'Please them, my eye,' the Wicked Witch said. 'You've got everything, Cinderella. You just snap your fingers, your fairy godmother comes along to give you everything you desire.'
>
> 'That's not true and you're not being fair at all! I don't have everything yet.'

The two exchange more barbs and the Wicked Witch says she is readying real parchments not embroidered in gold or silver, nor dipped in sweet smelling perfume. When Cinderella threatens to chop her head off, the Wicked Witch suggests they consult the Magic Mirror to see who is lying.

> 'Mirror, mirror on the wall. The Wicked Witch says I'm a bad and extravagant girl. I know I'm a good girl with a heart as white as snow. Tell me the truth.'
>
> 'Well honey,' the mirror replied. 'You surely ain't Snow White.'

Telling fairy tales

The above is typical of how Olivares would comment on Marcos and Imelda. Reading it now, one need not even know the specific circumstances that inspired the story at the time. Olivares said she drew inspiration from American humorist James Thurber, whose writing she admired. She particularly liked his wry humour, his sensitivity to human fears and foibles, and the timeless, aphoristic quality of his writing. Hers was pithy commentary embedded in a well-known fairy tale. And what a fairy tale Imelda's life was! One need only to mention shoes and the world thinks Imelda, not Cinderella. A final count by *Time* magazine in 1987 found that Imelda's wardrobe had 1,060 pairs of shoes, 508 floor-length gowns, 888 handbags, 71 pairs of sunglasses, 15 mink coats and 65 parasols (Ching 2010). But to Imelda, this is not extravagant. In an interview with Philippine Center for Investigative Journalism's Sheila Coronel (2006), Imelda Marcos said:

> They call me Imeldific, meaning extravagant, frivolous, excessive and vulgar. I said if you're committed to God, beauty and love, in a material world, you can be perceived as extravagant, excessive and even vulgar. [But] I have a responsibility. I have to set a standard.

This interview is reminiscent of another interview she granted some 24 years earlier to *Newsweek* magazine, and quoted by Babst (1982: 6) in her *Bulletin Today* column. On her lavish lifestyle, Marcos had said: 'I am always criticised for my jewelry; for what they call my lavish lifestyle, my extravagant frivolity. But I have always been criticised for my sense of beauty. I will continue to be a soldier for beauty because that is the only thing which feeds the human spirit.' With copy like this, who needs writers?

In the adaptation of the Norwegian fairy tale *Three Billy Goats Gruff*, Olivares tackled corruption. Ever the cheeky one, she writes: 'Gruff rhymes with some name that escapes me at the moment' (Olivares 1982b: 6). Graft, maybe? In any case, her story goes much the same way as the original, only the goats are not crossing a bridge but trying to get a feed from a nearby grassy hill owned by the Ugly Troll. When the Troll discovers the goats and accuses them of stealing, the littlest goat tries to deny it. Unfortunately, he had left little hoof marks on the hill and the Troll gobbles him up. The medium-sized goat who earlier had bleated his delight at being full cannot deny his crime either and the Troll gobbles him up as well. Finally, the Troll confronts the biggest of the goats, Gruff the Heavy, also known as Gruff the Biggie.

> 'You've been stealing almost all of my grass,' the Troll said to Gruff the Heavy.
>
> 'So what are you going to do about it?' roared Gruff the Heavy, then went about filling his sack with more grass, right under the watchful eye of the Troll.
>
> 'Why nothing,' the Troll answered, and offered an olive branch to Gruff the Heavy. The Troll and Gruff the Biggie feasted on more grass that night and got even fatter.
>
> Moral: With Trolls like that, blessed become the biggies for they shall continue to inherit all the grass (Olivares 1982b: 6).

Lamenting the lack of knowledge – of the self and society

The most successful stories Olivares wrote were those where she laments her own inadequacies, in understanding both herself and the goings-on in government and society. She portrays herself as confused and in need of her friendly psychiatrist. In 'The true, the good and the beautiful' (1982c), she is on her psychiatrist's Freudian couch:

> Having recurring dreams of the false, the bad and the ugly was cause enough for me to run to my psychiatrist.
>
> 'Doc, you gotta help me. I'm in real trouble.' I sobbed and immediately plopped down on his Freudian couch.
>
> 'What's the problem this time?'
>
> 'You gotta unify my three personalities, Doc. Whenever I read or hear news reports issued by government offices or reports focusing on government, *I* swallow everything as true. But Doc, *me* – my other

personality says that I am dumb to accept everything as true. Not only that, my other personality – *myself* – agrees with her and *myself* even said that the beautiful was only for show and the ugly is hidden through managed news reports.'

'Hmm, me and myself seem to be getting very negative. You have to accentuate the positive and throw out me and myself. They're garbage!' he answered.

'You mean government reports are pure garbage?' I asked incredulously.

'I didn't say that. I meant your two personalities are garbage if all they zero in is on the false, the bad and the ugly. Think beautiful thoughts,' the doctor advised me (emphasis in the original).

Olivares would have received the same advice from Imelda Marcos. Marcos had coined the slogan 'the true, the good and the beautiful' for the New Society. This, Imelda claims, is the secret to her own outer and inner beauty:

> I have such a great attitude because I really feel that everybody wakes up with, let us say, 1,000 points of energy. Because of my attitude, I see beautiful flowers. It energises me. Beautiful trees, beautiful people, beautiful conversation, beautiful friends, beautiful projects. By the time it is night time, I no longer have 1,000 points of energy. I have about a million (Coronel 2006).

In 'Me and my shadow' (1982c), Olivares explores the topic of government surveillance:

> It was one of those spooky days for me. Out there in broad daylight, I started to hear a voice which really scared the daylights out of me. I started muttering to myself: 'Lord, not me please. I don't have what it takes to be a Joan of Arc.'
>
> 'What a dope,' the voice said. 'And to think I have to be stuck with you the rest of my life.'
>
> I started to shake in my shoes. The figure shook as much as I did.
>
> 'Go away,' I croaked. 'I'm really scared.'
>
> 'I'd like to,' the voice said, 'but I can't. I can only leave you after sundown.' 'Relax,' the voice said, soothingly. 'I'm only your shadow.'
>
> 'Oh, for crying out loud,' I said as relief flooded through me. 'Why couldn't you have told me sooner? If you're only my shadow then you can't hurt me, because I'm stronger than you.'
>
> 'True,' the shadow answered. 'But I can look over your shoulder, check on what you're doing and curb your abuses.'

She demurs and suggests instead that the shadow tail erring politicians.

> 'That's exactly what we shadows are thinking of doing,' it answered as it sat when I sat. 'We're thinking of ways and means to shadow the different government ministries. You know, like placing them under surveillance.'

The shadow reveals the plan to form a coalition of shadows to check on the abuses of the majority party. Olivares uses the term fiscaliser, a word coined by Filipino lawmakers in the last century to mean critics of alleged government wrongdoing. It derives from the Spanish verb 'fiscalisar' meaning to criticise or to oversee.[1]

> 'No kidding,' I said, opening my eyes a little wider. 'So how do we get to know how effective a fiscaliser you shadows are? I have to remind myself that you're all politicians, too.'
>
> 'What have you got against politicians?' the shadow asked.
>
> 'Nothing much, except that someone once said that for a politician to be successful, he must be a Machiavelli and a Borgia, with Caesar's delusions. On top of that, he must have the gift of gab and grab.'

Olivares is skilful in her turns of phrase and unexpected plot twists, and always with biting accuracy and honesty. In 'MIA's culpa' (1982d), Olivares set her sight on the new Manila International Airport (MIA) built at the cost of hundreds of millions of pesos. At the time it was touted as comparable to Charles de Gaulle Airport in Paris, except that nothing worked. Using a fictional friend as a foil, she says:

> 'Hey listen. I didn't build this airport. I don't even have anything to do with its maintenance,' I replied defensively. 'But you have to admit, friend, we have a smashing-looking façade.'
>
> 'Great image! But how is your airport being maintained?' my friend asked as he unbuttoned his now soggy shirt. 'Maybe you don't have enough funds to maintain this airport.'
>
> 'You kidding? To get in, we have to pay ₱5.00. To get out, each departing passenger has to pay ₱50.00 for airport fees – that should cover the maintenance cost, don't you think?'
>
> 'Who's in charge of this airport anyway?'
>
> 'The chairman of the games and amusement board, Mr Tabuena,' I replied.
>
> 'Please tell him that airport maintenance is not a game and it's not amusing, either.'
>
> I promised I would.

In 'Bryant the Giant' (Olivares 1982e), Olivares narrates the story of a two-faced giant who always claimed he had a soft spot for children and who also loved his talking flowers. He had singing geraniums, tulips that gossiped, gladioli that brought only good tidings, and roses that, although pretty, always managed to prick him. Tired of all the noise and thinking they were persecuting him, he ordered them to be cut down and replaced with flowers that, when commanded, would say only the things Bryant wanted to hear. Soon the children stopped visiting, and this bothered Bryant.

> 'Why have the children been alienated from me?' he asked. Nobody really knew the answer. Only the cut flowers in his garden could have told him, but they had not been allowed to bloom and could no longer tell Bryant why the children had been alienated. There's a moral to this story, but somehow it escapes me at the moment.

Arthurian legends – and the search for the Holy Grail of pithy prose

Nothing was off-limits to Olivares in her search for literary vehicles in which to flex her pithy prose. One of her favourite story frames are the Arthurian legends; of King Arthur, his knights, Guinevere and Camelot. In 'Dragonland' (1982f), the setting has been modified to Changealot, where peasants and knights lived together.

> Changealot, as every student of mythical history knows, was a kingdom inhabited by peasants and knights of long ago. The peasants of Changealot are no different from the peasants of long ago. They worked for their living and comfort and they even worked day and night just to give some of their daily bread for their knights' upkeep, whose duty is to protect the poor, unarmed peasants from dragons and other dangerous elements that threatened their peace and their lives. The knights, on the other hand, were really ordinary peasants who had become extraordinary because they either slew dragons or promised to protect the rights of the peasants. Some knights became knights through bootlicking, but that's another story.

In this story, peasants were noticing more and more that Changealot was, indeed, changing a lot. They started to gripe that their knights had started to mint their armour in gold and not do their duty.

> One peasant actually went to a knight and demanded: 'Why aren't we being protected from the fire-snorting dragons? We give you most of the gold just to protect us and yet we find that your days are filled with meetings and your nights are spent with damsels who are not in distress and oftentimes when you are not with knights or damsels, you are off on a fact-finding crusade.'

Olivares is pointing to a news report that the great number of assemblymen and women of the Philippine parliament have been habitually absent during sessions (*Bulletin Today* 1982). Since there was often a lack of quorum, Filipinos had begun wondering how the laws, of which they had heard only after the fact, had ever been approved.

'The dragons have swelled to a dangerous number. They've bothered us too much. Why don't you do something about the dragons?'

'My dear man,' the knight replied. 'We've slain all the dragons, believe me. I've been all over the countryside and saw no dragons.'

'Impossible,' the peasant retorted. 'The dragons are still around. Just yesterday when I tried to get my horse out, there were too many dragons who demanded for gold. It was either the horse or the gold.'

'But you couldn't have seen the dragons,' the knight replied. 'If they breathed fire on you, you would have been completely burned, my dear man.'

'I have been burned many times by too many dragons,' the peasant replied. 'Every step of the way is being barred by dragons who insist on getting part of my hard-earned gold.'

'Perhaps what we need is to allow all the big dragons to revise their system. If we give the dragons the right to increase their fees and charges for horses or everything else, the other little dragons will no longer bother you.'

'The problem with dragons will not disappear,' the peasant replied. 'The little dragons will have to ask for more gold instead, and the peasants will be paying much more under the dragon's feet.'

The knight looked at the sundial. 'I'm off to another meeting. But really, I don't see why we shall be paying much more. But that's understandable. I'm a knight and you're only a peasant, so how can I expect you to understand these things?'

'Tell me,' the peasant said, 'where do you live?'

'In Dragonland, of course,' the knight replied.

'What's your name?' the peasant asked, pleasantly. 'Puff, the Magic Dragon, that masquerades as a knight.'

It is interesting that Olivares invokes the image of the uneducated peasant. The Philippines had been a Spanish colony for 300 years and the peasants had been kept ignorant by the Spanish colonial masters. When the Americans came in 1898, they spent the next 50 years educating the Filipino people in the intricacies of liberal democracy. This amounted to an education of a people in the 'American way' and, as Renato Constantino says in 'The miseducation of the Filipino' (1970), 'the pathetic results of this failure of Philippine education is a citizen amazingly naïve and trusting in its relations with foreigners, devoid of the capacity to feel indignation even in the face of insults to the nation, ready to acquiesce and even to help aliens in the despoliation of our national wealth'.

Knowing her target readership well

At the time of martial rule, the Philippines enjoyed a comparatively higher literacy rate than most of its Asian neighbours. The people were heavily dependent on radio and television for their news and information, as well as print media in the urban areas. Olivares's writing was addressed to the educated who read and enjoyed the Brothers Grimm fairy tales as children, or the Arthurian books and legends, or whose exposure to popular culture had been aided by the ability to write and speak in English. Her stories resonated not so much among the common folk as with society's elite, most of whom lost their riches to Marcos and his cronies.

Her stories also resonated and incensed the president and his first lady, so much so that the *Bulletin Today* publisher, Hans Menzi, was regularly being summoned to Malacañang Palace over this or that article Marcos deemed irritating (Mariano 1995). Following such visits, Menzi would return to the *Bulletin Toaday* offices to vent, and editors and columnists would consider themselves temporarily laid off work while the president cooled off. Olivares's column was a constant target. Each time, Menzi would come back and implore her to tone down her writing, or cool off on writing about Marcos, corruption, military abuse, and other controversial topics. It did not matter that she named no names in her stories nor that her stories, at least on the surface, were simply that – fairy tales and fables more fit for young readers than Manila's elite. However, in many cases the characters in her stories became a guessing game for the elite. In 'Idyll of kings' (1982g) Olivares brings up the issue of absenteeism in King Arthur's Round Table:

> One day, Sir Kay thought he had enough of idle knights. He asked the page of the castle to call the roll. 'Milords,' the page said, 'only 48 Knights of the Round Table are present out of a total of 181.'
>
> Immediately, Mordred stood and exclaimed: 'The other knights have become habitual absentees and according to the laws of the land, we must expel them from the Round Table.'
>
> 'There must be some credible excuse,' Sir Kay answered. 'Where is Merlin the Magician?'
>
> 'Sire,' the page replied. 'He has been lured by the spirit of Nimue, but he insists that Milord Mordred has no constitutional right with which to expel these knights.'
>
> 'Where is Sir Gawain?' asked Mordred, again taking the floor.
>
> 'He has been travelling on orders of the King, sire. He's off to the Thames.'

'Excused,' said Sir Kay. 'Now where is Sir Lionel?'

'Milord,' replied the page. 'He has been trapped in the enchanted forest of Morgana Le Fay for a body massage and an overnight stay.'

'Sir Galahad, I suppose, is still in search of the Holy Grail?' sneered Mordred.

'Aye, sir,' the page said. 'He is on a fact-finding mission again.'

'And Sir Lancelot du lac, where is he?'

'Sire, Sir Lancelot is with the Lady Guinevere, shining her shoes.'

'What? A knight boot polishing?'

'Sire,' replied the page. 'Don't let it be forgot, there once was a spot that Lancelot had to rub for happy-ever offering in Changealot.'

So who is Morgana? Who is Sir Galahad who by this account is off on another overseas trip? Who is the bootlicker? The coffee shops were full and abuzz with talk.

Another of Olivares's trademark styles was to have imaginary dialogues between values such as honour and conscience, or between fact and rumour, or between responsibility and hypocrisy. In 'Hypocrisy' (1982h), Olivares turns a visit to her hairdresser into an occasion to bump into a former classmate, Hypocrisy, to talk about their missing friends, Freedom and Habeas:

> Anyway, the other day, while I was having my hair done, I thought I heard Hypocrisy's booming voice all over the parlour. She was praising my old friend Freedom to high heavens. Having known Hypocrisy for a long time, I wondered what scenario Hypocrisy was putting on.
>
> 'Hypocrisy,' I yelled, my temper getting the better of me. 'What on earth are you up to again this time?'
>
> My old classmate looked at me straight in the eye and, without shame, she answered, 'Why nothing. All I've been saying to my hairdresser is that Freedom is alive and doing very well.'

Olivares disagrees and brings up her other classmate, Habeas.

> 'Well, do you remember that time when Habeas disappeared? That was also the time Freedom went into a coma.'
>
> 'Pooh,' Hypocrisy said with derision. 'She's alive and kicking and Habeas has been located. He is around, too. And Detention does not exist any more.'
>
> 'Strange, I hear from her every now and then. But anyway, let's talk about you. How are you doing?' I asked pleasantly.

'Pretty good. I say one thing and still mean another.'

Other mythical classmates and long-time friends were used by Olivares in her writings. In 'Down memory lane' (1982i), she laments her poor memory. Without exercising her memory cells, she writes, she could lose it all. Thank goodness for friends she could reminisce with:

> The other night, when my friends gathered for lunch, I asked them certain questions that required their memory cells to function. 'Do you remember the good old days?' I asked them.
>
> 'What good old days? We're having the good days now.'
>
> 'You're kidding,' I said. 'Times are hard. Money is scarce and prices are skyrocketing. How can you say we're enjoying the good times now?'
>
> 'We were all born yesterday,' they chorused.

Lambasting government ministers

Olivares could also come out with columns that were direct and without embellishment. In 'Let's talk turkey' (1982j), which was published on the tenth anniversary of the declaration of martial law, Olivares wasted no words in lambasting the then-minister-in-charge of the Office of Media Affairs, Gregorio Cendaña. He had come out in the media to explain that that particular date was declared a public working holiday for employees and workers who would report to work as 'an expression of gratitude for the changes brought about by the New Society' (ibid).

> I want to know what we Filipinos have to be grateful for on Thanksgiving Day. So let's talk turkey today. Should we be grateful that on 21 September 1972 – just like the Pilgrims in Plymouth who went into the forest to hunt for birds for a thanksgiving dinner – military men were fielded to round up Filipinos who were later branded as communists, subversives, seditious newspapermen and enemies of the government? Should we be thankful that the media were fully controlled by the government and no one could voice or articulate the silent pleas of those placed in a coop? The same person who languished for months and some for years in detention cells without being formally charged?

On journalism, she writes:

> Should we give our everlasting thanks for the 'historic' occasion that has changed the style of journalism? The style which now gives hosannas and prominent space to the powers that be – that same developmental style that curtails the media man's initiative to dig too deeply into political and socio-economic investigative reporting? The same developmental style of journalism that makes one think and write innocuously so as not to offend the powerful and select?

Olivares ends with an invitation to the minister:

> I'll eat turkey if the 'historic occasion' will be proven in history as turkey. But before I sit at a dinner table and express my gratitude on this our Thanksgiving Day, Mr Cendaña, I suggest we drop the gobbledygook and talk turkey instead.

The recipe for newspaper pie...

This review of Olivares' writings would not be complete without mention of her famous recipe for newspaper pie. In 'Guess who's coming to dinner' (1982k), she writes:

> Once in a restive while, I throw away my typewriter, get very domesticated, don an apron and head for the kitchen to bake my famous newspaper pie. Believe it or not, my friends have badgered me for its recipe and because cooking is not my metier, I have graciously given away the recipe to many of my good friends. Strangely enough, my friends say that I have not shared with them all my secrets in pie-making mainly because their pies – based on my recipe – just do not taste like mine. I find this very odd because the recipe is easy to follow and no spice has been deleted. The ingredients are all within reach. If one wants to save money and indulge in the local flavour, the main ingredients are the pages of the daily newspapers which could be had for 75 centavos. And depending on what newspaper page one stirs in a pan, the local flavour can be bland, sugary-sweet, all chopped up, or wickedly sexy and sensational.

Olivares cautions that the key to a good newspaper pie is to ensure guests do not suffer from indigestion:

> Therefore, depending on who's coming to dinner, the main ingredient can be either the front page, the editorial page, the funnies or any other page – as long as the page is agreeable with guests' dietary requirements.

To end, she shares a secret to serving members of the media:

> If members of the fourth estate are coming to dinner, offer your guests lots of water to wash down the after taste of the pie. If the pie taste is unpalatable, offer them a consolation dish. Serve your guests spaghetti with chopped meatballs. It's a dietary prescription these days.

Olivares finally had her fill of chopped meatballs in 1983 when her publisher, Hans Menzi, called her into his office. The president was unhappy yet again over something she had written. Once before, she had acquiesced to Menzi's request for her to stop writing anything remotely political in her column. She said:

> Hans said: 'Ninez, he's in a bad mood. Can you write about something else other than politics until he cools down?' So I wrote about sex ... sex among cockroaches, sex among snakes. ... Then he would come and say: 'Ok. It's

time. He's cool headed now.' So I started writing again (personal communication, 19 August 2014).

It was different this time. Menzi said Marcos was really angry and Olivares's writing was clearly directed against Marcos's human rights abuses, the blatant corruption within government and ever increasing censorship. In fact, Olivares and her fellow women journalists had been summoned to appear before the National Intelligence Board in Fort Bonifacio on 12 January 1983 to reply to questions by a military tribunal (Mojares 2006). In her biography, journalist Eugenia 'Eggie' Apostol recalls that it was 'scare tactics'. She recalled they were questioned on everything, from their private life, their religious beliefs, their income from writing, and also asked: 'By the way, are you a member of the Communist Party of the Philippines?' (ibid).

So when Menzi approached Ninez to ask if she could stop writing against the regime while the president cooled down, she declined. She told Menzi: 'You know I did it once. I'm willing to do it again for your sake. But what kind of journalist will I be if every time the president is mad at me because I am writing this stuff, I stop.' 'But I'm not firing you,' Menzi said.

Conclusion: The courage of Olivares and other 'contrarian' women journalists

Olivares was never afraid of losing her job. That was one of the reasons she wrote as she did. Unlike her male counterparts who were breadwinners, she was married and her husband could support her. Other 'brave' women journalists of the time said the same thing. Fellow *Bulletin Toaday* columnist Melinda Quintos-de Jesus (2012) said:

> The joke then was that the only journalists who had balls were women, apologies to the men please, like Joe Burgos and others like him. [But] unlike most male journalists we were not the sole breadwinners in our families, we did not depend on what we earned to keep the roof over our heads. It also helped that the custom and convention had kept us mostly out of the old boy cliques, which could have made it more difficult to break away from the pattern of press controls.

In the end, Olivares decided to leave the *Bulletin Toaday* and write for *Business Day*. Its publisher, Raul Locsin, assured her she would never be censored or forced to practise self-censorship.

Today, Olivares is herself a newspaper publisher. Dissatisfied with the daily newspapers for their blatant fawning over Cory Aquino, who succeeded Marcos following the People's Revolution in 1986, and then a succession of presidents, she set up the *Daily Tribune* in 2000 as the country's foremost contrarian press. She no longer writes in the style of fairy tales and fables but has reverted to straight, hard-hitting editorials critical of government officials and corrupt practices in government. These include the Aquino administration's partially unconstitutional Disbursement Acceleration Programme (DAP), and the graft-ridden Priority Development Assistance Fund (PDAF), commonly known as the 'pork barrel'.

She has faced multiple libel lawsuits but is unfazed. She said: 'I'm very comfortable with presidents who hate me. I have been very consistent in being an adversary. I always have an adversarial stance. It's the role of the press. I don't praise if they're doing their jobs right. I will always be contrarian. Someone's gotta do it' (personal communication, 19 August 2014).

Note

[1] The Philippines, having been a Spanish colony for 300 years, had a habit of bastardising and/or adopting Spanish words and then turning these into English (the Philippines was also under American rule for 50 years). This word does not appear in any English dictionary and is purely a creation of Filipino lawmakers from the English fiscal – of or relating to the public treasury or revenues, and the Spanish *fiscalizar* meaning to criticise or oversee

References

ABS-CBN News (2012) In his own words: Marcos on Martial Law, 21 September. Available online at http://www.abs-cbnnews.com/-depth/09/21/12/his-own-words-marcos-martial-law, accessed on 8 March 2015

Babst, Arlene (1982) Let the Lady do the talking, *Bulletin Today*, 16 September p. 6

Bulletin Today (1982) KBL scored for Batasan absenteeism, 23 January p. 1

Celoza, Albert (1997) *Ferdinand Marcos and the Philippines – The Political Economy of Authoritarianism*, Westport, CT: Praeger Publishers

Ching, Mark (2010) Cong. Imelda Marcos talks about her 'commitment to beauty', Philippine Entertainment Portal, 16 October. Available online at http://www.pep.ph/celeb/celeb_swatch/23129/cong-imelda-marcos-talks-about-her-commitment-to-beauty, accessed on 10 November 2014

Constantino, Renato (1970) The miseducation of the Filipino, Scribd. Available online at http://www.thefilipinomind.com/2006/03/making-of-americanized-filipino-minds_23.html, accessed on 12 November 2014

Coronel, Sheila (2006) 20 Filipinos 20 Years after People Power: Imelda Marcos, *I-Report PCIJ*. Available online at http://pcij.org/blog/wp-files/podcasts/Imelda.mp3, accessed on 10 November 2014

de Jesus, Melinda Quintos (2012) Women in media, In Medias Res, 7 March. Available online at http://www.cmfr-phil.org/inmediasres/women-in-media/In, accessed on 12 November 2014

Gleeck Jr, Lewis (1987) *President Marcos and the Philippine Political Culture*, Manila: Loyal Printing Inc.

IRAIA (2012) Martial law arrests and detentions by end of 1972, 23 September. Available online at http://wiki.iraia.net/mw/index.php?title=Martial_law_arrests_and_detentions_by_end-1972, accessed on 19 November 2014

Mariano, Gerardo (1995) Manila daily bulletin, Scribd, January. Available online at http://www.scribd.com/doc/54483950/Manila-Bulletin#scribd, accessed on 12 November 2014

Mojares, Resil (2006) Eugenia Apostol Biography. Ramon Magsaysay Awards. Available online at http://www.rmaf.org.ph/newrmaf/main/awardees/awardee/biography/139, accessed on 17 November 2014

Olivares, Ninez C. (1982a) The wicked witch, *Bulletin Today*, 18 September

Olivares, Ninez C. (1982b) Images in the rain, *Bulletin Today*, 25 July

Olivares, Ninez C. (1982c) Me and my shadow, *Bulletin Today*, 24 January

Olivares, Ninez C. (1982d) MIA's Culpa, *Bulletin Today*, 31 August

Olivares, Ninez C. (1982e) Bryant the Giant, *Bulletin Today*, 20 August

Olivares, Ninez C. (1982f) Dragonland, *Bulletin Today*, 4 September

Olivares, Ninez C. 1982g) Idyll of kings, *Bulletin Today*, 29 January

Olivares, Ninez C. (1982h) Hypocrisy, *Bulletin Today*, 12 September

Olivares, Ninez C. (1982i) Down memory lane, *Bulletin Today*, 12 February

Olivares, Ninez C. (1982j) Let's talk turkey, *Bulletin Today*, 21 September

Olivares, Ninez C. (1982k) Guess who's coming to dinner, *Bulletin Today*, 10 February

Rosenberg, David (ed.) (1979) *Marcos and Martial Law in the Philippines*, Ithaca, New York: Cornell University Press

Sin, Cardinal Jaime (1981) Papal visit and beatification of Lorenzo Ruiz, CBCP documents. Available online at http://www.cbcponline.net/documents/1980s/1980-papal_visit.html, accessed on 14 November 2014

Note on the contributor

Amy Forbes is Associate Dean, Learning and Teaching, and senior lecturer in journalism at James Cook University in Queensland, Australia. A journalist with more than 20 years' experience across television, print and online platforms in the Philippines, she is a Fulbright scholar. She is also the recipient of a 2014 Office for Learning and Teaching national award in Australia for Outstanding Contributions to Student Learning for leadership and excellence in developing and delivering a pioneering Work Integrated Learning-based curriculum in Multimedia Journalism.

Index

Begley, Adam, 65, 66, 67
Brand, Russell, 5, 70-84
Bulletin Today, 7, 169-185

Cacho-Olivares, Ninez, 7, 170-185
Charlie Hebdo, 2, 110, 158
Clarke, John, 2
Colbert, Steven, 2
Crónicas, 6, 110-121
Crook, Tim, 3, 8

Daily Mail, 74, 77, 83
Daily Telegraph, 64
Dickens, Charles, 3, 16, 19, 20, 24

El Jueves, 7, 156, 159-160, 161, 162, 163, 164, 165, 166, 167
El Papus, 7, 156, 178-158, 160, 161, 162, 163, 164, 165, 166, 167n, 168
L'Esquella de la Torratxa, 7, 138, 139, 145

Fernandes, Millôr, 6-7, 124-137
Fitzgerald, Scott, 88
Forbes, 47, 50
Ford, Corey, 28, 29, 30, 31, 36, 39
Frost, Chris, 1, 8

Gonzo, 5-6, 87, 89-90, 93, 94, 95, 96
Guardian, 22, 61, 62, 68, 71, 74, 80, 82, 83, 84

Harcup, Tony, 1, 8
Hensher, Philip, 64, 65, 66, 67
Hermano Lobo, 6, 7, 107, 156, 157, 160, 161, 162, 163, 165, 166

Identity, 4, 5, 27, 28, 29, 30, 32, 34, 38, 56, 57, 61, 67, 77, 78, 129, 138, 139, 141, 145, 146, 147, 148, 149
International Herald Tribune (*International New York Times*), 4, 41, 47, 50
Irony, 4, 6, 11, 28, 34, 35, 56, 60, 62, 63, 64, 74, 97, 110, 111, 112, 115, 116, 117-118, 127, 128, 130, 146, 147, 163, 164, 165, 166

Joseph, Sue, 1

Kipling, Rudyard, 3, 19, 24

La Campana, 139, 141, 151n
Leiren-Young, Mark, 1, 2, 8
Literary journalism, 2, 3, 6, 8, 23, 24, 50n, 51, 52, 97-109, 110-121
Los Angeles Times, 42, 43, 53

Malcolm, Janet, 59, 64
Mars-Jones, Adam, 62, 63, 64, 66, 68
Mercer, Rick, 2
Moliner, Empar, 6, 97, 105-107, 109
Montero, Rosa, 6, 97, 103-105, 107n, 108n, 109
Morris, Chris, 2

New Journalism, 5, 89-90, 96
New Yorker, 4, 8, 26-40, 55, 67, 71, 84, 131
New York Observer, 65
New York Review of Books, 54, 61, 67, 68
New York Times, 41, 42, 43, 44, 45, 48, 49, 51n, 52, 53, 54

Index

Oliver, John, 2
O Pasquim, 6, 124, 131-134, 136n, 137
Orwell, George 3, 4, 8, 10-25, 56, 57, 68, 88, 142, 151n

Papitu, 7, 138, 139, 140, 141, 142, 143, 144, 145, 146, 147, 148, 149
Parker, Dorothy, 3, 35, 36, 38, 40
Perelman, Sid, 26, 36
Pif-Paf, 6, 124, 125, 127-131, 133, 134, 136, 137
Por Favor, 6, 7, 107, 156, 158-159, 160, 161, 162, 163, 164, 165, 166, 167, 168
Pun, 27, 43, 127, 146

Remnick, David, 27, 40
Rieff, David, 5, 54-69
Rolling Stone, 5, 86, 87, 88, 92, 94, 95
Ross, Harold, 4, 26, 27, 28, 31, 32, 33, 34, 35, 38, 39, 40
Ross, Jonathan, 77

Sarcasm, 97, 102, 103, 112, 158, 163
Satire, 4, 6, 7, 16, 28, 30, 31, 97, 103, 110, 120, 130, 138, 139, 141, 142-144, 145, 146, 150, 153, 160, 166
Sex, 3, 17, 18, 35, 62, 79, 88, 94, 107, 146, 159, 164, 182

Shakespeare, William, 3, 4, 16, 19
Sontag, Susan, 5, 54, 55, 59, 60, 61, 62, 63, 64, 65, 66, 67, 68
Stewart, Jon, 2, 72
Stewart, Moira, 78

Thomas, Mark, 2
Thompson, Hunter S., 5-6, 8, 86-96
Thurber, James, 3, 26, 27, 28, 36, 37, 38n, 39, 40, 173
Torres, Maruja, 6, 97, 98-102, 103, 105, 107, 108n, 109, 157, 158, 159
Tribune (see also Orwell), 3, 12, 15, 21, 23, 68
Twain, Mark, 3, 19, 36, 89
Twitter, 2, 72

Vanity Fair, 29, 31, 39

Wall Street Journal, 41, 43, 53
Washington Post, 41, 42, 50, 51n, 52, 53
White, E. B., 26, 34, 36, 37
Wolfe, Tom, 5, 86, 89, 96

Yagoda, Ben, 4, 8, 26, 27, 29, 30, 32, 33, 34, 36, 38, 40
YouTube, 2, 71, 77, 90

www.ingramcontent.com/pod-product-compliance
Lightning Source LLC
Chambersburg PA
CBHW051056160426
43193CB00010B/1202